# Encyclopaedia of Cybernetics

# Encyclopaedia of Cybernetics

Translated from
the German
*Lexikon der Kybernetik*
by
**G Gilbertson** BA

Manchester University Press
Barnes & Noble Inc., New York

Original edition in German
(editor: Frau A Müller)


2085 Quickborn bei Hamburg
Heinrich-Lohse-Strasse 69


(translator: G Gilbertson)

Manchester University Press
316–324 Oxford Road
Manchester 13

GB SBN 7190 0308 3

USA

Barnes & Noble Inc.
105 Fifth Avenue
New York, NY 10003

Printed in Great Britain
by Butler & Tanner Ltd
Frome and London

## Translator's note

Without the assistance of specialists in many fields the present translation of the *Lexikon der Kybernetik* would have been impossible. My especial thanks are due to the following, all former colleagues at the University of Bradford: Dr C. K. Elliott (Management and Administration), Mr D. Nudds (Computer Laboratory), Dr A. Wright (School of Biology), Mr T. Sergent (School of Electrical Engineering).

It is emphasized that in an emerging discipline, some of the terminology will not prove completely acceptable to everybody. This was true of the original German edition and may prove even more so in translation. It has been not so much a case of literal translation as of finding the equivalent English usage in respect of certain terms and expressions.

The original contributors are not to be held necessarily responsible for these equivalents, but I have done my best to see that their meaning has been accurately interpreted. The majority have seen their articles and have taken the opportunity to make any necessary correction and revision for the English edition.

G Gilbertson BA

Interpreters' Institute
Universität des Saarlandes
Saarbrücken

February 1968

**The following arrangement is used in the Encyclopaedia:**

Term

(Synonym)

German

French

Russian

Simple explanation (in italics)

Precise scientific definition

Bibliography (in small type)

An asterisk before a term signifies that this term has its own entry alphabetically in the volume

**Absolute judgement**
Beurteilung, absolute
jugement absolu

———

*Co-ordination of appellation (colour names) or other reactions (pressing certain keys) with stimuli of a certain modulity (optically perceivable electromagnetic oscillations of various frequencies).*

Whilst in the relative judgement of *stimuli the relation between at least two stimuli leads to a *reaction of an organism (perhaps a 'larger-smaller' judgement), in an absolute judgement an identifying reaction is given to every element of a set group of distinguishable stimuli. A certain stimulus-repertory may possess an *entropy of *n* *bit. The system of co-ordinated reactions has an equally large entropy. By stimulus-change (equivocation) the experimentally comprehensible *transinformation between both systems can be smaller than *n* bit. By increasing the entropy of the stimulus system, this transinformation approaches a limit which can be interpreted as *channel capacity. Channel capacity is dependent on various variables. It clearly increases with the number of characteristics in which the stimuli vary, even if the variations of individual characteristics are dependent on each other. In variations of a single characteristic the maximal transinformation in all sensory areas is in the region of $\log_2 (7 \pm 2)$ bit.

GARNER, W. R.: Uncertainty and Structure as Psychological Concepts. J. Wiley, New York, London 1962.

**Absolute threshold**
Absolutschwelle
seuil absolu; valeur liminaire
порог абсолюный

*Originally a psycho-physical term for the smallest or largest discernible stimulus of a sensory modality; in general a value which with the specified probability of* $p < 1$ *creates a certain reaction under specified conditions.*

If $m_i$, $(i = 1, \ldots, k;)$ are symbols of objects (e.g. frequency, duration and pressure of sound signals) which in a certain group of test-subjects (e.g. 15-year-olds) under specified test conditions (e.g. instruction in attentiveness) produce a specified answer (e.g. *sound heard*) with a probability $O > p(A) < 1$, then the absolute threshold is that range given in units of the symbols (e.g. physical: c/s, s, W/cm², or psychological: mel subjective time-units, sone) in which $p(A)$ reaches a specified value. The necessary probability is generally reckoned as 0·5 (semi-threshold).

For physical values which produce an organic reaction, one uses the term *stimulus threshold.* With continua where it makes sense to talk of direction (cf. *difference threshold) one distinguishes an upper absolute threshold (overload-threshold) from a lower absolute threshold (e.g. effective, deadly dose; difficulty in carrying out tasks, calibrated according to mental age—cf. BINET, etc.). With sensory continua the lower absolute threshold, as the perception threshold, is equated with absolute zero on the perception scale (e.g. the lowest level of hearing).

TORGERSON, W. S.: Theory and methods of scaling. Wiley, New York, London 1960.

**Acceptance value**
Akzeptionswert
valeur d'acception
——

*A term used within the framework of cybernetic logic for a logical value which is chosen from a proffered alternative.*
The term acceptance value only has a meaning if there is also the possibility of refusing the proffered choice and of substituting this by a *rejection value. Acceptance value is therefore a concept which regards the classical system of double-valued logic as a subsystem in a morphogrammatic system. (cf. *morphogram). The point of the concept is: *rejection value.

**Access time**
Zugriffszeit
temps d'accès
время выборки

*A distinctive value of a *store.*
The time which elapses between the calling of a store address and the delivery of its content into a *register for further processing is called the access time.

SPEISER, A. P.: Digitale Rechenanlagen. Springer-Verlag, Berlin, Göttingen, Heidelberg 1961.

**Accumulator**
Akkumulator
accumulateur
сумматор; аккумулятор

*Part of the *arithmetic unit of a *digital computer.*
In an automatic *computer the accumulator takes over the function of the *adder in a manual calculator. In it the results (and intermediate results) of arithmetic *operations (addition, subtraction, multiplication) are formed. (The quotient in division arises in a separate arithmetic unit which corresponds to the rotation counting unit in a manual calculator.) Because of multiplication the number of places in the accumulator is twice the normal number in arithmetic quantities. The content of the accumulator is frequently made visible at the control desk or console of a computer; it is adjustable by means of some external control, such as rotary knobs or switches.

KNÖDEL, W.: Programmieren von Ziffernrechenanlagen. Springer-Verlag, Wien 1961.

**Action potential**
Aktionspotential; Spike
potentiel d'action
биопотенциал; биоэлектрический потенциал

*Transmitted electrical potential-variation when there is a supra-threshold stimulation of sensitive function units in the body.*
Sensitive function-units, such as nerve-cells, are influenced by stimulation in such a way that the functional *membrane which surrounds the cell is locally depolarized, and that the rest-potential resulting from the varying permeability of the membrane towards sodium and potassium ions is reduced (local potential-alteration proportional to the strength of the stimulus). If one oversteps the *threshold stimulus, the *excitation of the whole cell with a complete depolarization of the membrane sets in, and the much greater action-potential forms on the local potential-alteration. Action potential possesses a very rapid build up (duration approx. 0·1 m.secs.), i.e. the depolarization-phase, and a slower return (approx. 0·5 to 2 m.secs.) to the value of the rest-potential, i.e. the repolarization-phase, albeit with a different ion distribution. The original ion distribution is restored in a further recuperation phase with the help of a

relatively long chemical process (potassium-sodium pump). The recuperation phase represents a relative *refractory period of the cell, so that especially in the case of strong *stimuli of long duration, there is the possibility of several excitations (cf. *encoding). The amplitude of action potential is approx. 80–130 mV and is a function of the concentration-gradient of the ions involved. Depending on the method of recording, one or two phased action-potential can be measured.

MURALT, A. v.: Neue Ergebnisse der Nervenphysiologie. Springer-Verlag, Berlin, Göttingen, Heidelberg 1958.

**Action potential at a node of RANVIER**
Aktionspotential, mononodales
potentiel d'action mononodale
——

*Action potential at the node of a single nerve fibre.*

Mononodal action potential must be considered a basic element of action-potential and occurs at the node of RANVIER of a medullated nerve fibre. It has a very rapid build up (depolarization-phase), and exceptional peak, but in contrast to the multinodal *action potential and *compound action potential, a slow return phase (repolarization-phase). The latter is accentuated by the combined effect of several nodes, and the whole shape is systematically changed by the addition of further fibres with different speeds of conduction (cf. *compound action potential).

TASAKI, I.; TAKEUCHI, T.: Der am Ranvierschen Knoten entstehende Aktionsstrom und seine Bedeutung für die Erregungsleitung. Pflüg. Arch ges. Physiol. 244 (1941), pp. 696–711.

**Actual value; instantaneous value**
Istwert; Regelgrösse
valeur instantanée; valeur réelle
истинная величина; фактическое значение; действительная величина

*The value of a physical system measured at any particular moment. The actual value is brought closer to the *index value by *feedback control.*

OPPELT, W.: Kleines Handbuch technischer Regelvorgänge. Verlag Chemie, Weinheim 1956.

**Adaptation**
Adaptation
adaptation
адаптация

*Adaptation of the stimulation of a sensory cell to the strength of a stimulus by means of metabolic changes.*

The transformation of stimuli in *receptors or *synapses, which precedes encoding, always influences the metabolism of the sensory-cells in that it firstly provokes the formation of a stimulatory substance whose rate of formation is proportional to the strength of the stimulus. Dependent on the concentration of this stimulatory substance, which increases with a certain *time constant and is therefore somewhat delayed, a metabolic break-down sets in, by which the initial overshoot of the stimulatory substance can be reduced to a steady state proportional to the strength or frequency of the stimuli. Adaptation shifts the intensity threshold of the sensory-cells within the limits of its range and makes the best use of the difference threshold.

RANKE, O. P.: Allgemeine Physiologie der Sinnesorgane. In: Lehmann, G. (ed.): Handbuch der gesamten Arbeitsmedizin. Springer-Verlag, Berlin, Göttingen, Heidelberg 1960. KEIDEL, W. D.: Adaption, loss or gain of sensory information? In: Rosenblith, W. (ed.): Sensory Communication, pp. 319–338. M.I.T. Press and J. Wiley, London and New York 1961.

**Add**

**Adder**
Addierwerk
addeur
сумматор; суммирующее устройство

*Part of the *arithmetic unit which carries out the actual addition.*

In binary serial machines addition is achieved digit by digit: the corresponding stages, e.g. of the *operand register and the *accumulator together with the carry from the next lowest stage, form the input, and outputs are given once more to the accumulator and a delay unit. The whole process is, therefore, distinguished by the cycle 'shift setting of next position—adding', while the signs are evaluated separately beforehand. An adder of this type therefore has three inputs (binary digits *a*, *b* and the carry from the previous stage *c*) and two outputs (a result *s* and carry *u*), cf. diagram. An adder may be regarded as a logical circuit; from the table the switching functions result as follows:

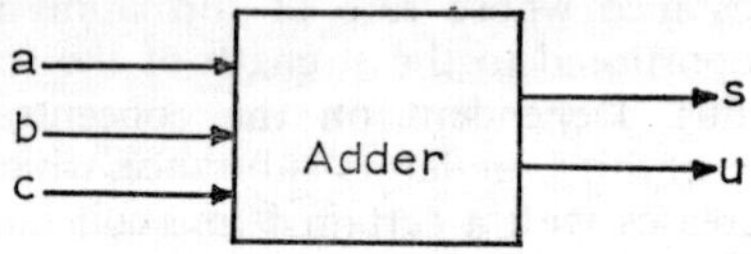


| a | b | c | s | u |
|---|---|---|---|---|
| 0 | 0 | 0 | 0 | 0 |
| 0 | 0 | 1 | 1 | 0 |
| 0 | 1 | 0 | 1 | 0 |
| 0 | 1 | 1 | 0 | 1 |
| 1 | 0 | 0 | 1 | 0 |
| 1 | 0 | 1 | 0 | 1 |
| 1 | 1 | 0 | 0 | 1 |
| 1 | 1 | 1 | 1 | 1 |

$$s = [a \mathbin{\&} (b \equiv c)] \vee [\bar{a} \mathbin{\&} (b \not\equiv c)]$$
$$u = (a \mathbin{\&} b) \vee (b \mathbin{\&} c) \vee (a \mathbin{\&} c)$$

With binary parallel machines adders of this type are organized in parallel; special care must be given to the carry. Decimal organized machines possess an adder in the form of a *translator.

STEINBUCH, K. (ed.): Taschenbuch der Nachrichtenverarbeitung. Springer-Verlag, Berlin, Göttingen, Heidelberg 1962.

**Address**
Adresse
adresse
адрес

*Code number by which information (data and *instructions) can be reached in the *memory (or *store) of a digital computer.*

In the store of a digital computer information is available in words (numerical data or instructions). Each individual word can be called on and entered into the *arithmetic unit. As a computer is not able to recognize the meaning or content of the stored information, the words are defined in the storage locations by use of the store address. This is also the case with intermediate results which await recall in auxiliary storage. (In certain types of memory, information can only be called on in blocks, i.e. in word groups, by using a block address.) In the instructions to the arithmetic unit, the address part gives the (data) address of that number which must be added to or subtracted from the content of the *accumulator. With *jump instructions it gives the address of the instruction which must subsequently be carried out. This is possible because with electronic arithmetic units the instructions are also stored in storage locations. In this way the execution of the instructions (the *progam) may be varied as required. With instruction addresses one must distinguish between (*a*) absolute addresses, i.e. real instruction and operation addresses, which give the real number of the storage location; (*b*) symbolic ad-

dresses. Here alphanumeric symbols are used for addressing, e.g. $\pi$. The computer translates these symbolic addresses into absolute addresses; (*c*) relative addresses. Here is given, for example, how many storage locations must be 'jumped' before the computer finds the next instruction. In absolute addressing, such a jump-address is given by its storage location.
In address modification one can modify absolute addresses by the content of *index registers; the content of such a (variable) register is added as a number to an absolute address in the address-section of an instruction. In this way absolute addresses can be modified during iterative computing processes (cf. *address modification).

KNÖDEL, W.: Programmieren von Ziffernrechenanlagen. Springer-Verlag, Wien 1961.

**Address modification**
Adressenmodifikation
modification d'adresse
модификация адреса; изменение адреса

*Alteration of the address section of an *instruction.*
A certain calculation often has to be carried out on several *operands of the same type. In this, however, it is not a question of allotting a location for each use of an *operation, but of repeatedly running through a single set of instructions. However, in order that with every cycle the next *operand may be used, the address sections of the corresponding instructions must be continually modified by the addition or subtraction of certain values. It is useful if this process follows automatically. With automatic address modification, the content of an *index register is added to or subtracted from the address section of the instruction in the *control unit before the execution of a modified instruction. The modified address thus becomes an effective address. The operands must be stored in a suitable sequence.

**Agnosia**
Agnosie
agnosie
агнозия

*Disturbance in the recognition of objects without defects in the peripheral sensitive or sensory mechanisms.*
A kind of agnosia is known for the following types of brain perception: visual agnosia or 'mind blindness', the inability to recognize objects visually. In the same way one speaks of tactile agnosia, and auditory agnosia or 'verbal deafness' in their varying forms, such as colour agnosia, agnosia of written characters (word blindness or alexia), agnosia with letters with figures and numbers.
Agnosia is caused by damage to the associative centres, whilst the primary receptor centres remain undamaged. Elementary *perception remains, yet cannot be used in the psychic life of the individual.

**ALGOL, algorithmic language**
ALGOL
ALGOL
международный язык программирования Алгол

*A problem-orientated, machine-independent programming language for the solution of mathematical-technical problems.*
ALGOL was created by representatives of several mathematical and scientific associations to obtain a formal *language for the standard formulation of *algorithms. Machine-dependent rules, such as instructions to the *compiler for the translation of a program written in ALGOL into *machine code, des-

cription of the *input and *output, regulations for the punching, etc., of the program, are not part of ALGOL. Compilers for ALGOL or a subset of ALGOL (possibly extended to include machine-dependent instructions) exist for a large number of *digital computers.

Report on the Algorithmic Language, Numerische Mathematik, Band 2, 1960.

**Algorithm**
Algorithmus
algorithme
алгорифм; алгоритм

*A general, clearly defined process for the automatic solution of all problems within a certain range. The *program of a *TURING machine is a precise formulation of this concept.*

The concept of the algorithm which has existed for centuries was given a precise mathematical formulation by CHURCH in 1936 (Church's thesis). All subsequent formulations turned out to be equivalent to this.

As far as the TURING machine is concerned the argument is as follows: Every algorithm can be represented in the form of a TURING table (or transition table).

According to WANG (1957) and LEE (1960) every TURING table is equivalent to a *program of elementary *instructions. When using the *alphabet $A = \{\Box, |\}$ one needs the instructions:

- $e$: clear the working cell to $\Box$
- $m$: mark the working cell with |
- $+$: take the cell on the right as the working cell
- $-$: take the cell on the left as the working cell
- $\mathscr{A}$ ($A$): branch off to the instruction marked $A$ if the content of the working cell is |, otherwise go over to the next instruction.

By means of the conditional expressions introduced by McCARTHY, algorithms can be simply formulated independently of a machine. In the conditional expression

$$p_1 \to a_1, p_2 \to a_2$$

$p_1$ and $p_2$ are predicates (cf. *Boolean algebra) and $a_1$ and $a_2$ are conditional or unconditional mathematical expressions. The bracket is to be interpreted in the following way: if $p_1$ is true, then $a_1$ must be evaluated, otherwise the second subexpression must be treated in the same way, e.g.

$$n! = (n = 0 \to 1, n \neq 0 \to n \cdot (n-1)!)$$

HERMES, H.: Aufzählbarkeit, Entscheidbarkeit, Berechenbarkeit. Springer-Verlag, Berlin, Göttingen, Heidelberg 1961, LEE, C. Y.: Automata and Finite Automata. Bell System Technical Journal 39 (1960). MCCARTHY, J.: A Basis for the Mathematical Theory of Computation. Proc. of Western Joint Computer Conference. 1960.

**All-or-none law**
Alles-oder-Nichts-Gesetz
loi du tout ou rien
закон 'все или ничего'; принцип 'все или ничего'

*A function unit within the body which is subject to the all-or-none law responds to every *stimulus above the threshold with an *excitation independent of the strength of the stimulus. Identity of liminal and maximal stimulus.*

The explanation of the validity of the all-or-none law in excitable function units of the body is given by the electrical processes of *excitation. The membrane which surrounds every sensitive cell is first locally depolarized by every *stimulus which does not fall within the *refractory period. When there is a stimulus above the threshold, this local depolarization and decrease of the rest-potential leads to an increase in the permeability of the membrane and to a further depolarization which is not locally limited; this very quickly leads to a sudden complete breakdown of the membrane-potential (cf. *action potential). Examples of the effect of the all-or-none law are the contraction of the heart muscles and the *encoding of strength of stimulus in pulse-frequency modulated action potential which are always of the same amplitude.

REIN, H.; SCHNEIDER, M.: Einführung in die Physiologie des Menschen. 11th edn. Springer-Verlag, Berlin, Göttingen, Heidelberg 1960.

**Alternation**
*see* *Disjunction (inclusive)

**Alpha waves**
Alpha-Wellen
ondes alpha
альфа лучи

*Regular sinusoidal shaped waves of the human electroencephalogram.*
These are recorded in the conscious state of the test-subject at rest and with closed eyes. When the eyes are opened the alpha waves disappear (i.e. the blocking reaction of the visual part of the brain). The *frequency of alpha waves is 8–12 c/s, their amplitude varies between 10 and 100, sometimes even 150 $\mu$V. As a rule alpha waves occur as a continuous series of elements of constant frequency and variable amplitude. Alpha waves start at the back of the head: their amplitude decreases by $\frac{1}{4}$–$\frac{1}{3}$ on the scalp. They often show a certain amplitude-asymmetry. In the dominant hemisphere they are less strongly developed. The first signs of alpha waves occur at the age of three; not until the age of 10–12 years do they form the whole *electrical activity.

**Alphabet**
Alphabet
alphabet
алфавит; азбука

An alphabet is an arranged set of *signs or *symbols which are elementary for the representation of *language or *grammar, from which complex linguistic expressions can be formed according to the rules of linguistic description.

**Alphanumerical**
Alphanumerisch
alphanumérique
буквенно—цифровой

Information in data-processing machines which contains besides numerical digits (0 . . . 9), other characters (mainly letters, but also for example = ; ? etc.) is called alphanumerical.

**Ambiguity**
Irrelevanz; Dissipation
ambiguité
диссипация

*A concept in mathematical *information theory.*
Let there be given two *fields of events $X$ and $Y$ in which $X$ is the field of its input signals, and $Y$ the field of its output signals. Then the average conditional information is $H_x(Y)$ (often also written $H(Y/X)$). The ambiguity is therefore equal to the uncertainty of the signal received when the transmitter signal is known. It reaches its maximum if *transinformation disappears. In the event of the channel degenerating into a *translator (introduced as a model) which encodes the *meanings of the field $X$ in the characters of the field $Y$, then the ambiguity becomes the expectancy value of the aesthetic information (cf. *informational aesthetics) on the

selected representation of the given meaning.

BERGER, E. R.; PILOTY, H.: Erläuterungen zu den in der Informationstheorie verwendeten Begriffen der mathematischen Statistik. NTZ Heft 1 (1963). FRANK, H.: Information et Pédagogie. Cybernética pt. 1 (1963).

**Amplifier**
Verstärker
amplificateur
усилитель; интенсификатор

By an amplifier is understood a system in which a local electrical output (voltage, current) is regulated by a signal input (voltage, current) in such a way that at the output of the amplifier an output signal is given which corresponds to the temporal variations of the voltage or current of the input signal, and which has an increased value compared to the value of the input signal. According to the type of amplifying element used, a distinction is made between transistor-amplifiers, valve-amplifiers, magnetic amplifiers and dielectric amplifiers. Mention must also be made of low-noise amplifiers recently developed: masers and parametric amplifiers. Amplifiers can also be sub-divided, according to the application of the output side, into voltage amplifiers, current amplifiers and power amplifiers. According to the frequency of the input signal, a distinction is made between AC and DC amplifiers, and in special cases pulse amplifiers. DC amplifiers are divided into high and low amplifiers, as well as wide and narrow band amplifiers.

**Amplitude filter**
Amplitudenfilter
filtre d'amplitude
амплитудный селектор

*A *filter which from a temporary process $s(t)$ lets through unaltered only those parts whose ordinate values satisfy specified conditions.*

The limiter is a special amplitude filter. An example of a limiter is a circuit which from $s(t)$ lets through unaltered only those parts whose ordinate values lie beneath an upper threshold $s_0$ (single-sided limit) while all values above $s_0$ appear at the output with the ordinate $s_0$.

**Analogous**
analog
analogue
аналогичный; подобный; непрерывно изменяющийся; аналоговый; моделированный

*Two or several different systems are called analogous if their *structures or their functions correspond to each other.*

Two systems are analogous if the terms of the first system correspond to the terms of the second (e.g. roads across a section of country and arteries in the body). So systems are analogous if they have either the same structure (used in this sense by G. S. HILAIRE) or the same function. In the latter sense (already used by CUVIER) the idea is used in the field of *cybernetics. (L. COUFFIGNAL).

**Analogue computer**
Analogrechner
calculatrice analogique
электронное моделирующее устройство; аналоговое устройство или машина; машина—аналог

*In contrast to the digital computer, the analogue computer is an instrument which processes continually changing variables of a system *analogous to the problem.*

Many problems in mathematics and technology, especially those which can be described by differential equations, can be treated and solved by turning the occurring variables into *analogous

electrical ones and by rebuilding their relation in an electrical model. This is done by the *programming of an electrical analogue computer in which time appears as the independent variable in a corresponding scale, but in which all dependent variables are represented by various electrical potentials. The *program consists of the connecting of these potentials by the use of summing and integrating amplifiers, multipliers, potentiometers for the input of constants, function generators, etc., whereby non-linear relations can normally be just as easily taken into account as linear ones. The actual calculation is done by setting the initial values and time functions on the program circuit.
The result consists of the variation with time of the dependent variables whose analogous potentials can be observed either for slow calculations on instruments or on multichannel recorders, or can be seen for a faster process by periodic repetition of the calculation process on oscillographs. The accuracy is determined, in contrast to digital computers, by the tolerance of the construction elements, constancy of the working values such as fixed potentials, gains, etc., and has therefore a limit at $10^{-3} \ldots 10^{-4}$. Ranges of use of analogue computers are given where continually variable values have a complex but known function-relationship, e.g. in control technology, network synthesis in oscillation experiments, in flight guidance instruments (cf. *simulator), etc.

Ernst, D.: Elektronische Analogrechner. R. Oldenbourg, München 1960. Korn, G. A. und Korn, T. M.: Elekrtonische Analogierechenmaschinen. Berliner Union, Stuttgart 1960.

**Analogy**
Analogie
analogie
аналогия; сходство; подобие

*Relationship or connection between corresponding values of two or more systems as well as in an extended sense between the two systems themselves.*
One must distinguish between structural and functional analogy, the latter being especially useful in *cybernetics. So in this sense analogy is the common function of two or more elements of two or more (analogous) mechanisms.
An analogy which has been built up on the basis of some already known attributes can be evaluated by the examination of new attributes which are thought to be common to the two systems. This method of deduction is called rational deduction by analogy.
The use of *models whose analogy with the system to be examined is only valid to a limited extent, represents a special case of the evaluation of analogy. It is either limited to the same function as the system, as for example in a case of a *simulator, or, as in the case of a model of a dam, is functional and structural. Here analogy becomes *similarity. Between these two extreme cases are many extended and utilizable analogies. In this way isomorphic machines are used in the representation of, for example, rheo-electric analogies.

Couffignal, L.: Kybernetische Grundbegriffe. Agis, Baden-Baden 1962. Ashby, W. R.: An Introduction to Cybernetics. Chapman & Hall, London 1956.

**Anticipation of a channel**
Vorgriff eines Kanals
anticipation d'un canal
предрешение канала

One talks of a *channel without anticipation if the probability

$$p_x(y_k = b),\ b \in B,\ k \text{ fixed}$$

does not depend on the characters

$$x_{k+1},\ x_{k+2},\ x_{k+3},\ \ldots$$

which arrive at the channel input after the point of time $k$.

GRELL, H. (ed.): Arbeiten zur Informationstheorie I. Dtsch. Vlg. d. Wissenschaften, Berlin 1957. HENZE, E.: Einführung in die Informationstheorie. Beiheft 3. Elektronische Datenverarbeitung, 2nd edition, Braunschweig 1965.

**Aphasia**
Aphasie
aphasie
афазия

*Originally defined by TROUSSEAU as the impossibility of verbal expression without the presence of any damage to the vocal system. More generally it can be regarded as the loss of use of symbols.*

Many types of aphasia are known; the most important are motor aphasia or aphemia (type PIERRE MARIE), sensory aphasia of WERNICKE and mixed aphasia (type BROCA).

Partial attacks of these systems are also known: difficulty in word-finding such as substantives (PITRES amnesic aphasia), selective loss of writing ability (agraphia) or of muscular ability of expression (amusia). Types of aphasia arise from injuries in the area of the arteria cerebrales media of the dominant hemisphere.

**Apperception**
Apperzeption
apperception
сознательное восприятие; апперцепция

Recording in the *short-term-memory of one section selected from the abundance of objects perceived at any one time (by means of attention) where it remains present in the consciousness for the *duration. Apperception is therefore the second phase of *perception connected with the consciousness.

**Apraxia**
Apraxie
apraxie
апраксия

A defect in mimicry (J. de DELAY); the person affected is incapable of carrying out any intended movement although no paralysis exists. A distinction exists between an ideational apraxia, which is seen predominantly in complex gestures in which the logical sequence of the components is disturbed, and an ideomotor apraxia, in which even the simplest movements cannot be executed. Limited types of apraxia are also known (buccofacial apraxia, similar to *limb-kinetic apraxia, agraphia.) Limited apraxia is connected with pre-frontal injuries (premotor area) of the predominantly affected hemisphere; generalized apraxia is caused by injuries to the parietal lobe or the corpus callosum.

**Arithmetic unit**
Rechenwerk
unité arithmétique
арифметическое устройство

*Used in the execution of calculations in a *computer.*

In the arithmetic unit the *operands taken from the *store are logically or arithmetically connected. Basic parts are the *accumulator and the *adder. Multiplication or division is carried out by continued addition or subtraction, or determined by the *translator. Subtraction is achieved by the addition of the complement.

SPEISER, A. P.: Digitale Rechenanlagen. Springer-Verlag, Berlin, Göttingen, Heidelberg 1961.

**Assembler**
Assembler
programme d'assemblage
собиратель

*Program for the translation of a program written in a machine-orientated pseudo-language, into a machine-code.*

An assembler produces a *program written in a *machine-code by substituting each instruction of the program written in the pseudo-language by an instruction in the machine-code or a sub-routine written in the machine-code. The translation process consists of a given correspondence between instructions of the pseudo-language and instructions of the machine-code (cf. *programming language).

**Association**
Assoziation
association
ассоциация

*Provable connections in man as a result of certain patterns of behaviour between stimulus-data and mental images as their psychical correlates or between mental images themselves.*

Most theories of learning start from the assumption that in learning connections are created between stimulus-data and behaviour tendencies. These connections are designated associations. Also, relationships between stimuli and reactions such as are simulated in a *perceptron, a class of cybernetic instruments by ROSENBLATT and his colleagues, or even in the *learning matrix of STEINBUCH, are called associations. Of especial interest in psychological research are associations between different mental images. In most of the experiments in this field test subjects are given words to which they must react by naming their spontaneous ideas. An extensive agreement has been found between the responses of various test subjects. It is assumed that the connections which are thereby shown play a decisive role in the creation of thought processes. The analysis of the type of relation between the stimulus-word and the reaction-word shows a preponderance of an antithesis-relation in adults. In children, or in a tired condition, or under the influence of alcohol the number of reactions using similar sounding words increases (Klang-association).

The reaction time in these types of experiment clearly shows a stochastic dependency on the *frequency of the respective relation. Particularly short reaction times are found not only with the most common associations, but moreover also when the range of possible reactions is limited by some instruction (such as: 'Give the opposite'). This is termed a *controlled* association, in contrast to *free* association. Both results are compatible by the assumption that the reaction time is dependent on the *entropy of the possible reactions of the scheme with a given stimulus-word.

Association experiments are used predominantly for the comprehension of connotations of concepts (cf. *semantic differential) and for gaining a diagnostically important insight into the individual structures of associative connections.

ESTES, W. K.: Toward a statistical theory of learning. Psychological Review 65 (1958). HILGARD, E. R.: Theories of learning. Appleton-Century Crofts, New York, 1956. ROSENBLATT, F.: The Perceptron: a probabilistic model for information storage and organization in the brain. Psychological Review 6/5 (1958).

**Ataxia**
Ataxie
ataxie
атаксия; некоординированность движений

*Disturbances in the co-ordination of*

*voluntary movements connected with damage of the pertinent control system.* This may be injured in the layer of proprioceptive sensibility (tabetic ataxia, syndrome of the long fibres of DEJERDIN) as well as in the area of the cerebellum (cerebellar ataxia) or of the labyrinthine mechanisms for posture control (ataxia of the inner ear).
Ataxia is rarer when there is damage to the medial surface of the frontal lobes (BURN's frontal ataxia) or of the corpus callosum cerebri (ZINGERLE). A distinction is made between static ataxia (in connection with the control of muscle contractions which are responsible for posture) and dynamic ataxia, which is evident in the execution of voluntary movements.

**Autocorrelation function**
Autokorrelationsfunktion
fonction d'autocorrélation
автокорреляционная функция

Autocorrelation function is the *correlation function of a stationary random (stochastic) process (with the parameter quantity $T = (-\infty, \infty)$ for example):

$$\varphi(\tau) = E\{X_t X_{t+\tau}\} = \lim_{T\to\infty} \frac{1}{2T} \int_{-T}^{T} X_t X_{t+\tau} dt.$$

DAVENPORT, W. B.; ROOT, W. L.: An Introduction to the Theory of Random Signals and Noise. McGraw Hill, New York 1958.

**Automation**
Automation
automation
автоматизация

*Combination of automatic processes which replaces work done by people, especially in the field of industry. Automation is interpreted in different ways by different authors.*
(1) Automation is the execution by machines of certain mental tasks. (2) Automation is the use of automata to raise the economic efficiency of a business.
The use of automata is called automation. Moreover, when these automata, as individual units of a system, are combined by automatic processes in such a way that the whole system is under its own control, then this too is automation. Through the development of automation we have in the last few years experienced a new industrial boom. The first industrial revolution (in the nineteenth century) replaced the power of the worker by a machine which controlled the tool; the second industrial revolution replaces the brain-power of the worker (calculation, control, etc.).

WIENER, N.: Mensch und Menschmaschine. Metzner, Frankfurt/M. 1952.

**Automaton**
Automat
automate; mécanisme automatique
автомат

*Machine whose actions are produced by automatic control: also the mathematical *model which serves to describe this machine (cf. *automaton, finite; *TURING machines). By automation one understands the taking over by automatons of actions previously carried out by humans.*
In mathematical theory, the behaviour of automatons is described by the use of *Boolean algebra. Mathematical methods permit the selection of the most economical automatons from those of similar performance. Auto-control is regulated by a *program.

**Automaton, finite**
endlicher Automat
automate finalisé
конечный автомат

*Mathematical model for the description of sequential circuits and neuron networks which possess a finite number of discrete states.*

A finite automaton can be considered as a 'black box' which answers questions by 'yes' or 'no'. The questions are finite sequences of characters of a finite *alphabet. The characters are read by the automaton sequentially. A finite automaton has a finite number of possible internal states. One state is called the original state. Every further state is clearly defined by the preceding state and the character read in this state. The states fall into two classes, $R$ and $F$. In each state the automaton shows (e.g. by the flashing or non-flashing of a lamp) to which class the state belongs. If, after reading a series of characters, the automaton is in a state for the $R$ class, then this is to be taken as the answer 'yes'. A finite automaton with the alphabet

$$A = \{a_1 \ldots, a_m\}$$

and the state-set

$$Q = \{q_1 \ldots, q_n\}$$

can be represented by a diagram.

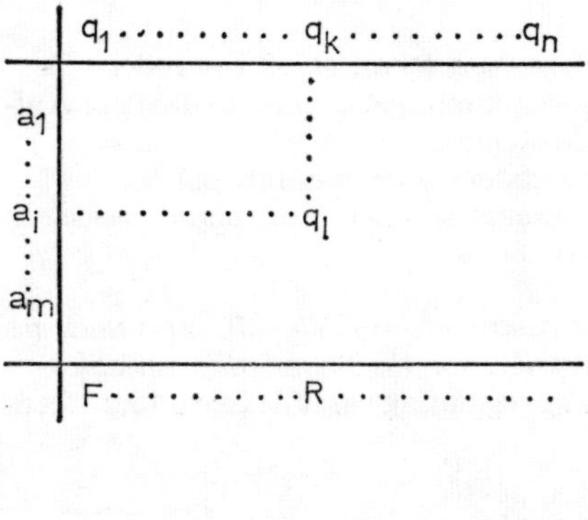


If the character $a_i$ is read in the state $q_k$ then the automaton goes over to state $q_l$. The last section of the table gives the class division.

A *graph can replace a table. Points on the plain correspond to states, and arrows to state transitions. So state $q_k$ is connected with state $q_i$ by the arrow $a_i$. The set of all characters-sequences which lead the automaton from the original state to a state in class $R$ is called the behaviour of the automaton. Automata with the same behaviour give the same responses to the same input-sequences. For every finite automaton there is one of the same behaviour which has a minimal number of states.

A set of character-sequences represents exactly the behaviour of a finite automaton if it (the set) is regular. The concept 'regular set' is defined thus:

1 Every finite set $U$ of character sequences is regular.
2 The set $UV$ of character-sequences which are formed by the concatenation of the sequences from the regular sequences of $U$ and $V$ is regular.
3 The union $U \cup V$ of two regular sets $U$ and $V$ is regular
4 The iterate $U^* = L \cup U \cup UU \cup UUU \cup \ldots$ ($L$ is the empty set) of a regular set $U$ is regular
5 No set is regular unless it is on the basis of 1, 2, 3 or 4.

SHANNON, C. E.; MCCARTHY, J.: Automata Studies, Princeton University Press, 1956. GILL, A.: Introduction to the Theory of Finite-State Machines. McGraw Hill, New York 1962.

**Autonomic nervous system**
autonomes Nervensystem
grand sympathique
——

*The autonomic nervous system consists of the total of peripheral nerve-paths which ennervate the smooth muscle system and glands.*

The autonomic nervous system comprises the sympathetic system, which arises in the thoracic and lumbar regions of the spinal cord, and the parasympathetic system, which is formed from the cranial parasympathetic outflow and the sacral-parasympathetic outflow. These two systems are distinguished by both anatomical distribution and by chemical function: schematically all preganglionic fibres are cholinergic, the sympathetic post-ganglionic fibres are adrenergic and the para-sympathetic post-ganglionic fibres are cholinergic.

In contrast to the *central nervous system which influences conscious activities, the autonomic nervous system assures the control of the vegetative functions.

**Axon**

Axon

axone

аксон

*Stimulus conductor leading from the neuron.*

Nerve cells or *neurons consist of a cell-body, several *dendrites which branch off from it and a longer fibre (the axon) leading to an effector-organ or to other nerve cells; there the axon splits up into several synaptic ends (cf. *synapse). In lower animals these fibres are non-medullated, i.e. they have practically no myelin-sheath isolating the axon from the surrounding tissue; they have a continuous stimulus-conduction and therefore conduct correspondingly slowly—approx. 1 m/sec. In vertebrates, axons do have an isolating myelin (fatty)-sheath which is interrupted at regular intervals at the node of RANVIER. (cf. *action potential at a node of RANVIER). The primary stimulus-process in this nerve fibre is limited to the nodes (saltatory stimulus-conduction) and occurs at a much greater speed—5–100 m/sec., since between the nodes (internodes) the stimulus-conduction is not dependent on chemical processes and relatively slow ion movements.

ECCLES, J. C.: The physiology of nerve cells. The Johns Hopkins Press, Baltimore 1957. Handbook of Physiology. Vol. 1 Neurophysiology. (Ed. FIELD, J.; MAGOUN, H. W.; HALL, V. E.) Am. Physiol. Soc., Williams and Wilkins Co, Baltimore 1959.

# B

**Band width**

Bandbreite

bande passante

ширина полосы частот; полоса пропускания

*See* *Frequency range

**Bang-bang servo; on-off controller**

Zweipunktregler; Ein-Aus-Regler; Auf-Zu-Regler

régulateur à deux points paliers

двухпозиционный или двухступенчатый регулятор

*A controller in which only two values are possible for the *regulating variable.*

The regulating variable (see under *feedback control system) is adjusted alternately to one or the other value (i.e. index value or actual value) corresponding to the deviation of the actual value from the index value of the controlled condition. With the same rhythm the controlled condition hovers around the *index value. In temperature control, for example, the temperature can be measured with a contact thermometer, which switches off the heating when the index value is reached, and switches it on when the temperature sinks below the index value.

OLDENBOURG, R. C.; SARTORIUS, H.: Dynamik selbsttätiger Regelungen. Band 1. R. Oldenbourg, München 1951. OPPELT, W.: Kleines Handbuch technischer Regelvorgänge. Verlag-Chemie, Weinheim 1960.

**Behaviour determination; regulation of behaviour**
Verhaltenssteuerung
processus régulateurs du comportement
регулирование поведения

*The tracing back of the variability of patterns of behaviour of an organism to definable classes of determining conditions.*

The idea that the behaviour of an organism can be traced back to a set of determining conditions which in practice can never be completely registered is one of the basic principles of psychological research. HOFSTÄTTER gives at least six distinguishable classes; inborn constitution, acquired need, results of learning processes, ideas of social values, and the perceived picture of the situation at hand. These interacting conditions determine behaviour and set an *index value of the condition which the determined behaviour will produce. In many cases this index value cannot be equated to a sort of 'psychic *homeostasis'. If an organism has shown determined behaviour, then *perception enables some control over the difference between the state reached as a consequence of the behaviour and the appropriate index value. If a deviation is registered, then one or more of the conditions determining the behaviour alter by a learning process. This leads to an alteration of the index value or of the *probability of the behaviour shown in an identical situation, or to both. Behaviour determination can therefore be represented as a process in a special model of a *feedback control system.

HOFSTÄTTER, P. R.: Theoretische Grundlagen der Verhaltenssteuerung. Psychologische Rundschau 13/3 (1962).

**Behaviourism**
Behaviorismus
béhaviorisme, théorie du comportement
бихевиорисм

*Defines the observable behaviour of organisms in describable situations as a subject of psychology.*

Behaviourism was first developed by WATSON (1908). He turned against, amongst other things, the old lines taken by psychology which regarded the investigation of experience and sensation as a subject of their science. Experience and sensation cannot however be regarded as behaviour in the sense of behaviourism, as it does not satisfy the demands for independent observation by various observers. The task of behaviouristic psychology is the comprehension of functional connections between *stimuli and *reactions. In this, nervous, visceral or the motor reactions are often considered as new stimuli in stimulus-reaction chains. The aim of molecular behaviourism is the most complete comprehension possible of all members of chains of this type. In present-day psychology a moderate molar behaviourism plays an important role. It looks for *random or *stochastic dependencies between output stimuli, which are given outside the organism, and end-reactions by which the organism makes contact with its surroundings. The organism itself is considered as a *black box*. For unobserved processes in the organism, hypotheses are developed. Models of this type should be constructed as simply as possible, should permit no possibility of contradiction, must embrace all phenomena of a well-defined area and lead to forecasts of behaviour (hypotheses, theories, theorems) which empirically are incapable of being falsified. Behaviouristic psychology, in its research methods and way of thinking, has the character of an experimental natural science on the basis of a hypothetico-deductive methodology.

HOFSTÄTTER, P. R.: Psychologie. Fischer Lexikon 6, Frankfurt/M. 1957.

**Beta waves**
Beta-Wellen
ondes bèta
бета—лучи

*Low amplitude sinusoidal waves in the human *electroencephalogram (stronger when they occur in *electrocorticogram).*
The amplitude of beta waves is 50–100 $\mu$V, their average frequency 14–25 c/s. They are produced asynchronously in both hemispheres, mainly in irregular bursts. Their origin is on the level of the medial and frontal regions.
Beta waves disappear during sleep, and can be blocked during consciousness by a movement—clenching the fist, passive mobility of the arm. Beta waves are connected with the motor function; they do not exist before the age of 13–15 years.

**Binary**
Binär
binaire
бинарный

Binary is the characteristic of a system which can only accept two (different) states or values ('alternatives'). This means that the result of tossing a coin is binary: heads or tails.
Numbers whose position-representation has radix 2 are called binary numbers. Such a system needs only the two digits 0 and 1 to represent its numbers. Electrotechnical conditions are also binary: switches and relays are either in the states 'on' or 'off'. Such states can be interpreted with the help of a binary number system.

**Binary digit**
Binärzeichen
bit
бинарная единица; двоичная цифра

**Character from a *repertory of two signs.*
In information processing the following are used:
1 for the written representation of binary numbers normally the figures 1 and 0. Where confusion with decimal figures is possible, one may choose any other pair of characters, e.g. *Q* and *L* (occasionally the letters *O* and *L* are used).
2 for technically concrete representation the following are chosen: e.g. punching/non-punching (punch cards, punched tape), voltage/no voltage, positive voltage/negative voltage, current/no current (switch positions), magnetization-directions opposed to each other.

In propositional logic (cf. *propositional functions) the abbreviations *T* (true) and *F* (false) are usual.

**Binary number**
Dualzahl
nombre binaire
двоичные числа

*A number whose position-representation uses the radix of 2.*

Example: the number 57 is represented in the positional system with the radix 10 which is familiar to us as:

$$5 \times 10^1 + 7 \times 10^0 = 57.$$

In a system with the radix 2 it is represented as follows:

$$1 \times 2^5 + 1 \times 2^4 + 1 \times 2^3 + 0 \times 2^2 + 0 \times 2^1 + 1 \times 2^0 = 111001.$$

The binary system needs only the figures 0 and 1 for number representation, recently designated *O* and *L* to enable differentiation. The advantages are: simple arithmetic and simple technical realization (switch, relay, valves in computers). The disadvantages are: relatively small numbers specified by many figures, and translation into and from the decimal system is very time-consuming.

As early as 1703 LEIBNITZ recognized the advantages of binary numbers, and they were introduced into the technology of *computers by K. ZUSE. In computers they simplify construction and increase the speed of calculation.

**Biological regulation; control and regulation of biological phenomena**
Regelung, biologische
régulation biologique
биорегулирование

*The ability of living organisms to maintain certain values or states approximately constant (i.e. usually within fairly close limits, as exceeding these limits would mean serious disturbances for the process of life). Biological regulation also includes all methods and mechanisms by which this is achieved.*

After C. BERNARD had pointed out the constancy of the internal milieu, it was recognized that the maintenance of the physiological state, under the name *homeostasis, was one of the most important subjects of biological research. One must also mention the theory of biological control based on R. WAGNER (1925) and the general principle of feedback control systems introduced in 1940 by H. SCHMIDT.

To-day it is thought that biological control occurs on the same principles as technical control (cg. *feedback control system); however, the system is far more complicated, as a great many factors participate in the regulation, so that one can in fact talk of the reciprocal action and hierarchy of several feedback control systems. The controlling signals are transmitted in higher forms of life by, amongst other things, the nervous system and hormones (H. DRISCHEL uses the expression 'vegetative system' for the total of components of an organism which participates in control). Animals are open systems, and the maintenance of equilibria can be regarded as the basis of metabolic regulation. Moreover, the regulation of growth is an important special case of biological regulation. The following may be regarded as examples of controlled conditions in physiology: level of sugar in the blood, concentration of hydrogen ions and body temperature (in warm-blooded animals). Even in elementary processes of the single cell, where one cannot talk of nervous or hormonal conductions, several control mechanisms can be found (e.g. by the feedback of chemical reactions). On the other hand, processes such as directional and positional stabilization, keeping the body in an upright position, or, more generally, the achievement of a goal, despite external disturbances, could not occur without some sort of regulation. These few examples may suffice to establish that the cybernetic principle of regulation by feedback is of fundamental importance for the whole of biology, including psychology of behaviour.

MITTELSTAEDT, H. (ed.): Regelungsvorgänge in der Biologie. R. Oldenbourg. München 1956. DRISCHEL, H.: Baustein einer dynamischen Theorie der vegetativen Regulation. Wissenschaftliche Zeitschrift der Universität Greifswald Jahrgang II (1952/53). Mathematisch-naturwissenschaftliche Reihe, No. 2. WAGNER, R.: Probleme und Beispiele biologischer Regelung. Thieme, Stuttgart 1954.

**Bit**
Bit
bit
бит; бинарная единица; двоичная цифра

*Element of binary *encoding unit of *information.*

Bit (from 'binary digit') denotes an element in a binary code. If for example $E$ is encoded by 01010, then one says that 5 bits have been used for its encoding; 'bit' also means the unit of *information introduced by SHANNON after a suggestion by TUKEY. 1 bit is that information which contains an event contained within a probability field in which it (i.e. the event) has the probability $\frac{1}{2}$.

SHANNON, C. E.: A mathematical Theory of Communication. Bell System Technical Journal 27 (1948) pp. 379–423, 623–56.

**Blockdiagram**
Blockschaltbild
organigramme; schéma fonctionnel
блок—схема; блочная схема; скелетная схема

*Graphic method for the symbolic representation of functional relationships. It greatly facilitates the surveying of complicated systems.*

A blockdiagram consists of rectangles, triangles, circles, etc. and so-called blocks which are connected by arrowed lines. All blockdiagrams can be placed between two extremes. (1) Abbreviated or simplified blockdiagram. In this case each block can represent a piece of apparatus or a set of equations. The connecting lines show which blocks influence each other, and the arrows in which direction the influence takes place (see diagram 1).

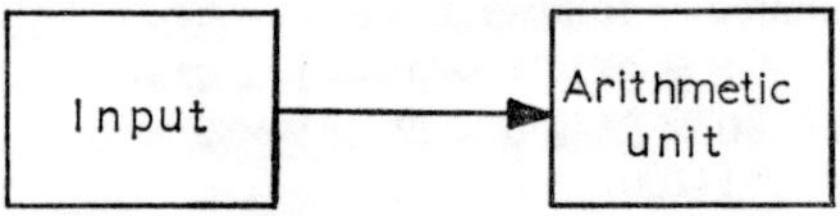


1 Blockdiagram

(2) Detailed or exact block diagram; in this case each connecting line represents a physical or mathematical variable. The lines which flow into one block are called the input variables of this block, and the lines leading outwards the output variables. The block itself represents the function which produces the output variables (see diagram 2).

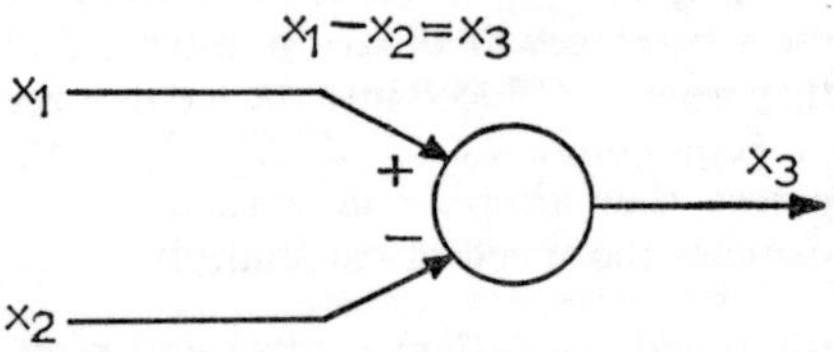


2 Blockdiagram

The representation of the block is so chosen that it gives some hint of the block function. In some cases the complementary type of representation is also used and called the signal-flow diagram. In this the functions are represented by connecting lines and the variables by circles (see diagram 3).

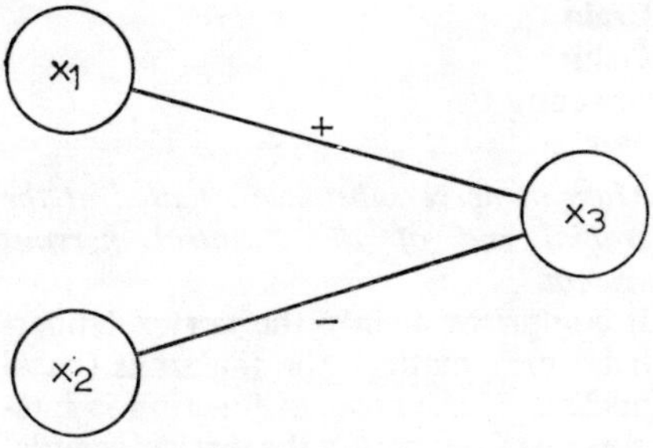


3 Blockdiagram

HASSENSTEIN, B.: Die bisherige Rolle der Kybernetik in der biologischen Forschung. Naturw. Rdsch. 13 (1960) pp. 319–55, 373–82, 419–24. OPPELT, W.: Kleines Handbuch technischer Regelvorgänge. Verlag Chemie, Weinheim 1956.

**Boolean algebra**
BOOLEsche Algebra
algèbre Booléenne
алгебра Буля

*Formal system (cf. *languages, formalized), with two binary operations. Interpretations are set theory, propositional logic and switch-theory.*

A set $B$ of elements in which two binary operations $+$ and $\cdot$ are admitted, is a Boolean algebra if the following conditions are fulfilled:

(1) the operations are commutative:

$$a + b = b + a, a \cdot b = b \cdot a$$

(2) each operation possesses a unit-element:

$$a + 0 = a, a \cdot 1 = a$$

(3) the operations are distributive:

$$a \cdot (b + c) = (a \cdot b) + (a \cdot c),$$
$$a + (b \cdot c) = (a + b) \cdot (a + c)$$

(4) for every $a$ there is an $a'$ with

$$a + a' = 1, a \cdot a' = 0$$

The symbol '=' is not an operation in the formal system, but belongs to syntax-language (cf. *languages, formalized).

From the conditions (1)–(4) results the associativity of the operations

$$(a + b) + c = a + (b + c),$$
$$(a \cdot b) \cdot c = a \cdot (b \cdot c),$$

and the uniqueness of the element $a'$ and also $(a')' = a$. From reasons of symmetry the duality-principle is valid: a formula remains correct if the functions $+$ and $\cdot$ as well as the unit-elements 0 and 1 are interchanged. Important identities are:

$$a + a = a, a + 1 = 1,$$
$$a + (a \cdot b) = a,$$
$$0' = 1, (a \cdot b)' = a' + b'$$

and the dual cases:

$$a \cdot a = a, a \cdot 0 = 0, a \cdot (a + b) = a,$$
$$1' = 0, (a + b)' = a' \cdot b'$$

A Boolean function $f(\alpha)$ is an expression which can be formed from the variable $\alpha$ and the constants $a, b, \ldots$ from $B$ by a finite number of operations of the type $+$, $\cdot$, and $'$.

For every Boolean function the following decomposition is valid:

$$f(\alpha) = f(1) \cdot \alpha + f(0) \cdot \alpha'$$

If follows that two Boolean functions $f(\alpha)$ and $g(\alpha)$ are exactly identical if $f(0) = g(0)$ and $f(1) = g(1)$. Corresponding considerations are valid for functions in several variables. By this, every Boolean function can be changed into an additive and dually into a multiplicative normal form. An interpretation of Boolean algebra is the algebra of sets. The sub-sets of a set form a Boolean algebra with respect to the union $\cup$ and the intersection $\cap$. Every Boolean algebra can be represented by certain subsets of a set with the connectives $\cap$ and $\cup$.

In propositional logic all propositions are assumed to have one of the two truth-values 'true' or 'false'. With *disjunction and *conjunction as operations the propositions form a Boolean algebra. It follows from the above decomposition in connection with the extentionality of the logical connectives that every *propositional function can be represented by a truth-table. If a truth-value is assigned to every proposition, then one obtains a mapping into a two-elemental Boolean algebra which consists of the symbols $T$ and $F$ (i.e. true and false).

In predicate logic propositions are formed from nouns and predicates. A proposition is true if and only if the predicate in question applies to the object defined by the noun. The predicate can be represented by the propositional form $p(x)$ (with a free variable $x$). By $\forall x\, p(x)$) is denoted the proposition that $p$ is true for every $x$ of a certain class of objects and from $\exists x\, p(x)$ the proposition that $p$ is true for at least one $x$. The quantifiers $\exists x$ and $\forall x$ are called existential and universal quantifiers. In a more restricted predicate calculus the use of quantifiers is limited to sets of objects. A third interpretation of Boolean algebra is *switching algebra. Switches have two stable states. The functions $+$ and $\cdot$ denote parallel and series-switching. Each circuit is described by a Boolean function. In minimizing switching circuits use is made of the set theoretical interpretation of Boolean algebra. The notation for the connectives is not uniform. In switching algebra one finds, for example, instead of $+$, $\cdot$ and $'$ the logical symbols $\vee$, $\wedge$, $-$, or $\vee$, &, $\sim$.

WHITESITT, J. E.: Boolean Algebra and its Applications. Addison-Wesley Publ. Co., Reading Mass./London 1961. LORENZEN, P.: Formale Logik. Gruyter, Berlin 1958. WEYH, U.: Elemente der Schaltungsalgebra. R. Oldenbourg, München 1961.

**Brain**
Gehirn
cerveau
мозг

*Mass of nerve substance situated at the cranial end of the *central nervous system.*

It comprises mainly the cortex (superficial grey matter), the thalamus (basal nucleus whose especial function is integration of the brain), the lenticulocaudal nuclei (which play an important part in the regulation of muscle-tone, of voluntary movements and posture), the hypothalamus (despite its small volume an essential part of the autonomic system). In family history there is clearly a relation between the differentiation of the brain and that of psychic behaviour. This does not mean, however, that cerebral structures produce consciousness: how can the mind have a physical location?

**BUNSEN-ROSCOE law**
BUNSEN-ROSCOE-Gesetz
loi de BUNSEN-ROSCOE
закон Бунзена—Роско

From experiments on the photo-chemical production of chloro-oxyhydrogen gas BUNSEN and ROSCOE (1857) deduced the law that the photo-chemical production $A$ depends only on the product from the intensity $I$ of the radiation and the length of radiation $t$, in other words:

$$A = f(I \times t).$$

This law is valid for a large number of photo-chemical reactions in limited fields of $I$ and $t$, but not without exception. For example, for the blacking of photo-plates the following is valid

$$S = \log (c \times I^{\gamma_1} \times t^{\gamma_2})$$

Here $I$ and $t$ are not interchangeable.

**Calling sequence**
Rampe
séquence d'appel
Rampe
———

*Connected with a *jump-instruction to a *sub-routine, a group of parameters which deliver necessary information to the sub-routine.*

Frequently sub-routines are kept so flexible that some parameters only need to be known at entry. Examples of parameters of this type are: addresses of *operands, length of number-fields, values of variables, etc. These values are taken up by the sub-routine at locations known to it. As the exit address in the main routine is known to the sub-routine, parameters are stored in cells which follow the jump-out instructions, i.e. they are placed ready in a calling sequence. The sub-routine can calculate the addresses of these cells and take over the parameters. The sub-routine returns to the main routine after the calling sequence.

**Capacity** (I); **capacitance**
Kapazität
capacité
емкость

*A physical value, the capacity of a condensor.*

If a direct voltage $U$ is applied to two electrodes which are insulated from each other by a non-conductor (i.e. a capacitor) then they receive the electrical charge $Q$. This charge is proportional to the voltage applied:

$$Q \sim U$$
$$Q = C \cdot U$$

The proportionality factor

$$C = \frac{Q}{U}$$

is called the capacity of the condensor. This is not dependent on the current applied, but only on the geometrical shape and arrangement of the electrodes, as well as on the characteristics of the material of the non-conductor. It is measured in Farad (F). Usually the following sub-units are used:

$$1\text{pf (picofarad)} = 10^{-12}F$$
$$1\text{nf (nanofarad)} = 10^{-9}F$$
$$1\mu\text{f (microfarad)} = 10^{-6}F$$

KÜPFMÜLLER, K.: Einführung in die theoretische Elektrotechnik. Springer-Verlag, Berlin, Göttingen, Heidelberg 1957. WESTPHAL, W. H.: Physik. Springer-Verlag, Berlin, Göttingen, Heidelberg 1956. GERTHSEN, Chr.: Physik. Springer-Verlag, Berlin, Göttingen, Heidelberg 1956.

**Capacity** (II); **storage capacity**
Kapazität
capacité de mémoire
емкость памяти

*Size of a store.*

The capacity of a *store is a measure of the amount of information which can be held in the store. It may be given in *bit, *characters, or *words.

SPEISER, A. P.: Digitale Rechenanlagen. Springer-Verlag, Berlin, Göttingen, Heidelberg 1961.

**Captain**
Kapitän
capitaine
капитан

*Paradigm for the level or instance of goal-setting (normative decision) in a social-science system (see *social science); one of the four cybernetical levels (see *cybernetics, levels of).*

The transition from a technical science to actual techniques consists of an effective approach to a pre-given goal (see *index value, set-point). A goal is represented and set by a character with a pragmatic *semiotic-aspect; the assertion of the binding-force of the goal is an *imperative. Its binding force can be logically traced back to facts, although other goal-settings must continually be referred to (deduction of steering instructions by the pilot from actual and index-values). As syllogisms are only avoidable if non-deductable basic-imperatives (fundamental commands, final goals, postulates) are accepted, (although it is not the job of the pilot-level to confirm these), then the level of the captain must be introduced as the source of the goal (imperatives).

This corresponds to the view of a system which observes its own information-reception and information-processing, and in so doing realizes that it does not necessarily have to steer towards the goal towards which it is at present steering, but that it can steer towards another. This presupposes that the behaviour of the system is not completely determined by the information at present being recorded and by the information gained from experience which it has stored, but also depends on index-values (motives, voluntary decisions, resolutions) which are felt to be variable at any time without external influence. So long as a system of this sort is active, it presupposes *freedom, even if in a contemplative state it feels it is casually determined (i.e. not by aims). As conscious information-processing in man corresponds to a system of this sort, the existence of goals (and hence of captain-decisions) is an essential precondition in informational sciences.

On the other hand, the level of captain does not exist in a technical system. Machines do not determine their goals themselves, but are constructed by the organization of all available materials in such a way that they help to achieve those goals set by man (cf. *techniques). This is also true in the highest stage of cybernetical machine-techniques, where it is a question of the technical imitation of the function of the *pilot type 3 by self-organizing machines (cf. *self-organization). For only if the index values are pre-given can any judgement whatever be made as to whether such systems adapt their behaviour to their environment in such a way that the index values are approached. It lies in the nature of machines that they do not have a captain-level—this is supplied by the operator.

In natural machines or other natural systems, (e.g. organisms), the existence of a captain-level within or outside the system can generally be contested. The scientific investigation of these systems can be carried out in a strictly casual-analytical way. Even non-vitalic biology permits teleology as a *regulative principle of research*. For heuristic reasons biological cybernetics considers it especially useful to regard the systems which it has to investigate as if captain-decisions (approach to index values) should be realized in them (especially by closed-loop control). But this leads to the dispute as to whether the subsequent casual-analytical (Darwinistic) solution of the hypothetical goals of organs of living creatures is not, in principle, also possible for the goals of man, so that for the external observer (never for man, as he is himself pursuing goals) a captain-level would never exist.

It follows from the definitions of *techniques and captain that there can be a technical imitation of the functions of *oarsman, *steersman and *pilot but no complete technical imitation of the function of captain. For every technical measure helps to achieve a definite goal by methods other than by direct personal effort. To strive for an objectivization (technical imitation) of the captain-function would amount to not wanting to determine the goal oneself. The goal of not setting any more goals (but to achieve them technically by dicing and socially by voting) is, however, *per se* a goal which has been set and which can be revoked at any time.

FRANK, H.: Über die wissenschaftliche und die ideologische Komponente im Mass der Freiheit. Zeitschrift für Philos. Forschung, Band XVI (1962).

**Centering (character centering)**
*See* *Character centering

**Central nervous system**
Zentralnervensystem
système nerveux central
центральная нервная система

The central nervous system consists of two parts: the brain and the spinal cord. A distinction is made between the twelve pairs of cranial nerves which arise in the brain and the 31 pairs (in humans) of spinal nerves. With the exception of the optic nerves, these, together with their sub-divisions, form the peripheral nervous system, whose main function consists of conducting in both directions the information processed in the central nervous system.
The central nervous system contains white and grey matter. The latter is formed by a large collection of cell-bodies of the *neurons, while the white matter consists of *axons which conduct nerve-pulses over distances which are quite long compared to the dimensions of the cell-bodies. The main function of the spinal cord can be regarded as the transmission of information, although it also produces motor activity as a reaction to sensory stimuli. Lower animals still show complex behaviour even when the brain is removed. The great brain is surrounded by the *cerebral cortex which is a layer of grey matter 2–3 mm thick. By electrical stimulation of the cerebral cortex during brain operations, it was shown that discrete centres of the cortex are connected to special functions in various parts of the body, such as sight, hearing, sensation and motor activity. No special function for the frontal centres could be ascertained by electrical stimulation, yet it must be remembered that injuries to this area may alter personality. It is highly probable that the grey matter is concerned with the phenomenon of *intelligence and *learning; the physical nature of these is not really known.

ROHRACHER, H.: Die Arbeitsweise des Gehirns u. die psychischen Vorgänge. J. A. Barth, München 1953.

**Cerebellum**
Kleinhirn
cervelet
мозжечок

*Nerve-mass situated in the fossa occipitales at the exit of the large transmission-pathways. The cerebellum receives sensory, mainly proprioceptive information, controls movements and the tone of muscles.*
The function of the cerebellum lies in the maintenance of normal co-ordination of the muscles and the continuous control of motor-activity dependent on the information which is delivered from the proprioceptive receptors, as well as from the collaterals of the cortical motor-neurons (cortical-pontocerebellar path). In addition, the cerebellum performs the function of a *feed-back

centre; its efferent paths reach the motor-centres of the cerebral cortex and also the nuclei of the extra-pyramidal paths.
The clinical symptoms of injuries to the cerebellum are disturbances such as intention-tremor, dysmetria and adiadochokinesis.

**Cerebral Cortex**
*See* *Cortex (of brain)

**Channel**
Kanal
canal
канал

*A physical system which can transmit *signals in a spatial or temporal direction.*
A physical system in which a signal occurs is called a channel if at least one of the following conditions is fulfilled:
1 The signal can be produced by external influences on a sub-system of the physical system under discussion (i.e. channel input), and be observed—perhaps in a changed form—in at least one further sub-system (i.e. channel output) which is at some physical distance from it. (Space-channel ≡ transfer channel).
2 The signal can be produced by external influence on the physical system at a time $t_i$ and be observed in this system at a later time $t_k$. (Time-channel, e.g. *store and *memory). If both of these conditions are fulfilled, then one talks of a time-space-channel.
Mathematically, a channel $(A, p_x, B)$ is given by the input-alphabet $A$, by the output-alphabet $B$ and the family of probability-distributions

$$p_x(S) = P\{y \in S / x \in A^I\}$$

In this, $x$ is a *message of the *message-space $A^I$ of input-messages, and $y \in B^I$ a message from the message-space $B^I$ of output-messages.

FRANK, H.: Zum Problem des vorbewussten Gedächtnisses. Grundlagenstudien Bd. 2, Heft 1 (1962). GRELL, H. (ed.): Arbeiten zur Informationstheorie. Bd. 1 & 2, Akademie-Verlag, Berlin 1957.

**Channel, stationary**
Kanal, stationärer
canal stationnaire
стационарный канал

A channel is called stationary if it is invariant (cf. *invariance) to shifts in its statistical characteristics. If $T$ is the shift-operator:

$$Tx = x',\ x = \{\ldots x_{-1}, x_0, x_1, x_2, \ldots\}$$
$$x' = \{\ldots x_0, x_1, x_2, x_3, \ldots\}$$

then $q_{Tx}(TS) = q_x(S)$ should be the probability distributions of the channel for all input-messages $x$ and all $q$-measurable sets $S$ of output messages.

GRELL, H. (ed.): Arbeiten zur Informationstheorie I. Dtsch. Vlg. d. Wissenschaften, Berlin 1957. HENZE, E.: Einführung in die Informationstheorie. Beiheft 3. Elektronische Datenverarbeitung. 1963.

**Channel capacity**
Kanalkapazität
capacité du canal
пропускная способность канала (связи); емкость канала

*Upper limit of the tranfer-rate of *messages, i.e. a measure for the *information which a *channel can store or can transfer per time-unit or per character.*
A time-channel which retains messages as signals from a time $t_i$ to a time $t_k$ has as its channel capacity the upper limit of the average *transinformation. The corresponding definition is applied to space-channels (transfer capacity or average transinformation-flow in *bit per character*), or it is divided by the average time-delay of the transferred characters (transfer capacity in *bit per time-unit*).

Informationstheorie/Begriffe, NTG Entwurf 1962 NTZ Heft 1 (1963) pp. 46–9.

**Character; sign**
Zeichen
signe
знак; сигнал

*That which refers to something else (the so-called *referent, i.e. the source or meaning of the character), or more precisely the function of the reference itself. A component part of a *message. Examples: letters, mathematical symbols, gestures, or a flag on the palace of a head of state as a sign that he or she is in residence.*
A character is always connected with the *perception of a *signal which, deputizing for another perception-object, refers to this as the so-called referent. This function of referring, or of showing, can be equated to a character. Also (as in the normal mathematical definition of cardinal numbers) a character can be defined as the set of signals which in a given situation are equivalent to a given signal, i.e. which refer to the same referent. In both cases, a clear distinction must be made between signals and characters: a character, not the signal, exceeds the range of competence of traditional physical information-theory, in so far as it must take into account not only the physically definable signal but also its receiver, whether the signal is as a location of the referent-function of the signal or as a criterion of the equivalence of different signals.
Characters are classified into 'indications', or 'signs of . . .', and 'representations', or 'signs for . . .'; each of these is further sub-divided. In the former, the cause is the referent; in the latter, the meaning allotted to it (its designate).
Three *semiotic aspects are distinguished in a character or sign: the syntactical, the semantical and the pragmatical. This distinction roughly corresponds to that made between *semiotics in *syntax, *semantics and pragmatics.

MALDONADO, T.: Beitrag zur Terminologie der Semiotik. Hochschule für Gestaltung, Ulm 1961.
FRANK, H.: Kybernetik, Brücke zwischen den Wissenchaften. Umschau, Frankfurt Part 1, 2nd edn. 1962.

**Character centering**
Zeichenzentrierung
centrage des signes
центрирование (центровка) образов

*The reproduction of a *character in a position most suitable for recognition.*
In order to be as economical as possible in recognition circuits, in many types of *character readers the character is put into a position in the reproduction store which is precisely defined for the character concerned.

STEINBUCH, K.; KAZMIERCZAK, H.: Grundlagen und Anwendungen der automatischen Zeichenerkennung. In: Jahrbuch des elektrischen Fernmeldewesens. 1960/61.

**Character reader; reading machine**
Zeichenleser; Lesemaschine
machine à lire
читающий автомат

*Character readers are machines which automatically allot the appropriate meaning to hand- or machine-written characters.*
There are two types:
1 Optical character readers: the character which is in optical contrast is scanned, usually stored, and then recognized by one of these processes: stencil-process, probe-process, correlation-process, potential-process, stroke-analysis, contour-sequence-process, etc.
2 Magnetic character readers: the printing of specially shaped characters with magnetic ink greatly simplifies the scanning and recognition process. This is limited mainly to a one-dimensional

scanning process which produces a voltage which varies according to the characters scanned. Recognition normally occurs after a correlation process. Magnetic character readers are of the greatest importance in the work of banks, where the highest accuracy in recognition is essential.

STEINBUCH, K.; KAZMIERCZAK, H.: Grundlagen und Anwendungen der automatischen Zeichenerkennung. In: Jahrbuch des elektrischen Fernmeldewesens. 1960/61. STEINBUCH, K.: Automatische Zeichenerkennung. In: Taschenbuch der Nachrichtenverarbeitung. Springer-Verlag, Berlin, Göttingen, Heidelberg 1962.

**Character recognition; pattern recognition**
Zeichenerkennung, automatische
reconnaissance automatique des signes
распознавание образов; узнавание образов

*The allocation of a meaning to a stimulus-distribution recorded by a suitable receptor.*

The essence of character recognition lies in *one* definite meaning being allotted to whole classes of patterns (invariant classes).

The machine (see *character reader) must therefore not only allot to the prototype of a pattern (letters, numbers, a picture) the meaning given to it, but also recognize all possible disturbed characters (including hand-written ones) which deviate from the prototype.

The process of character recognition consists of the characters in a parallel or series-decision (see *parallel system and *series system) being examined for the existence of certain describing features, and of a meaning being allocated to them on the basis of these existent and non-existent characteristics. Automatic character recognition is simplified by a limitation to certain standardized *type fonts or by printing magnetic characters (cf. *magnetic ink font).

STEINBUCH, K.; KAZMIERCZAK, H.: Grundlagen und Anwendungen der automatischen Zeichenerkennung. In: Jahrbuch des elektrischen Fernmeldewesens. 1960/61.

**Characteristic curve**
Kennlinie
caractéristique
характеристика; характеристическая кривая; график

*Graphic representation of the connection between two physical variables.*

If one measures a variable $I$ (e.g. the current through a *diode) as a function of a second variable $U$ (e.g. the voltage across the diode) and records the function $I = f(U)$ in a co-ordinate system, then the resultant curve is called a characteristic curve.

KÜPFMÜLLER, K.: Einführung in die theoretische Elektrotechnik. Springer-Verlag, Berlin, Göttingen, Heidelberg 1957.

**Chorea**
Chorea
chorée
хорея

*Disease which is characterized by sudden involuntary movements and which affects particularly the neck and limbs.*

The main forms of chorea are acute chorea (SYDENHAM), an infectious aetiology (observable in children and young people), and chronic chorea (HUNTINGDON, an hereditary (and) family disease, accompanied by psychic disturbances in adults). Chorea is connected with injuries to the grey central nuclei adjacent to the neostriatum. An electromyographic plotting of chorea-induced movement localizes the muscle-groups involved, without the participation of antagonistic muscles (in contrast to aetiototic movements).

**Clock; clock generator**
Taktgeber; Taktgenerator
métronome; horloge
главные электрочасы; задающий генератор

A generator producing clock pulses which control the temporal sequence of the program execution in data processing systems.

**Clock track**
Taktspur
trace d'impulsion
тактовая дорожка

A special track in *magnetic drum stores, *magnetic tape stores or *magnetic disc stores which contains clock pulses and serves as a *clock during writing or reading.

**Closed loop control**
*See under* *Feedback control system

**COBOL: common business orientated language**
COBOL
COBOL
кобол

*A problem-orientated *programming language for the treatment of business problems.*

COBOL was created by the American Codasyl-group (Conference on Data Systems Languages) for an easily readable formulation of programmes (with special facilities for data descriptions). The demand for readability leads to a great redundancy in the available instructions. The language used is English, but translations are being worked on by groups which are connected with Codasyl.

A COBOL program consists of a procedure section (containing the instructions of the program), a data section (with description of the applied *input- and *output-instructions), a machine section (containing the description of the computer used) and an identification section (for the naming and documentation of the program). If the computer is changed, only the machine section is altered for the same program. COBOL compilers exist for a whole range of computers, especially for those which can be used for business problems.

Department of Defense: Report to Conference on Data Systems Languages Including Revised Specifications for a Common Business Oriented Language (COBOL), Washington, D.C. 1961. SCHAPPERT, H.: Algorithmische Sprachen—eine Einführung in die Programmsprache COBOL.ADL-Nachrichten, Heft 20, 22, 23 (1962).

**Code**
Code
code
код

*A not necessarily reversible definite relation between two quantities of characters (letters, numbers, symbols), or a formula by which information is encoded. Also the character-system used for this encoding. (In this sense language and script are also code-systems.)*

Two classes of code can be distinguished:

1 non-error-detecting code: in which one tries to get along with a minimum of code-elements (see *encoding) for each code-word, e.g. non-redundant code (see *redundancy). In general the falsification of a code-element in a code-word caused by disturbances leads to another valid code-word, so that code-word-error can remain undetected.

Example:

| Decimal number code | Non-error detecting binary code |
|---|---|
| 0 | 0 0 0 |
| 1 | 0 0 1 |
| 2 | 0 1 0 |
| 3 | 0 1 1 |
| 4 | 1 0 0 |
| 5 | 1 0 1 |
| 6 | 1 1 0 |
| 7 | 1 1 1 |

2 error-detecting code: such codes are distinguished from non-error detecting codes by the increased binary-digit redundancy. Further differences exist between: (*a*) systematic code: a code in which one increases the protection from unknown code-word-errors by the rational addition of redundant code elements to the information-carrying elements of a code-word or block. They permit the detection of code-element-errors (see *error-detection) or their correction (see *error correction). If the statistics of the code-element errors are known (they can be obtained by measurements in the transmission channel), then for a given probability of undetected code-word-errors one can develop optimal codes with regard to transmission speed. (*b*) non systematic code: a differentiation between binary-digits which carry information and those which only contribute to protection is not possible. An example of error-detecting, but in the above sense non-systematic, codes is given by the so-called ($q$ out of $n$) codes, which are distinguished by equally-weighted code words ($q$ = number of binary 1s per code word with $n$ positions = weight).

BERGER, E. R.: Nachrichtentheorie und Codierung. In.: Steinbuch, K. (ed.): Taschenbuch der Nachrichtenverarbeitung. Springer-Verlag, Berlin, Göttingen, Heidelberg 1962.

**Coding (in nervous system)**
Codierung, sinnesphysiologische
codage
кодирование (физиол.)

*Method of relating a conducted nervous excitation to a stimulus or to a condition of excitation of *synapses. In general, the non-perceivable information-transformation in a receptor.*

The encoding-positions, normally *receptors and *neurons are put into a state of excitation which involves metabolic change (ionic exchange). This excitation is at first proportional to the strength of the stimulus through the simultaneous process of adaptation. At a functional boundary-membrane between the receptor or the *synapse and the nerve fibre leading away, the coding occurs into a series of pulse-frequency modulated signals of short ionic shocks (cf. *action potential) of the same amplitude, whereby high pulse-frequencies (max. 800/s to 1000/s) are related to the strengths of stimulus. This membrane has a characteristic curve for the dependence of permeability on the ionic concentration and from this can produce oscillations during the return to the resting state. The speed of these oscillations and also the number of conducted impulses is dependent on the strength of stimulus and on supplementary effects influencing metabolism in the sense of *facilitation or *inhibition. Coding in the information-processing system of the body achieves a satisfactory information-transfer even when there is a partial suppression in conduction, or variations in metabolism.

KEIDEL, W. D.: Codierung, Signalleitung und Decodierung in der Sinnesphysiologie. Aufnahme und Verarbeitung von Nachrichten in Organismen. Hirzel, Stuttgart 1961. KEIDEL, W. D.: Sinnesphysiologie. In: Marchionini und Spier (eds.): Handbuch der Dermatologie (Supplement). Springer-Verlag, Berlin, Göttingen, Heidelberg 1962.

### Coherent
Kohärent
cohérent
когерентный

*Oscillations with constant phase-relations are coherent; oscillations with variable phase-relations are non-coherent. Also used as a term for the phase-relation of generators.*

Originally the term was applied predominantly to light-waves; coherent light-waves are prone to interference. Lately coherent has also been used in pulse-systems technology. Independent technical generators generally produce non-coherent pulse-sequences. Coherence is induced by mutual influence. Electronic data-processing equipment (cf. *information-processing) works almost entirely with coherent pulse-trains (cf. *clock-generator). On the other hand, mainly non-coherent pulse-trains are used in the nervous-system. The distinction between coherent and non-coherent pulse-trains is an important one, as their processing follows different rules.

BOTTLINGER, K. F.; LADENBURG, R.; LAUE, M. von; SCHULZ, H.: Wellenoptik und Polarisation. Handb. d. Experimentalphysik Bd. 18. Wien, W.; Harms, F. (ed.), Springer Berlin 1928. THEWLIS, J. (ed.): Encyclopaedic dictionary of physics. Oxford, London, New York, Paris 1961. JENIK, F.: Die Überlagerung von Impulsfolgen in Systemen mit einer Schwelle. AEÜ 16 (1962).

### Communication
Kommunikation
communication
коммуникация; сообщение; связь

The original meaning of communication is a physical transmission passing from one point (temporal or spatial) to another. Often, however, the meaning of communication is limited to the transmission of a message (cf. *theory of information). Communication takes place between a transmitter and a receiver via a channel as the conductor. The physical channel can be any system of notification through time or space, or any clear *transformation between two temporal-spatial systems $A(x,y,z,t)$ and $A'(x',y',z',t')$.

SHANNON, C. E.: Mathematical Theory of Communication. Univ. Illinois Press, Urbana 1948. BRILLOUIN, L.: Science and information theory. Academic press, New York 1962. CHERRY, C.: Kommunikationsforschung—eine neue Wissenschaft. (trans. P. Müller) S. Fischer Verlag, Frankfurt/M. 1963. MOLES, A. A.: Théorie informationnelle de la perception. In: Le concept d'information dans les sciences contemporaines. Gauthier-Villars, Paris 1963.

### Compiler
Compiler
compilateur
программирующая программа; компилирующая программа

*Program for the translation of a program written in a pseudo-language which is not machine-orientated into a *machine-code.*

If there is no clear correspondence between instructions of the pseudo-language (cf. *pseudo-code) and instructions of the machine code of the computer envisaged for the execution of the program (pseudo-language is not machine-orientated) then a transformation of the syntax of the pseudo-language is necessary. Often the translation can only be completed during the execution of the already translated section of the program, especially when the program itself provides the information necessary for the translation.

### Complexity
Komplexität
complexité
комплексность

*A general metric characteristic of a system or organism which consists of a combination of parts, and is independent of the physical nature of this system or organism.*

The general theory of systems allows the definition of the degree of complexity of various organisms by a measurable variable, its arrangement into a hierarchy and hence their comparison. This measurable value is called complexity. This concept is only applicable to those organisms which have a rather large number of component parts whose individual features lose their importance in comparison to their contribution to the whole. The concept of complexity is therefore a statistical one.

A more precise analysis of organisms shows that the structure of a system cannot be defined solely by the enumeration of the parts of the system, i.e. a sufficiently large system contains more *information than the mere listing of parts of this system. The concept of complexity is therefore connected to the information contained in that message which the organism as a whole represents to the observer. In fact, the degree of effort necessary to define the structure of an organism depends on both the number of the elements of the organism and on the degree of connection between these elements. Therefore, complexity and information are two closely related values. One ought really to distinguish between the complexity of an organism and its complication. Reciprocally it is possible to consider the information of a given message as the complexity of the assembly of its parts, whereas complication is a characteristic of this message more or less near SHANNON'S maximal information Ho. A complicated organism is an organism whose characteristics can only be given if those of all the individual organs are known: it is linked with the maximal information one could have in a message where all characters are different.

There are as many types of complexity possible as there are ways of observing the organism. Of these, two are of especial interest: (1) structural complexity, or constructional complexity, is of interest to anyone who has to construct the organism or the message from the various given elements. One has a *repertory of elements available which are assembled according to more or less predictable connective-laws. Just as in information-theory, one defines the frequency of occurrence of the various element-categories and calculates the structural complexity $C_s$ according to the equation

$$C_s = - N . \sum_n p_i \log_2 p_i$$

in which $p_i$ stands for the probability of the occurrence of the i-th element-category. (2) functional complexity; this refers to the total of elemental-actions which the organism is capable of carrying out. They occur with a given frequency, and are connected to each other by various relations, (e.g. a typewriter). Functional complexity $C_f$ is defined by a formula of the same form as for $C_s$, but one must here refer to the repertory of elemental-actions which are possible.

Complexity therefore represents a universal value for the characterization of an organism. It allows one to measure this organism in a continuum independently of its physical dimensions.

NEUMANN, J. von: Cerebral mechanisms in behaviour. Wiley, New York 1957. MOLES, A. A.: Information theory and aesthetical perception. University of Illinois Press 1966. MOLES, A. A.: Über konstruktionelle und instrumentelle Komplexität. Grundlagenstudien Band 1, Heft 2 (1960). ASHBY, W. R.: An Introduction to Cybernetics. Chapman & Hall, London 1956.

**Compound action potential**
Summenaktionspotential
potentiel total d'action
суммарный потенциал

*The potential which arises by summation of the action potentials of the single fibres of a nerve.*
The pathways of excitation-conduction in the body, called *nerves, consist of, amongst other things, a bundle of several parallel individual fibres. After *encoding, these conduct the information at varying speeds with the help of their *action potentials, which are always of the same value but of variable sequence-frequency. The value of compound action potential is dependent on the sequence-frequency of the action potentials of the single fibres and on the varying speed of conduction (synchronization, also with regard to the receptor latencies) in the individual fibres; so despite complicated encoding short-circuiting of the stimulus parameters is possible. Single- or two-phased action potentials can be obtained on the method of recording.

ERLANGER, J.; GASSER, H. S.: Electrical Signs of Nervous Activity. Univ. Penn. Press, Philadelphia 1937. MURALT, A. von: Die Signalübermittlung in Nerven. Birkhäuser, Basel 1946.

**Computability; theory of computation**
Berechenbarkeit
calculabilité
исчисляемость; вычислимость
*Solvability of a mathematical problem by a non-continuous or terminating *algorithm.*
A function is computable if there is a *TURING machine which, after a finite number of steps, gives the correct function-value for any argument written on the tape.
Computable functions are therefore in principle realizable on stored-program *computers.
The set of computable functions can be enumerated, i.e. it can be placed in (1–1) correspondence with the set of natural numbers. This is however no longer true for the set of functions in the general sense. This latter is of a higher order. It is therefore an exception if a function is computable.

HERMES, H.: Aufzählbarkeit, Entscheidbarkeit, Berechenbarkeit. Springer-Verlag, Berlin, Göttingen, Heidelberg 1961. LORENZEN, P.: Metamathematik. Bibliographisches Institut, Mannheim 1962.

**Computer (digital); computing machine**
Rechenautomat; Digitalrechner; Computer
calculatrice; machine à calculer automatique; computer
вычислительная машина; счетно- решающее устройство

*An electronic computing machine which works with numbers (i.e. digital); it automatically executes calculations according to a program.*
The *arithmetic unit carries out the basic arithmetic *operations as well as some logical operations on digitally encoded data taken from the *store. The results of the calculating operations are fed into the *store. In the *control-unit the instructions establish the operations to be carried out, as well as the *addresses of the locations from which the *operands (numbers or instructions) must be taken, or to which results (numbers or modified instructions) must be fed. The instructions are read sequentially by the control unit from the store; the sequence of instructions forms the program, which together with the data is fed into the store via the input unit before the start of the calculation. The output unit delivers the results of the calculation in numerical form.

GÜNTSCH, F. R.: Einführung in die Programmierung digitaler Rechenautomaten. De Gruyter, Berlin 1960. SPEISER, A. P.: Digitale Rechenanlagen. Springer-Verlag, Berlin, Göttingen, Heidelberg 1961. RUTISHAUSER, H.; SPEISER, A. P.; STIEFEL, E.: Programmgesteuerte digitale Rechengeräte. Birkhäuser, Basel and Stuttgart 1951.

## Computing time

Rechenzeit
temps de calcul
время исчисления

The time which a (mathematical, technical or economic) problem needs to be processed in a program-controlled *computer depends (*a*) on the time necessary for the input and output of data and of the program, (*b*) on the actual speed of calculation (operation speed) of the electronic equipment, (*c*) on the construction of the equipment as *serial operation or *parallel operation and (*d*) on the type of information stores which are called upon during the program (these are distinguished by *access times which vary in length).
The addition-time of a machine is the time necessary to add a machine-word (a number or an instruction) in the *accumulator of the computer. The average addition-time is to-day of the order of a micro-second. But when comparing different machines, a comparison of the addition-times is not an infallible standard.
A typical computer, for example the I.C.T. 1905, has the following computing times:
Addition, subtraction, clearing instructions: (*a*) fixed point: 7 $\mu$secs. (*b*) floating point: 12 $\mu$secs. Multiplication: (*a*) fixed point: 40 $\mu$secs. (*b*) floating point: 29 $\mu$secs. Division: (*a*) fixed point: 44 $\mu$secs. (*b*) floating point: 51 $\mu$secs. *Jump-instructions: 3 $\mu$secs.

KNÖDEL, W.: Programmieren von Ziffernrechenanlagen. Springer-Verlag, Wien 1961.

## Concept formation

Begriffsbildung
conceptualisation; formation de concepts
выработка понятий; образование понятий

*In the process of concept formation an organism learns to respond with the same reaction to all the stimuli which have a specified characteristic or a specified characteristic configuration in common.*
Let us examine the repertory of all possible stimuli of which each individual stimulus may or may not possess one or more characteristic. If all these $2^n$ stimuli are equally probable, then the stimulus repertory has an *entropy of *n* *bit. The stimuli are now repeatedly offered to the organism in random series (cf. *random number). It should learn by this to answer each stimulus with one of the total of *m* reactions ($m < 2^n$). When the stimuli occur, intermediary information (i.e. entropy) is transferred via the stimulus system, and *transinformation via the reaction system. The difference between the two is irrelevant information for the organism. Concept formation is rendered more difficult by such irrelevant information. Relevant transinformation can be divided into additive components, each of which gives the section which is transferred by the condition of a single characteristic or a combination of several characteristics. Concept formation is facilitated by a large information-section which is transferred by single characteristics, not combinations. In addition there are influences of the entropy of the reaction-system and of certain series-characteristics in the stimulus-presentation.

GARNER, W. R.: Uncertainty and Structure as Psychological Concepts. J. Wiley, New York, London 1962.

**Conditioning, classical (Pavlovian)**
Konditionierung, klassische
conditionnement classique
условный рефлекс

After the repeated pairing within a short period of time of a reflex-triggering stimulus (the showing of food) with a neutral stimulus (bell) a stage is reached where the reflexive-behaviour (saliva-flow) can also be triggered off solely by using the conditioned stimulus (bell). PAVLOV, who was the first (in 1927) to study in detail the evoking of specified reflexes (classical conditioning) noted the following conditions:
1 There must be a reflex arc.
2 The stimulus to be conditioned must occur within a sufficiently short space of time to the original trigger.
3 Accidental uncontrolled stimuli must be excluded as far as possible.
4 The stimulus to be conditioned must not be part of an already extant reflex, whose reaction interferes with the behaviour demanded.
Experiments with human test-subjects often make use of the lid-closing reflex (shutting of the eye-lids in the event of a blast of air) or of the psycho-galvanic skin-reflex. In almost all cases the best results are achieved if the new stimulus precedes the original trigger by 0·5 seconds. But the possibility of classical conditioning can still be shown when the new stimulus is offered after the triggering stimulus (see footnote). Classical conditioning can also be built on already conditioned reflexes. So chains arise which in experiments with animals can only be demonstrated up to three or four orders, if it is a question of a behaviour which can help to avoid injury (e.g. withdrawing a paw from an electric shock as a reflex). The intensity and probability of the occurrence of a particular reaction to the conditioned stimulus decrease with time and as a function of the number of activations of the conditioned reflex unless an occasional reconditioning by the repetitions of the combined offering of stimulus and original trigger takes place.

*Translator's note:* more modern research casts some doubt on the validity of this statement.

HILGARD, E. R.: Theories of Learning. Appleton-Century Crofts. New York 1956. HOFSTÄTTER, P. R.: Psychologie. Fischer Lexikon 6, Frankfurt 1957.

**Conditioning, instrumental; operant conditioning**
Konditionierung, instrumentale
conditionnement instrumental
———

If an organism which is subject to the tension of need (such as hunger) shows a certain behaviour (e.g. the pushing of a lever) at a certain *stimulus (e.g. the ringing of a bell), and this mode of behaviour leads to a reduction of the need (e.g. feeding), then there results a connection between stimulus and *reaction, which leads to an increase in the probability of the occurrence of the rewarded behaviour in the same output situation. The essential difference from Pavlovian *conditioning is that instrumental conditioning creates a connection between stimulus and reaction without presupposing the previous existence of a connection of another stimulus to the same reaction in the form of a reflex. A conditioned response can always be interpreted as a (mode of) behaviour which can be regarded as an instrument or operation for achieving a goal (e.g. feeding) or for avoiding some danger (e.g. electric shock). At the start of a conditioning process, the organism shows a random series of behavioural acts which ceases with the *correct* reaction and the subsequent reward (phase of *learning by *trial and error). If a conditioned response repeatedly leads to no reduction of the need-tension by reward or evasion of danger then the connection between stimulus and response which has been built up is suppressed.

The concept of instrumental conditioning explains many observable learning processes, whose interpretation by classical (Pavlovian) conditioning leads to a wide range of supplementary assumptions which cannot always be checked empirically. In instrumental conditioning, need-tension is often produced by social motives (especially in man). So a large part of children's learning can be interpreted as instrumental conditioning; the force behind this can be regarded as the need for parental recognition or the desire to avoid being punished by lack of affection.

HILGARD, E. R.: Theories of Learning. Appleton-Century Crofts. New York 1956. HOFSTÄTTER, P. R.: Psychologie. Fischer Lexikon 6, Frankfurt 1957.

**Conjunction**
Konjunktion
conjonction
конъюнкция; логическое умножение

*Binary *logical connective with the symbol ∧ or · and the meaning 'and'.*
Truth-table:

| | | | | |
|---|---|---|---|---|
| $a$ | $T$ | $T$ | $F$ | $F$ |
| $b$ | $T$ | $F$ | $T$ | $F$ |
| $a \wedge b$ | $T$ | $F$ | $F$ | $F$ |

Conjunction can be expressed in terms of *negation and *disjunction:

$$a \wedge b = \overline{\bar{a} \vee \bar{b}}$$

In information technology the symbol & is also common.

**Consciousness**
Bewusstsein
conscience
сознание

*A fundamental principle of philosophy (together with 'existence') for which no rational definition can be given, as its content is more immediately familiar to us than anything else.*

Thinking, feeling and wishing are combined in human beings with consciousness and are called 'conscious processes'. Consciousness is the essence of the awareness of all possible consciousness-contents. Awareness, which ROHRACHER calls 'consciousness-immanent self-observation', has no effect on thinking, feeling and wishing. Consciousness is therefore not communicable, but only evident on the basis of one's own actual consciousness-contents. Accordingly there is no way of proving that apart from one's self anyone else possesses consciousness, nor is there any way of disproving that a cybernetic machine possesses consciousness, yet everyone is convinced that every other human being possesses consciousness and that no machine does. *Cybernetics distinguishes itself by the very fact that it describes processes of *transformation of signs (information), that is, of data which cannot be defined without recourse to the concept of consciousness, into processes to which no consciousness as such is attributed (physiological and technical processes); the reference to consciousness-processes, which are understood by *introspection, results therefore only from heuristic reasons. *Information-psychology attaches to the total of the actually conscious an imaginary (fictitious) *short-term memory which retains consciousness-objects for the *duration.

The cybernetic metaphysics of G. GÜNTHER tries to escape from the 'as if' of technical and physiological processing of 'signs' by extending dualistic metaphysics, which recognize only 'Being (Existence)' and 'Consciousness' as metaphysical instances, by the introduction of *information as a third metaphysical instance. On the other hand the consciousness-theory of K. STEINBUCH tries to admit as valid only 'Existence' and 'Information', as levels of metaphysics, and to understand 'consciousness' as the designation for the reflexivity of consciousness-processes, or more precisely, for the iterability of characters which can always be designated by new characters. By this, of course, only one of ROHRACHER's two forms of self-observation is covered, namely 'reversive' self-observation (cf. *introspection) which has an influence on the observed consciousness-contents, but not however 'consciousness-immanent' self-observation, which was described in theoretical form as a feedback-free distorted reflection of the contents of the short-term memory (which was thought of as having a physiological foundation) on another level, namely the consciousness. This distorted-mirror theory (FRANK) therefore remains closely wedded to dualistic metaphysics, at least in the form of a theory.

ROHRACHER, H.: Einführung in die Psychologie. Urban & Schwarzenberg, Wien (Innsbruck 7th edn.) 1960. GÜNTHER, G.: Bewusstsein und Maschine. 2nd edn. Agis, Baden-Baden 1963. STEINBUCH, K.: Bewusstsein und Kybernetik. Grundlagenstudien Band 3, Heft 1 (1962). FRANK, H.: Kausalität und Information als Problemkomplex einer Philosophie der Kybernetik. Grundlagenstudien Band 3, Heft 1 (1962).

**Control engineering**
Regelungstechnik
technique de régulation
техника регулирования; техника управления

*The technology of the design and production of feedback control systems.*

Usually the basic characteristics of the controlled system are given by its purpose (steam boiler, machine-tools, aeroplane). The task of control engineering then consists of the design of suitable regulators which will keep the deviation of the controlled condition from the index value down to a permissible level. (cf. *feedback control system).

DIN 19226. Normblatt über Benennungen und Begriffe der Regelungstechnik. 1954 (Entwurf einer Neufassung Mai 1962). LEONHARD, A.: Die selbsttätige Regelung. Springer-Verlag, Berlin, Göttingen, Heidelberg 1957. OLDENBOURG, R. C.; SARTORIUS, H.: Dynamik selbsttätiger Regelungen. Band 1, R. Oldenbourg, München 1951. OPPELT, W.: Kleines Handbuch technischer Regelvorgänge. Verlag Chemie, Weinheim 1960. SOLODOWNIKOW, W. W.: Grundlagen der selbsttätigen Regelung. R. Oldenbourg, München and Berlin 1959.

**Control loop**
*See under* *Feedback control system

**Control unit**
Kommandowerk
unité de contrôle
управляющее устройство; командное устройство

*The control unit of a computer controls the read-out of instructions from the store and their execution.*

*Instructions are read by the control unit from the *store in the sequence established in the *program. In certain cases *index registers modify the address of a store location contained in the address-section of the instruction (cf. *address modification). In addition, the control unit starts the execution of the operation (given in the operation part of the instruction) in the *arithmetic unit, *the store, or *the input or *output equipment. With *jump instructions a test is made of whether the jump condition has been fulfilled.

SPEISER, A. P.: Digitale Rechenanlagen. Springer-Verlag, Berlin, Göttingen, Heidelberg 1961.

**Control value**
*See* *Index value

**Controlled condition**
Regelgrösse
grandeur réglée
регулируемая величина; управляемая величина

*See* *Index value *and* *Feedback control system (section 1)

**Controlled system**
Regelstrecke
installation réglée
объект регулирования

*See under* *Feedback control system, especially section 1.

**Core memory; core store**
Ferritkernspeicher
mémoire à tores magnétiques
запоминающее устройство на ферритах

*A store constructed from magnetic cores for the storage of binary coded information.*

Core stores are built from a matrix arrangement of magnetic cores (0·5 mm-thick rings with a diameter of 1 to 2 mm, of a ferro-magnetic material). All cores in a core store have horizontal, vertical and diagonal wires running through them (line-, column-, and reading wires). As a result of its two defined magnetic states every magnetic core represents a store-location for the storage of a binary character for any desired length of time. The magnetic state of a magnetic core is changed by coincident electrical signals on the column- and line-wires linked with the core. This means that access can be made to each individual store cell and that its store content can be called upon or changed individually. Core stores are used in *computers as working stores because of their very short *access time.

SPEISER, A. P.: Digitale Rechenanlagen. Springer-Verlag, Berlin, Göttingen, Heidelberg 1961.

**Correcting element**
Stellglied
organe de régage
исполнительный элемент; регулирующий орган

*See under* *Feedback control system, esp. sections 3 and 4.

**Correlation; correlation function**
Korrelationsfunktion
corrélation; fonction de corrélation
функция корреляции

The correlation of two *random variables shows the degree of their dependence. In classical probability calculation one regards the correlation coefficient in the treatment of *stochastic processes and their applications (e.g. in information theory) as correlation.

Let $\{X_t,\ t\epsilon\ (-\infty,\ \infty)\}$ be a stationary stochastic process; then

$$\varphi(\tau) = E\{X_t X_{t+\tau}\} = \lim_{T\to\infty} \frac{1}{2T}\int_{-T}^{T} X_t X_{t+\tau}\,dt$$

is called its correlation. It is

$$|\varphi(\tau)| < \varphi(o),\ \lim_{\tau\to\pm\infty}\varphi(\tau) = E\{1X_\tau 1^2\}$$

and $\varphi(\tau) = \varphi(\tau)$.

In probability calculation $E\{X_\tau X_{t+\tau}\}$ is also called co-variance function.

Correlation function is usually taken to mean *autocorrelation function, which is in fact a special case of *cross correlation function in which the two correlated functions are identical.

ROSENBLATT, M.: Random Processes. Oxford Univ. Press, New York 1962.

**Correlation coefficient**
Korrelationskoeffizient
coefficient de corrélation
коэффициент корреляции

The correlation coefficient is the normalized *correlation of co-variance

$$r = \frac{E\{(X-E\{X\})(Y-E\{Y\})\}}{[E\{(X-E\{X\})^2\}E\{(Y-E\{Y\})^2\}]^{1/2}},$$

$$-1 \leq r \leq +1.$$

It is a measure of the dependence of the *random variables $X$ and $Y$. For independent random variables $r = 0$, and the variables are then called uncorrelated. Uncorrelated random variables are, however, not necessarily independent. In correlation functions of stochastic processes the term normalized correlation function is preferred.

RÉNYI, A.: Wahrscheinlichkeitsrechnung. VEB Wissenschaft, Berlin 1962.

**Cortex, cerebral**
Hirnrinde
écorce cérébrale
мозговая кора

*Outer layer of grey-matter (nerve-cells and plexus) which surrounds the surface of the brain.*

The cortex is connected to the sections beneath it by fibres which run in both directions. The distribution of cells and fibres changes according to the physiological character of the part of the cortex concerned. Different zones are known: projection-zone, sensory-zone, motor-zone, association-zone, and aphasia-zone. The importance of the cerebral localization should not be underestimated: but important psychical functions (intellectual performance, *memory, etc.) represent the activity of the whole brain.

**Counter**
Zähler; Zählwerk
compteur
счетчик; пересчетное устройство

*A device for counting events.*

$N = z^n$ events, mainly electrical signals, can be counted by $n$ counting stages, each of which can adopt one after the other one out of $z$ states, if the counting-stages are connected in series in such a way that the $k^{th}$ stage adopts its original state after running through all $z$ states, and simultaneously sends a counting-pulse (carry) to the $(k+1)^{th}$ stage, while the signals to be counted (the counting-pulses) are fed to the first counting stage. Normally decimal counters (with $z = 10$) and binary counters ($z = 2$) are used. The following are used as counting-stages: electro-mechanical circuit elements (cf. *relay) or electronic elements (counting tubes, bi-stable flip-flop circuits (cf. *multivibrator)). Reversible counters can count upwards or downwards as required.

**Creativity**
Creativität
créativité
способность создания

*A special ability of the mind to reorganize the elements of a field of perception in an original fashion, enabling the execution of operations in some kind of phenomenal field.*

This definition presupposes:

1 The existence of a perception field of

the individual, i.e. of a picture which he has at any one moment of his surroundings and of a series of cultural elements (Knowledge or mental forms).
2 The existence of phenomenal or pragmatic field, e.g. of an experimental field within which the researcher or artist is capable of working, either directly (as with an experimentor) or via an intermediary, such as could be the case with an engineer or business executive. This phenomenal field may be the optical range of a microscope, the material treated by an artist, social space, etc.
3 Finally this definition presupposes that the perception field can be divided into simple elements which can be formed into a combination (structuralistic hypotheses). These elements may be words, semantemes, morphemes, melemes, etc.
Creativity is therefore a mental ability which every individual possesses to some extent. In some, however, it is extremely well developed and forms the basic presupposition for their work. It can be measured according to the above definition by the *originality of the effective perception field, i.e. by the conditional perception content corresponding to the number of possible arrangements of the elements of the perception field.

WERTHEIMER, M.: Productive Thinking. Harper, New York 1945. MOLES, A. A.: La création scientifique. Kistner, Geneva 1958.

**Cross correlation function**
Kreuzkorrelationsfunktion
fonction de corrélation inverse

Cross correlation function is a measure for the correlation (cf. *correlation function) between two stationary stochastic processes

$\{X_t \mid -\infty \leqslant t \leqslant \infty\}$ and $\{Y_t \mid -\infty \leqslant t \leqslant \infty\}$

$$\Psi_{XY}(\tau) = E\{X_t Y_{t+\tau}\} = \lim_{T\to\infty} \frac{1}{2T} \int_{-T}^{T} X_t Y_{t+\tau}\, dt$$

$$\Psi_{YX}(\tau) = E\{X_{t+\tau} Y_t\} = \lim_{T\to\infty} \frac{1}{2T} \int_{-T}^{T} \left( X_{t+\tau} Y_t \right) dt$$

DAVENPORT, W. B.; ROOT, W. L.: An Introduction to the Theory of Random Signals and Noise. McGraw Hill, New York 1958.

**Cryotron**
Cryotron
cryotron
криотрон

*Switch- and memory-store element for binary signals.*
In a cryotron the dependence of the critical temperature on an external magnetic field is used for the purposes of switching-and memory-storing. Several natural elements and many alloys become superconductors at temperatures between 0°K and 20°K. The temperature at which superconduction occurs is called the jump-temperature. At jump-temperature the electrical resistance of the pertinent cryogenic element falls to exactly 0$\Omega$. By a suitable alteration of the external magnetic field the resistance can be switched to and fro between zero and a finite value. In principle the cryotron consists of two cryogenic elements. The element which functions as the electrical conductor for the gate current is surrounded by a coil, which consists of an element with a higher jump-temperature. A frequent combination is Ta and Nb.
At the temperature of liquid helium (4·2°K) the coil of Nb which produces the magnetic field is superconductive even with large magnetic field strengths.

The gate-circuit of Ta is superconductive for field strengths up to approx. 40 Oe. For greater field strengths the gate-circuit is interrupted because of the finite resistance. By suitable series or parallel circuits of several cryotrons, logical circuits and flip-flops can be realized in a comparatively easy fashion. It is of great advantage that the internal part of the circuit only consumes power when the circuits are switched.

BUCK, D. A.: The Cryotron—A Superconductive Computer Component. Proc. IRE 44 (1956) pp. 482–493.

**Cybernetical pedagogics**
Pädagogik, kybernetische
pédagogie cybernétique
кибернетическая педагогика

*Branch of *informational sciences (for example, in the technical field, of cybernetical *social sciences) which tries to understand pedagogical questions abstractly as a flow of information between the teaching system (no matter whether this is a teacher or a *teaching machine) and the learning system (pupil or *learning machine). Also a term for the pedagogic application of *information psychology, or in general for every application of cybernetic thought to pedagogic needs.*

FRANK, H.: Kybernetische Grundlagen der Pädagogik. Agis, Baden-Baden 1962. FRANK, H. (ed.): Lehrmaschinen in kybernetischer und pädagogischer Sicht. Klett und R. Oldenbourg, Stuttgart and München 1963.

**Cybernetics**
Kybernetik
cybernetique
кибернетика

*Collective term for the efforts—which have arisen in connection with the development of program-controlled *computers, sometimes called rather misleadingly 'electronic brains'—to understand problems of various specialist scientific and technical fields, especially in biology and information technology, as special cases of the same range of problems (*information processing, control).*
The definitions suggested by the various authors vary greatly. It is however agreed that information theory as a mathematical tool is as much a part of cybernetics as is the theory of biological and sociological control processes. Normally the theory of *TURING machines*, of *learning machines*, etc., is also included, as well as any application of information theory to informational psychology, informational aesthetics, etc. From the point of view of philosophy, cybernetics is nearly always concerned with the reproduction of conscious processes in systems which are not credited with consciousness (technical or biological systems), with the fictive recognition of conscious processes in such systems for heuristic purposes, or with the adoption of terminology developed therein to describe conscious processes (particularly in informational psychology, cybernetical pedagogics and cybernetical sociology). The various authors do not agree, however, on whether cybernetics exerts some influence on environment, hence falling under the heading of *technique* (SCHMIDT), whether it is a form of description of environment and hence a science (WIENER), or whether it embraces both forms of treatment of environment (FRANK). It is agreed, however, that, on account of its calculative methodology, cybernetics cannot be considered as one of the humanities, as these strive towards a direct, intuitive insight into the phenomena of the mind by avoiding calculations.
Cybernetics was founded independently

by H. SCHMIDT (1941) and N. WIENER (1948): the latter was the first to use the term 'cybernetics'. The origin of the word is the Greek *κυβερνητης*. It is debatable whether translation by 'steersman' or by 'pilot' is precise, as the present-day distinction between these mutually dependent functions could not be made in the ancient world. Cybernetics is concerned with the analysis or reproduction of the functions of *steersman* and *pilot*. *κυβερνητης* is connected with Plato's *κγβερνητικη* (art of control of steering or control) Ampére's 'cybernétique' (theory of patterns of behaviour in government) and the concept of cybernetics in theology (dogma of leadership of the Church). Moreover, from the Latin 'gubernare' and the French 'gouverneur' has evolved the English word 'governor' which, since Watt, has had the technical meaning of 'centrifugal governor' alongside its original political meaning. With this in mind, WIENER applied the term 'cybernetics' to 'the entire field of control and communication theory, whether in machines or animals.' SCHMIDT insists on the definition in his earlier essay attached to his interpretation of the history of techniques: 'Cybernetics is the construction of technical systems in order to objectivise our basic psycho-physical relation to physical nature'. In an attempt to combine the abundance of definitions which, in part, cancel each other out, FRANK gives the following definition: 'Cybernetics is the calculative theory and the constructional technique of information, of information processing and of information processing systems'. In addition to this definition, an attempt at the systematic classification of cybernetics leads to the distinction of formal (general, abstract) cybernetics from three types of material (regional) cybernetics, and finally to three corresponding areas of cybernetical technique. While formal cybernetics does not yet demand the concrete form of the information processing systems being examined, but is content with their structure, engineering cybernetics (theory of information processing, of control, etc.), bio-cybernetics (neurophysiology, theory of biological control, etc.) and informational science (science of communication, anthropo-cybernetics) concentrate, as branches of material cybernetics, on systems which can best be described in physical, physiological or psychological concepts. Correspondingly, technical cybernetics is subdivided into cybernetical machine techniques, cybernetical bio-techniques (medicine, zoo-techniques) and cybernetical social science.

SCHMIDT, H.: Denkschrift zur Gründung eines Instituts für Regelungstechnik. Verlag Schnelle, Quickborn. 2nd edn. 1961. WIENER, N.: Cybernetics or control and communication in the animal and the machine. Hermann and Co., The Technology Press and John Wiley and Sons, Paris, Cambridge, New York 1948. FRANK, H. (ed.): Kybernetik-Brücke zwischen den Wissenschaften. Umschau-Verlag, Frankfurt/M., 5th edn. 1965. FRANK, H.: Kybernetik und Philosophie. Duncker and Humbolt, Berlin 1966.

**Cybernetics, levels of**
kybernetische Instanzen
instances cybernétiques

---

The functional behaviour of man can be classified under: (*a*) setting of a goal; (*b*) planning (in the sense of the development of methods to achieve this goal; (*c*) co-ordination (in the sense of the guidance or control of an existing supply of energy as a function of a planned sub-instruction; and (*d*) physical performance in pursuing the goal set. Each of these function-classes is given a level

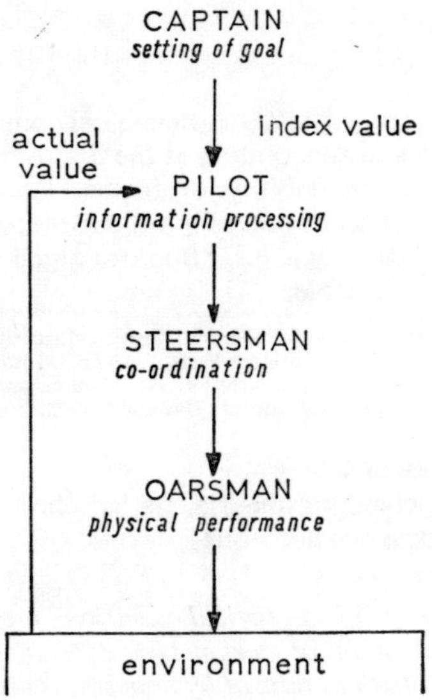


1 Levels of cybernetics

or instance by which they are carried out.
The usual example or paradigm is formed from the naval functions of (1) *captain, (2) *pilot, (3) *steersman, (4) *oarsman, since this explains the origin of the term *cybernetics* and illustrates the idea of a feedback control system which was originally the basic principle of cybernetics; it also produces a graphic representation of the isomorphy of various systems with which cybernetics is concerned (compare diagram 1 with diagram 2).

Ducrocq, A.: Die Entwicklung der Kybernetik. Europ. Verlagsanst., Frankfurt/M. 1959. Frank, H.: Kybernetik—Wesen und Wertung. In: Alsleben, K. (ed.): Kybernetik und Organisation. Schnelle, Quickborn bei Hamburg 1963.

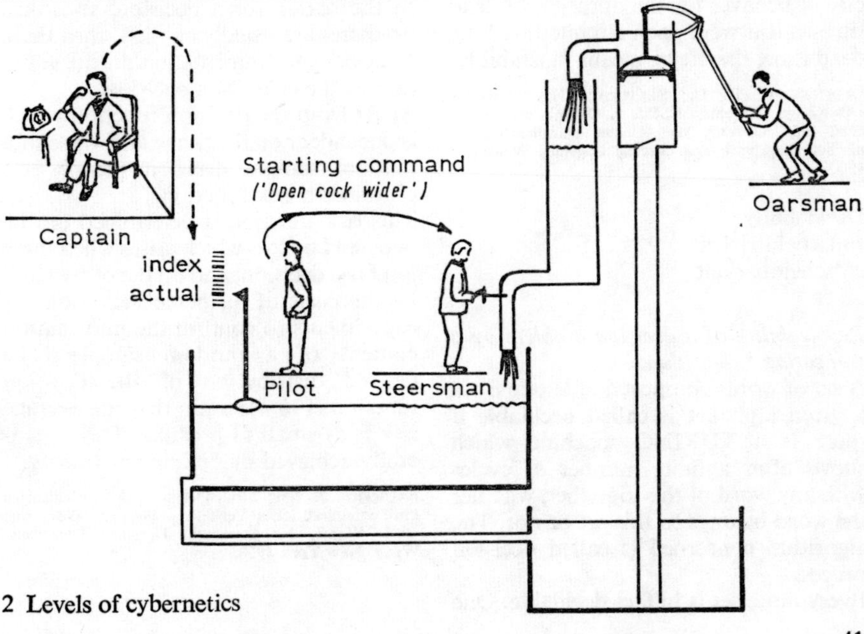


2 Levels of cybernetics

# D

**Data processing**
Datenverarbeitung
traitement des données
переработка информации; обработка данных

*See under* *Information processing

**Dead time**
Totzeit
temps mort
«мёртвое» время

*A period of time between an alteration of the input of an open-circuited *feedback control system or feedback circuit and the occurrence of its effect at the output.*
The cause of dead time is the finite transmission speed of the transmission elements in the circuit. After the occurrence of a disturbance, a closed loop circuit behaves for the duration of dead time as if it were open circuited. A long dead time, therefore, means *instability.

OLDENBOURG, R. C.; SARTORIUS, H.: Dynamik selbsttätiger Regelungen. Bd. 1. Oldenbourg, München 1951. OPPELT, W.: Kleines Handbuch technischer Regelvorgänge. Verlag Chemie, Weinheim 1960.

**Decidability**
Entscheidbarkeit
entscheidbarkeit

——

*Resolvability of a decision problem by a truncating *algorithm.*
A set of words composed of letters from a given alphabet is called decidable if there is a TURING machine which shows after a finite number of cycles with any word of this alphabet, whether the word belongs to this set or not. The algorithm concerned is called decision process.
Every finite set is in fact decidable. One of the greatest mathematical achievements of this century is the discovery of the undecidability of formal systems, e.g. the set of generally valid formulae of predicate logic (cf. *Boolean algebra) is not decidable.

HERMES, H.: Aufzählbarkeit, Entscheidbarkeit, Berechenbarkeit. Springer-Verlag, Berlin, Göttingen, Heidelberg 1961. LORENZEN, P.: Metamathematik. Bibliographisches Institut, Mannheim 1962.

**Decision theory**
Entscheidungstheorie, statistische
théorie des décisions

——

*Theory of statistical decision process (evaluation of parameters of statistical distribution, tests of hypotheses, choice of random samples for statistical experiments).*
In the search for a decision, statistical processes are usually applied when there is *incomplete* *information on the situation or the effect of a decision.
Apart from the decision function which is dependent on the range and value of a random sample, decision theory also examines a risk function.
This risk function is determined on the one hand by loss which arises when there is a false decision, and on the other hand by the costs of further observations or experiments to confirm the information content of a random sample. The desired distribution of the decision function is to ascertain that the average risk is as small as possible. This is generally achieved by *minimax strategy.

NEUMANN, J. von; MORGENSTERN, O.: Spieltheorie und wirtschaftliches Verhalten. Physica, Würzburg 1961. WALD, A.: Statistical Decision Functions. Wiley, New York 1950.

**Decoding**
Decodierung, nachrichtentechnische
decodage
декодирование } информационно-
дешифрирование } логическое

*The extraction of any *information from suitably coded *signals (acoustic, optic, electrical, etc.)*

In the information theory sense decoding is understood as the extraction of an information element, which usually belongs to a larger *repertory, from a number of information elements which stem from a (usually) smaller repertory. Decoding represents the reverse process of *encoding.

BERGER, E. R.: Nachrichtentheorie und Codierung. In: Steinbuch, K. (ed.): Taschenbuch der Nachrichtenverarbeitung. Springer-Verlag, Berlin, Göttingen, Heidelberg 1962.

**Decoding (of sensory information)**
Decodierung, sinnesphysiologische
decodage
декодирование

*Conversion of the pulse-frequency-modulated excitation conducted in the nerve into excitation-states of synapses.*

Decoding in the *synapses is attained (by a chemical mechanism) in such a way that the first action potential of a pulse-frequency-modulated series to arrive releases an excitation substance whose concentration, because of autocatalysis sinks so slowly that the next signal causes a build-up of the concentration of the excitation substance. The more frequently the signals arrive, the larger is the peak concentration (of the excitation substance) (cf. *summation). In central-nervous decoding there is therefore no simple form of *information proportional to the impulse strength. As several nerve fibres reach a synapse and only one leaves it (reduction process) and as a result of the interconnection of the information conduction system in the sense of a *focalized-diffused-excitation there results a nonlinear behaviour of the biological information processing systems, so that the highest decoding systems which comprise several synapse-cell populations work on the principle of local and temporal intervention (cf. *probabilistic approach) or probably show the ability of autocorrelation (cf. *autocorrelation function). Generally a renewed *encoding occurs in the boundary-membrane between synapse and the following nerve fibre.

NACHMANSOHN, D.: Die Rolle des Acetylcholins in den Elementarvorgängen der Nervenleitung. Ergebn. Physiol. 48 (1955) pp. 575–683. KEIDEL, W. D.: Codierung, Signalleitung und Decodierung in der Sinnesphysiologie. Aufnahme und Verarbeitung von Nachrichten in Organismen. Hirzel, Stuttgart 1961.

**Delay line store**
Laufzeitspeicher
mémoire à ligne à retard
электронная (кольцевая) схема задержки; электронная линия задержки; линия задержки; цепочка задержки

*Dynamic store-elements in digital *computers in which information circulates in closed circuits until summoned. A delay line ensures a defined delay.*

The *pulses of a word are read by an *amplifier at the end of the delay line and written in again at the start if the store is not to be cleared. The number of *bits which can be stored results from the product of transit time and pulse-frequency; the maximum *access time is the transit time. The following can be used as delay line stores: coaxial transmission lines, chains of inductances and capacities for electronic storage, as well as mercury lines and quartz plates and magnetostrictive wires for the storage of sound-waves which have longer transit times because of their slower distribution speed. They all have in common the disadvantage that the information can only be maintained by constant energy-input (regeneration of the pulses which are altered by unavoidable energy-losses); for this reason, magnetic stores (*core stores, *magnetic tape store, *magnetic disc store and *magnetic drum store) have recently become far more popular. A *cryotron is a variation of a delay line store.

BILLING, H.; OEHLMANN, H.: Laufzeitspeicher. In: Steinbuch, K. (ed.): Taschenbuch der Nachrichtenverarbeitung, para. 4.9 Springer-Verlag, Berlin, Göttingen, Heidelberg 1962. SPEISER, A. P.: Digitale Rechenanlagen. Springer-Verlag, Berlin, Göttingen, Heidelberg 1961.

**Delay time**
*See under* **Transit time**

**Delta waves**
Delta-Wellen
ondes delta
дельта лучи

*Slow, generally irregular, sinusoidal waves of the human *electroencephalogram of variable shape and frequency.*
Delta waves are polymorphic and polyrhythmic. Their frequency lies between 0·5 and 3 c/s, their amplitude between 100 and 150 $\mu$V. They represent the total electrical activity of the brain of a child up to the age of 3 years, and their frequency increases with increasing age. They emit from every part of the scalp; there is no synchronization between the two hemispheres. In a pathological condition, delta waves give an indication of important changes in the development of the EEG, together with the disappearance of physiological rhythms at their points of origin.

**Dendrite**
Dendrit
dendrite
дендрит

*Section of a *neuron.*
Nerve cells or neurons consist of a cell-body, several dendrites branching off from it, and the longer nerve fibre (the *axon) which leads to the effector organ or to the other nerve cells. At the dendrites, which are web-like, relatively short continuations of the cell-bodies, several nerve fibres leading inwards from other nerve cells terminate at *synapses. Dendrites therefore increase the catchment area of the nerve cells.

ECCLES, J. C.: The physiology of the nerve cells. The John Hopkin Press, Baltimore 1957. ECCLES, J. C.: The Mechanism of Synaptic Transmission. Ergeb. der Physiol. 51 (1961) pp. 300–429.

**Describing function**
Beschreibungsfunktion
fonction descriptive
описательная функция

*Description of the transfer behaviour of a nonlinear unit.*
A nonlinear unit is excited by a sinusoidal input *oscillation $x(\omega) = Xe^{j\omega t}$. The fundamental of the output oscillation given by the nonlinear unit is $y(\omega) = Ye^{j(\omega t+\alpha)}$. The *frequency response of the nonlinear unit is dependent both on the frequency $\omega$ as well as on the amplitude $X$ of the input oscillation. This relation $N(\omega, X)$ is designated 'describing function' and is defined by:

$$N(\omega, X) = \frac{y(\omega)}{x(\omega)} = \frac{Y}{X} e^{j\alpha} = Ae^{j\alpha}$$

The describing function is represented by a family of curves with $X$ and $Y$ as parameters.

OPPELT, W.: Kleines Handbuch technischer Regelvorgänge. Verlag Chemie, Weinheim 1956.

**Descriptor**
Deskriptor
descriptor
дескриптор

*Is used in conjunction with *information retrieval.*

By descriptor one understands semantical information units whose coded representation is capable of being machine-processed. Each of these units represents a defined fact. A general definition is: a descriptor is the classification mark of the semantic function of the description of a defined fact (cf. *semiotic aspects of signs).

The information complex of a subject is split up by a finite number of such descriptors, which together form the descriptor list, into sub areas. The characterization of the content of a document can be achieved by the statement of appropriate descriptors which are chosen from the given descriptor list. For the mechanical treatment of documentary information it is advisable to represent descriptors in numerical form (i.e. a descriptor number represents a descriptor).

The following points are essential:

1 a descriptor is always an element of a given descriptor list
2 a descriptor can of course be characterized by a 'catch-word' but it then includes all synonyms and concept-paraphrases of the 'catch-word'
3 a descriptor can in fact comprise essentially different 'catch-words', if these are included in the paraphrasing of the facts characterized by them.
4 descriptor is essentially not synonymous with 'catch-word, slogan'.

**Deviation**
Regelabweichung
écarte de réglage
рассогласование; отклонение регулируемойвеличины; оцибка регулирования

*Difference between the *index value and the *actual value of the *controlled condition.*

**Didactics, mechanical**
Didaktik, mechanische
apprentissage méchanique
механическая дидактика

If a self-organizing (cf. *self-organization) receiver has to store a given text (cf. *mechanical memory), then it can minimize the *information of this text by a suitable arrangement. If for example the text $z_1 z_2 z_3 \ldots z_m$, has to be memorized and is composed of $q$ words each with $p$ letters, then the receiver can first store the information $q \cdot p \cdot \log_2 p$ on the basis of the letter repertory and then on the basis of the word repertory the information $q - \log_2 q$. The total information to be stored,

$$J = q\text{-}p \log_2 p + q \cdot \log_2 q$$
$$= m \cdot \log_2 p + q \cdot \log_2 q$$

reaches its minimum if the following relation is valid:

$$\log_2 p = \frac{1\text{-}p}{\ln 2} + \log_2 m$$

From this relation it follows, for example, that a text of length $m = 10$ must be stored in groups of two, a text of length 20 on the other hand in groups of three. The methods of mechanical didactics have a practical use in the learning by heart of simple facts (series of figures, series of letters and foreign languages, etc.).

CUBE, F. von: Über ein Verfahren der mechanischen Didaktik. Grundlagenstudien aus Kybernetik und Geisteswissenschaft, Heft 1 (1961).

**Difference limen; just noticeable difference**
*See* *Differential threshold

**Difference matrix**
Unterscheidungsmatrix
matrice des distances de Hamming
матрица различения

*A concept from informational encoding.*
A table of the *HAMMING distances between each code word of a binary code and every other word.
An example of a difference matrix results from observing the HAMMING distance.

**Differential threshold (DT); difference limen (DL); just noticeable difference (JND); liminal difference**
Unterschiedsschwelle
seuil différentiel; différence liminaire
порог различимости

*Originally a psycho-physical term for the smallest perceptible difference of stimulus; now generally used for the divergence of values which is sufficient to be able to differentiate between circumstances or facts with a specified probability.*
If $m_i$ ($i = 1, \ldots, k$) are the co-ordinates of a fact, of a referent or an output stimulus or standard stimulus $S$, e.g. the three valences of a colour, in a $k$ dimensional feature space (cf. *threshold) and $m_i'$ the co-ordinates of the facts $S'$, which in comparison to $S$ are answered by test-subjects (e.g. 10-week-old rats) under specified test conditions with the required probability $p(A) < 1$ by specified reaction $A$ (e.g. inhibition of a reaction conditioned to $S$), then the difference threshold of $S$ concerning the features $m_i$ is equal to the difference vectors $\Delta_i = m_i - m_i'$. In contrast to *absolute threshold, difference threshold always refers to comparative judgements or reactions. The required probability $p(A)$ is established according to the type of reaction classes permitted. It is mainly 0·5 if 'equal' judgements or equivalent reactions can occur, 0·75 if these are excluded. Besides the assessments 'equal-unequal' the usual reactions 'smaller-equal-larger' are adjusted to the pertinent object-features (e.g. redder, louder, brighter, more beautiful, etc.). According to the subjective direction of the feature-continua (e.g. higher social status, artistic value, pitch) or even the increase in value of physical features, a differentiation is made between an upper and a lower difference threshold, depending on whether a noticeable increase or a noticeable decrease was ascertained. The one-dimensional relative difference threshold of a fact $S$ is the quotient of the upper threshold and the feature value of $S$. If the relationship is formed from physical feature values it is approximately constant in the average range of many sensory continua (WEBER'S law). The thesis of the metric equivalence of the differential thresholds is the basis of *FECHNER'S law, which was used, for example, in the construction of the Phon-scale.

TORGERSON, W. S.: Theory and methods of scaling. Wiley, New York and London 1960.

**Digital**
Digital
digital
цифровой

By a digital machine one understands a machine which works numerically, and which gives its results in figures and therefore to the nearest unit. Examples: milometer of a vehicle, counting units in calculators and cash registers.
The opposite of digital machines are analogue machines such as slide-rules,

clocks, and physical measuring devices whose 'arms' are in continuous motion. Examples: speedometers in vehicles, heating-element ammeter.
One of the oldest digital machines is the abacus whose balls slide on wires or rails.

**Digital computer**
*See* *Computer (digital)

**Diode**
Diode
diode
диод

*An electronic element in which an electric current can flow in one specified direction.*
One must make a distinction between high-vacuum diodes and semi-conductor diodes. The former are *vacuum tubes with two electrodes (cathode and anode) in which a stream of electrons can only flow from the (heated) cathode to the anode. A semi-conductor diode is formed at the junction of *p* and *n* semi-conductor materials, the current flow being from *p* to *n* zones. A charge carrier transport occurs if the *p* zone is positive with respect to the *n* zone. When polarity is reversed a very small reverse current flows.

**Discrimination**
Diskriminierung (Unterscheidung)
discrimination
дискриминация; различение

*An organism discriminates between two impulse-data $S_1$ and $S_2$ if it reacts with different behaviour-patterns $R_1$ or $R_2$ when they occur.*
Discrimination presupposes that the impulse data can be distinguished and that the organism is capable of discrimination. Discriminability is a function of *perception. It exists between two impulses $S_1$ and $S_2$ if they are spaced on a similarity-continuum at a distance of at least the amount of the *differential threshold. The value of this threshold is a function of the ability of the perceiving organism to discriminate on the relevant similarity-continuum. On the basis of *generalization and *concept formation, every organism reacts at first to a new *stimulus $S_n$ with a high probability with a reaction $R_a$, which is conditioned to that stimulus $S_a$ which has a maximum similarity to $S_n$ or which shows a feature-configuration corresponding to that of $S_n$. If this reaction does not lead to a reduction of the given need-tension (cf. *conditioning, instrumental), then other reactions are shown until a conditioning of $S_n$ to a new reaction $R_n$ occurs. By this type of 'differential reward' of the given reactions a discrimination is built up between $S_n$ and $S_a$. Mathematical models for discrimination have been developed from quantity-theoretical assessments in, for example, the *learning theories of ESTES and of BUSH and MOSTELLER.

LUCE, R. D.: Developments in Mathematical Psychology. Glencoe, Illinois 1960. HILGARD, E. R.: Theories of Learning. Appleton-Century Crofts, New York 1956.

**Disjunction (exclusive)**
*See* *Non-equivalence

**Disjunction (inclusive); alternation; inclusive OR**
Disjunktion
disjonction; ou inclusif
дизъюнкция; логическое сложение

*A binary logical connective with the symbol* $\vee$ or $+$ *and the meaning 'or' in the sense of 'vel' (and/or).*

Truth-value table:

| | | | | |
|---|---|---|---|---|
| $a$ | $T$ | $T$ | $F$ | $F$ |
| $b$ | $T$ | $F$ | $T$ | $F$ |
| $a \vee b$ | $T$ | $T$ | $T$ | $F$ |

Disjunction can be traced back to *negation and *conjunction:

$$a \vee b = \overline{\bar{a} \wedge \bar{b}}$$

**Disturbance; perturbance**
Störgrösse
grandeur perturbatrice
величина помех; (внешнее) возмущающее воздействие

Every observation of a phenomenon leads to the differentiation of a given number of variables which may be referred to a co-ordinate system of a configuration space. Disturbance is the name given to every variable whose variations cannot be forecast by the observer in their dependence on time at the instant of observation by means of functional associations known to him. In order to be able to describe the phenomenon as it really is, he must accept the existence of one or more complementary variables which by the very phenomenon of disturbance evade any law. In communication processes white noise is an example of disturbance. The concept of disturbance is therefore linked with the concept of uncertainty which exists at a given time for a given observer. In a *feedback control system disturbance is that variable which fluctuates independently of the other variables which determine the state of the system in a characteristic fashion. Here disturbance appears as the independent variable.

MEYER-EPPLER, W.: Grundlagen und Anwendungen der Informationstheorie. Springer-Verlag, Berlin, Göttingen, Heidelberg 1959.

**Drum store**
*See* *Magnetic drum store

**Duration**
Gegenwartsdauer
durée de présence
время существования

*Time during which the content of perception remains present in the consciousness without concentration being directed to it.*
A definition of duration can still only be approximated, as it is presumably not independent of the respective consciousness-content. Experiments on the ability to reproduce numbers which were heard incidentally during the reading of a text resulted in an evaluation of duration at a maximum of 10 seconds. Duration enables one, for example, to count the chimes of a bell in retrospect. Information psychology interprets duration as a type of store which is attached to the consciousness, and which introduces a hypothetical short-term memory for this purpose.

FRANK, H.: Kybernetische Grundlagen der Pädagogik.—Eine Einführung in die Informationspsychologie, Tel. 5. Agis, Baden-Baden 1962.

**Elective entropy**
Entropie, elektive
entropie élective

———

*A mathematical measure for a finite scheme (a repertory of a finite number of elements with a distribution of probability or *frequency) in which in contrast to selective entropy the probabilities or the frequencies are shown as mutual elections (or mutual relations) of the elements.*
The concept of elective entropy arises from the problems of sociometry and by mathematization becomes a central concept for further fields (plays, drama, etc.).
There are three possibilities for elective entropy:

1 that of elements (*entropy of groups);
2 that of choice classes on the basis of probabilities;
3 that of choice classes on the basis of frequencies.

CUBE, F. von; GUNZENHÄUSER, R.: Über den Begriff der Gruppenentropie. (Soziometrie und Kommunikation), Schnelle, Quickborn b. Hamburg 1963.

**Elective entropy of choice classes**
Entropie der Wahlklassen, elektive
entropie élective des classes de choix

*A measurement for a system of elements which stand in mutual relationship and which elect each other.*
If one takes as the basis of the definition of such a measurement not the elements themselves (i.e. the selectors) but the classes of those elected $i$ times ($i = 0, 1, \ldots, n\text{-}1$) and if one defines as the probability $p_i$ of a choice group ($i$) that probability which corresponds to a *stochastic process (cf. BERNOULLI):

$$p_i = \binom{n-1}{i} . p^i . q^{n-1-i} \; (i = 0, 1, \ldots, n-1)$$
$$p = k/(n-1); \; q = 1 - p,$$

and if one defines as $h_i$ the actual *frequency of the occurrence of the choice group elements, then the following expression is such a measurement, called elective entropy of choice classes, on the basis of probabilities:

$$EEW = \sum_i h_i \cdot \log_2 \frac{1}{p_i} \text{ with } \begin{cases} \sum_i h_i = 1 \\ \sum_i p_i = 1 \end{cases}$$

In *information theory this formula corresponds to the average information of a text based on a known repertory; the text elements have a probability $p_i$ given by the finite scheme, and occur in the text with the actual frequency $h_i$.
A corresponding measurement, elective entropy of choice classes on the basis of frequency, may be defined by the following expression:

$$EKH = \sum_i h_i \cdot \log_2 \frac{1}{h_i} \text{ with } \sum_i h_i = 1$$

(this term was introduced by A. A. MOLES under the concept of complexity of an organism).

CUBE, F. von; GUNZENHÄUSER, R.: Über den Begriff der Gruppenentropie. (Soziometrie und Kommunikation), Schnelle, Quickborn b. Hamburg 1963.
MOLES, A. A.: Über konstruktionelle und instrumentelle Komplexität. Grundlagenstudien aus Kybernetik und Geisteswissenschaft, 1/2 1960.

**Electrocorticogram**
Elektrocorticogramm
électrocorticogramme
электрокортикограмма

*Recording of the variations of potential-differences of cerebral origin (cf. *electroencephalogram) by electrodes which during a brain operation are introduced directly into the brain convolution.*

The electrocorticogram has the advantage over the electroencephalogram of recording beta waves without the interference of the superficial tissue, (i.e. perincephalic fluid, skull and scalp) and facilitates the observations of fast processes at low amplitude (cf. *beta waves).

**Electroencephalogram**
Elektroencephalogramm (EEG)
électroencéphalogramme
электроэнцефалограмма

*Recording of the variations of the potential-differences which are caused by the activity of the *neurons of the *brain by the use of electrodes attached to the scalp. The electrodes are arranged in pairs or used in conjunction with a reference-electrode (bipolar or monopolar method). This means that all brain activity can be systematically examined.*
Electrical activity recorded in this way can be attributed to the cortical and subcortical neuron circuits; it is modulated by activities of meso-diencephalic origin (system of the reticular thalamus, active reticular formation).

**Electronic**
elektronisch
électronique
электронный

A wide concept used to cover all electrical principles, which are applied in the recording, transmission and processing of information, especially in contrast to electro-mechanical devices. Electronic circuit elements are valves, transistors, diodes, etc.; electro-mechanical ones are relays, switches, motors, etc.

**Electronic brain**
Elektronengehirn
cerveau mécanique
электронный мозг

A rather misleading name (it is not the electrons which form the basic difference between the type of machine meant and the brain) for cybernetic machines (cf. *techniques) whose most important parts are program-controlled computers. The word is supposed to give rise to the idea that 'electronic brains' can be the regulating section (the 'brain') of a comprehensive system which includes even classical (i.e. energy transforming) machines: the so-called robot. The popular conception of a robot as a puppet-like machine is completely false: it could not be distinguished from the other parts of a completely automatic control system.

POLETAJEW, J. A.: Kybernetik. Dtsch. Vlg. d. Wissenschaften, Berlin 1962.

**Encoding**
Codierung, nachrichtentechnische
codage
кодирование

*Every representation of a *message by suitable *signals (acoustic, optic or electric). In the information sense the representation of a single message-element (mainly taken from a larger repertory) by several information elements which have been taken from a (usually) smaller repertory.*
In choosing the most suitable encoding process several criteria must be considered:
1 The information elements selected for encoding should be capable of being combined or transferred as easily as possible. From this requisite stems the supreme importance of the *binary digit for technical encoding purposes.
2 The representation of the information should result with the smallest possible number of elements. Of encoding processes which come close to these de-

mands, redundancy-saving encoding processes must be mentioned, especially the processes of SHANNON, FANO, and HUFFMANN as well as the process of controlled code-change. The codes which result from these are distinguished by the differing length of their words. For this a shorter code-word is coordinated to the more frequently occurring information elements which are to be encoded, and a correspondingly longer code word to the more infrequent information elements.

3 The information elements should be transmitted with the optimum speed and with a given assurance against code-word errors. Protected codes fulfil this condition (cf. *code, *error detection and *error-correction). To obtain them, further redundant binary positions are added during encoding to the information-carrying binary positions of the unprotected code-word according to certain, mostly algebraic, rules, so that the code-word length is increased. In contrast to redundancy-saving codes protected codes are distinguished by the equal length of their words. The most well-known are those code-groups which can be treated together algebraically by the rules of group theory, and whose encoding and decoding are relatively simple.

The number of binary-character errors per code-word which have to be detected or corrected depends on the HAMMING-distance achieved in the protected code by the increase in redundancy.

Just as the protection of single code-words can be achieved by a redundancy increase, the protection of blocks (several code-words) can similarly be carried out. In block protection the inspection positions are normally obtained from the addition of the *weights* of the lines and of the columns of the blocks on an even or an uneven number (weight of a line or a column = the number of the binary positions within the line or column which are occupied by binary 1s). This digit addition is also called *parity check*. Example: Block protection by addition to an even digit total within the lines.

| Block | | | Digit total |
|---|---|---|---|
| 0 | 0 | 1 | 1 |
| 0 | 1 | 1 | 2 |
| 1 | 0 | 0 | 1 |
| 1 | 1 | 1 | 3 |

Unprotected block

| Block | | | | Digit total |
|---|---|---|---|---|
| 0 | 0 | 1 | 1 | 2 |
| 0 | 1 | 1 | 0 | 2 |
| 1 | 0 | 0 | 1 | 2 |
| 1 | 1 | 1 | 1 | 4 |

Protected block

4 The information which has to be transmitted should be kept in coded form. Generally the information is first changed into a seemingly meaningless text with the help of a code translator. This is then encoded into a form suitable for transmission.

BERGER, E. R.: Nachrichtentheorie und Codierung. In: Steinbuch, K. (ed.): Taschenbuch der Nachrichtenverarbeitung. Springer-Verlag, Berlin, Göttingen, Heidelberg 1962. SHANNON, C. E.: Communication in the Presence of Noise. Proc. IRE 37 (1949) pp. 10–21. FANO, R. M.: The Transmission of Information. MIT-Report No. 65 (1949). HUFFMAN, D.: A Method for the Construction of Minimum Redundancy Codes. Proc. IRE 40 (1952) pp. 1098–1101. FRANK, H.: Kybernetische Grundlagen der Pädagogik. Mathematischer Teil. Agis, Baden-Baden 1962. STEINBUCH, K.: Codierung für gestörte Kanäle. NTF 19 (1960) pp. 47–55.

**Endocrine system**
Endokrines System
système endocrinien
система желез внутренней секреции; внутрисекреторная система

*System of communication in the body which is effected by special substances (hormones) introduced into the blood. Hormones influence tissues far away from the hormone-producers (glands).*

The endocrine system is one of the three communication systems in the body. The others are the *nerve system and the communication system which controls the growth of cells (cf. biological *regeneration). Communication by the diffusion of hormones exists in lower organisms without nerve systems, but is just as important in higher forms of life. Hormones are produced in glands without ducts and delivered from them into the blood (endocrine glands, hormone glands), in contrast to glands with ducts which produce saliva, digestive juices, etc., and conduct these directly to the mouth, stomach, etc. Hormone production is controlled partially by the nervous system, but is influenced predominantly by other hormones and by chemical parameters in the blood, such as blood sugar level. The endocrine system controls growth and sexual development; disorders of the endocrine system induce abnormal symptoms such as giants or dwarfs. If the thyroid gland underproduces, the result is cretinism (retardation of mental and physical development). Clinical treatment is possible here with the help of oral administration of thyroid extracts. Adrenalin is produced by excitement and thus prepares the body for emergency measures.

**Engram**
Engramm
engramme
энграмма

*Suggested by SEMON to denote the alteration to the nervous system which occurs during impression of memory.*

It is assumed that impressions of this type exist, as information must have a location at the moment it is being processed in the brain. It is, however, very difficult to carry out experiments on the principle of engram. It can be easily calculated that the human brain stores several million *bit, (i.e. the brain can take in more than $10^7$ equi-probable situations. The principle of generalized complementarity (BOHR) and that of finite classes (ELSASSER) make experiments with such a complex system even more difficult.

**Entropy**
Entropie
entropie
энтропия

In *information theory a definition of the expectancy-value:

$$H(p_1, p_2, \ldots, p_n) = -\sum_{i=1}^{n} p_i \log_2 p_i$$

of the *information content $I_i$ of an event $A_i$ of a finite field of events or probability field with $n$ elementary events $\{A_i\}$, $i = 1, 2, \ldots, n$ with

$$I_i = -\log_2 p_i, p_i = P(A_i).$$

The entropy of a source or the average information content of this source is obtained from the entropy $H_n$ of the finite probability field of all $n$-words of this source (series of $n$-letters of the alphabet of this source) by the limiting condition:

$$H = \lim_{n \to \infty} \frac{H_n}{n}.$$

Conditional entropies are formed analogously as defined unspecified or absolute entropies, with the corresponding conditional probabilities. As the term entropy is used in thermodynamics for an expression which formally agrees, yet which is different in dimension, various suggestions have been made that, to avoid confusion, 'uncertainty' be used in information theory; this avoids contestable philosophical arguments.

GRELL, H. (ed.): Arbeiten zur Informationstheorie I. Akademie-Verlag, Berlin 1957. HENZE, E.: Einführung in die Informationstheorie, Beiheft 3, Elektronischen Datenverarbeitung, Braunschweig 1963.

**Entropy, elective**
*See* *Elective entropy

**Entropy of groups**
Gruppenentropie
entropie des groupes
групповая энтропия

*Measurement of a system of elements which 'elect' each other in a general sense.*
Elective entropy of elements or entropy of groups is defined in the following way: if one bases a *repertory on $n$ different elements, in which each element makes $k$ elections from the other $n-1$ elements, and if one specifies these numbers of *elections* $v_i$ by relative *frequencies

$$h_i \ (i = 1, 2, \ldots, n),$$

then by the entropy of groups of this system one understands the expression $EE = \sum_{i=1}^{m} h_i \times \log_2 \frac{1}{h_i}$. $EE$ depends on $n$ and $k$.

CUBE, F. von; GUNZENHÄUSER, R.: Über die Entropie von Gruppen. Schnelle, Quickborn b. Hamburg 1963.

**Equivalence (material equivalence)**
Äquivalenz
équivalence
эквивалентность; равноценность

*Binary *logical connective with the symbol $\equiv$ or $\leftrightarrow$. Two statements are equivalent to each other if their entry in the truth table has value T.*
Truth table:

| | | | | |
|---|---|---|---|---|
| $a$ | $T$ | $T$ | $F$ | $F$ |
| $b$ | $T$ | $F$ | $T$ | $F$ |
| $a \equiv b$ | $T$ | $F$ | $F$ | $T$ |

The expression in terms of *negation, *disjunction and *conjunction (cf. *Boolean algebra) is as follows:

$$a \equiv b = (a \wedge b) \vee (\bar{a} \wedge \bar{b})$$

**Equivocation**
Äquivokation
équivoquation
двусмысленность; эквивокация

*Concept of mathematical *information theory.*
Two *probability fields are given as $X$, $Y$ in which $X$ is the probability field of the input signals of a channel, and $Y$ is the field of its output signals. Then the conditional *information designated $H_Y(X)$ often also written $H(X/Y)$ is called equivocation. Equivocation is therefore equal to the *uncertainty of the transmitted signal with a known reception signal. Equivocation reaches its maximum if and when the *transinformation (*transmitted information) disappears. If the channel deteriorates into a *translator (introduced as a model) which translates the super *characters of the field $Y$ into the *characters of the field $X$ which are perceptible (cf. *apperception) then equivocation becomes the expectancy value of the aesthetic information (cf. *informational aesthetics) about the

selected representation of the super-character by subcharacters.

BERGER, E. R.; PILOTY, H.: Erläuterungen zu den in der Informationstheorie verwendeten Begriffen der mathematischen Statistik. N.T.Z. Heft 1 (1963). FRANK, H.: Kybernetik und Ästhetik. In: Jubiläumsband der Tschechischen Akademie der Wissenschaften zum 15. Erscheinungsjahr der 'Cybernetics' von Norbert Wiener, Prag 1963. FRANK, H.: Information et Pédagogie. Cybernetica 6 (1963).

**Error correction**
Fehlerkorrektur
correction d'erreur
поправка ошибок

*Automatic correction of false code-words in *decoding and code-checking in information transmission and *information processing systems.*

The prerequisite for error correction is a sufficiently large binary-location redundancy (*HAMMING distance) in the blocks or *code-words used (cf. *encoding). Three basic principles of error-correction have evolved:

1 Localization of the incorrect binary-location. With the help of various parity checks on information carrying and redundant binary locations within the block or individual code-words, one or more false binary locations can be localized and corrected by *negation. Example: the receiving-side parity check on an even total results in an uneven total in the second line and the fourth column. This means that the binary character at the point of intersection of this line and this column must be incorrect, and therefore can be corrected by negation ($1 \rightarrow 0$).

2 Similarity-decoding (i.e. list-decoding, comparison decoding). The basis of similarity decoding is the graphic interpretation of the code-words as the nodes of an information-space (HAMMING distance). The protection of a code with $m$ locations with $N$ code-words by $k$ check-points is synonymous with the selection of $N$ code-words from the repertory of all $N' = 2^{m+k} = 2^n$ code-words. The $N$ code-words are then valid code-words for transmission and receiving sides, while the remaining $N'$-$N$ code-words are meaningless. Selection has to be so arranged that in the $n$ dimensional information space the HAMMING distance between the valid code-words is a maximum. Then every valid code-word is surrounded by several similar but meaningless code-words. The HAMMING distance represents a measure for this similarity. The smaller it is, the more similar are the code-words under consideration. Error-correction through similarity decoding uses this fact and corrects a received incorrect code-word into the code-word which is most valid in the above sense. For decoding, use can be made of, for example, an 'electric' list (cf. *translator) of all valid and meaningless code-words and collate them to the valid code-words (list-decoding); or of a reduced 'electric' list of all valid code-words with a post-controlled extreme value circuit (cf. *learning matrix in testing phase). In such a circuit the most similar valid code-word is selected in parallel operation by the comparison of the offered code-word with all valid code-words stored in the translator.

3 Probability decoding. This is a question of a principle of error correction rarely applied in decoding. As a criterion for the translation of a meaningless code-word into a valid code-word one does not use similarity in the sense of the least HAMMING distance, but the conditioned probability $p(x_j/y_r)$ that the received meaningless code-word $y_r$ has resulted from the valid code-word $x_j$. This type of correction is possible if the *a priori* probability of the valid

code-words $x_j$ varies greatly and if no clear similarity decoding is possible, as various meaningless code-words belong at the same time to the correction area of different valid code-words. (This is always the case if a meaningless code-word has the same HAMMING distance to two or more valid code-words. This case occurs if the HAMMING distance $d$ of the code used is an even number.)

| | 1 | 2 | 3 | 4 | QSP |
|---|---|---|---|---|---|
| 1 | 0 | 0 | 1 | 1 | 2 |
| 2 | 0 | 1 | 1 | 0 | 2 |
| 3 | 1 | 0 | 0 | 1 | 2 |
| 4 | 1 | 1 | 1 | 1 | 4 |
| 5 | 0 | 0 | 1 | 1 | 2 |
| QSP = | 2 | 2 | 4 | 4 | |

Transmitted block

| | 1 | 2 | 3 | 4 | QSP |
|---|---|---|---|---|---|
| 1 | 0 | 0 | 1 | 1 | 2 |
| 2 | 0 | 1 | 1 | 1 | 3 |
| 3 | 1 | 0 | 0 | 1 | 2 |
| 4 | 1 | 1 | 1 | 1 | 4 |
| 5 | 0 | 0 | 1 | 1 | 2 |
| QSP = | 2 | 2 | 4 | 5 | |

Received block
QSP: parity check

BERGER, E. R.: Nachrichtentheorie und Codierung. In: Steinbuch, K. (ed.): Taschenbuch der Nachrichtenverarbeitung. Springer-Verlag, Berlin, Göttingen, Heidelberg 1962.

**Error detection**
Fehlererkennung
detection des erreurs
опознавание ошибок

*In binary codes the recognition of errors in transmission.*
Redundant information *codes are used in data-processing or in data-transmission to increase protection against errors. In a non-redundant code incorrect transmission of a code-word element always results in a decoding error: the receiver is incapable of deciding whether the word which has been received represents information from the transmitter or whether it has been falsified by the *channel. The introduction of *redundancy, e.g. by the equivocation of parity-check digits, reduces the *probability of identifying errors in the channel (cf. *irrelevance) with information of the transmitter, (cf. *transinformation). Systems with pure error detection are, in the event of an error, directed to check back and repeat the transmitted word. Further redundant digits in the code enable *error correction to be carried out. A measure for possible error detection or error correction in binary codes is *HAMMING distance $d$, the minimum distance as the sum of different binary digits between any two code-words. If desired, double-error correction or quadruple-error detection is possible when $d = 5$.

BERGER, E. R.: Nachrichtentheorie und Codierung. In: Steinbuch, K. (ed.): Taschenbuch der Nachrichtenverarbeitung. Springer-Verlag, Berlin, Göttingen, Heidelberg 1962.

**Evoked response**
Rindenpotential
potential cortical
потенциал коры головного мозга

*Variations in potential which occur at the cortex of the great brain as a result of the excitation of peripheral parts of a sensory-organ system.*
Evoked response which arises (e.g. by *autocorrelation) via the excitation states of several *neurons represents the end product of the information processing within the specific and non-specific system between peripheral sensory cells

and the cortex of the great brain. Essentially it consists of a large surface-positive variation in potential, with an average duration of 10 msec. and a latency of, for example, 8–15 msec. in hearing.

Every sensory organ possesses a more or less sharply defined specific projection area in the cortex where the above primary evoked response can be recorded, after stimulation, directly on the cortex. Secondary evoked responses with a larger latency (30 msec.) can be found when there is only slight or even no narcosis at several non-specific locations in the cortex; at the same time the primary evoked responses (e.g. of a conscious animal) become more complex and extended. In humans, complex evoked responses with several components can be detected on the outside of the undamaged scalp with the help of electronic recording devices; in this, an average approximately di-phased component with a latency of 75–150 msec. is fundamental as well as the component corresponding to the secondary evoked responses.

FIELD, J.; MAGOUN, H. W.; HALL, V. E. (eds.): Handbook of Physiology, Neurophysiology. Vol. I. Am. Physiol. Soc., Washington 1959.

**Exclusive disjunction**
*See* *Non-equivalence

**Excitation**
Erregung, physiologische
excitation
возбуждение (физиол)

*Primary biological response to a *stimulus.*
Excitable function units, such as nervous and muscular tissues, are capable of excitation through the difference of ionic concentration, caused by metabolic processes, between the ınternal and external media of a cell surrounded by a functional *membrane. Excitation consists of (*a*) a depolarization of this membrane; when the stimuli are weak, this depolarization is initially local and dependent on the strength of the stimulus; and (*b*) the subsequent measurable decrease in the rest-potential. If however, a certain stimulus-threshold is exceeded, then the cell responds by a complete and rapid depolarization. The much larger *action potential is built up on the local response and the excitation processes proceed independently of the type, duration and strength of the stimulus (cf. *all-or-none law). During depolarization and the subsequent slower repolarization-phase, complicated ionic-shifts occur as a result of the changing permeability of the functional membrane towards potassium and sodium ions. An excitation is not limited to the stimulus-location, but is conducted at a certain speed along a fibre in both directions (cf. *axon).

MURALT, A. von: Neuere Ergebnisse der Nervenphysiologie. Springer-Verlag, Berlin, Göttingen, Heidelberg 1958.

**Extinction**
Verlernen
oubli

---

*A reduction in the strength of an *association, formed by learning (cf. *conditioning), between a pre-given *stimulus and an appropriate *reaction.*

In the process of conditioning, an association is formed between a stimulus and a reaction and is expressed in an increase of the probability of the occurrence of this reaction to the given stimulus. This process is reversed after completion of learning. After classical conditioning (cf. *conditioning, classical) this process is slowed down if during learning only one part of the material offered by the initially neutral stimulus is followed by the reaction release. Accordingly, after instrumental conditioning (cf. *conditioning, instrumental) the extinction is slowed down if the offered reinforcement (punishment, diversion of danger, announcement of success) has not always followed the behaviour (partial reinforcement). The process of extinction, measured by the variation of the probability of the occurrence of the corresponding reaction with the stimulus examined, independent of the time elapsed since conditioning, is usually exponential. By a subsequent conditioning of the same or a similar stimulus with a different pattern of behaviour the extinction of the original association is accelerated. Various theories accept as an explanatory principle that the association created by conditioning is retained by new associations in which parts of the pertinent stimulus or reaction participate. Another theory states that the execution of every behaviour amplifies a specifically allotted inhibition-potential. This amplification of inhibition, which leads to extinction, is masked during the conditioning process itself by the effects of the given rewards. There exist many other theories.

HILGARD, E. R.: Theories of learning. Appleton-Century Crofts, New York 1956. HOFSTÄTTER, P. R.: Psychologie. Fischer Lexikon 6, Frankfurt 1957. LUCE, R. D.: Developments in mathematical psychology. Glencoe, Illinois 1960.

# F

**Facilitation**
Bahnung
facilitation
формирование

*Effect which furthers excitation through networks of information conductors in the body.*

The excitation-increasing effect of facilitation influences (for example, in afferent paths coming from higher centres) the metabolic processes of the elements responsible for encoding. In addition excitations of the unspecific *system (formatio reticularis) have a directive and inhibitive influence on the cortical fields, although electronic potential-alteration and synchronization-effects have an essential role in this.

Facilitation is also generally attainable through training (conditioning) (cf. *conditioning, classical or Pavlovian). Facilitation, as well as *inhibition is a decisive piece of equipment in the sensory-organ system for contrast-formation and application of attentiveness.

BREMER, F.: Neurogenic factors influencing the evoked potentials of the cerebral cortex. In: Rosenblith, W. (ed.): Sensory Communication. Wiley, New York 1961. HERNÁNDEZ-PEÓN, R.: Reticular Mechanisms of Sensory Control. In: Rosenblith, W. (ed.): Sensory Communication. Wiley, New York 1961.

**Factor analysis**
Faktorenanalyse
analyse factorielle
факториальный анализ

*A mathematical model for the analysis of random variables expressed as weighted sums of statistically independent components.*

Models and methods of factor analysis were developed initially in psychology in the field of experiments dealing with intelligence. The results of psychological intelligence tests show that positive correlations (cf. *correlation coefficient) exist between the tests themselves. From this it is clear that these tests measure, to a certain degree, a common feature called factor. Each observation can therefore be divided into a component which originates from the factor, and into a component specific to the test. The model of multiple factor analysis (THURSTONE) which is to-day applied in the widest range of sciences goes further. Observations of a normally distributed random variable are analysed into components which result from several statistically independent factors, and into a component which includes a factor specific to the variable and random errors. Only those factors are definable which participate in the occurrence of several of the $k$ observed variables. For every combination of a variable with a factor, a weight or loading $a_{ij}$ must be calculated. If one multiplies the theoretical factor values of an observation of the $k$ variables by the appropriate loadings of the $i^{th}$ variable, then the sum of the products gives the magnitude of the $i^{th}$ variable in the observation. The loadings give the relative importance of every factor for the individual variables, and form the matrix $A$. Let the matrix $R$ contain the correlation between the variables and (in the leading diagonal) estimates of the proportion of variance not due to the specific factor. Factor analysis is then the solution of the equation $AA' = R$ for $A$. $A$ should be of order $k \cdot m$ ($k$ variables, $m$ factors), the $m$ columns should be orthogonal to each other, and $m$ should be as small as possible, bearing in mind the estimation errors in the definition of $R$. $A$ has infinitely many possible values. Secondary conditions which determine $A$ constitute the various methods of solution. In order to be able to interpret discovered factors on the basis of the variables examined, mainly orthogonal, transformations of $A$ are executed (rotation of the factor-matrix). Non-orthogonal transformations are much rarer and rather controversial.

HARMANN, H. H.: Modern Factor Analysis. Univ. Chicago Press 1960.

**FECHNER's law**
FECHNERsches Gesetz
loi de FECHNER
Закон Вебера-Фехнера

*See under* *Psychophysics

**Feedback**
Rückkopplung
———
обратная связь

*A system is a feedback system if it consists of two or more sub-systems which are connected to a circuit in such a way that an output value of each sub-system is an input of value the following sub-system (cf. blockdiagram). There is at least one directional system (cf. *feedback, absence of) an amplifier, so that a certain directional effect exists in the circuit.*

There are two principal forms for the causal relationship in which several objects can stand: an open chain of effect and a closed loop of effect. (A causal relationship must be thought of as the relation of variable characteristics of objects or of physical variables). In the open causal chain one object affects a second, and this affects yet another, and so on. In a closed loop, one object similarly affects a second, but this second object (or a later one) then affects the first; an object affects itself via another; every variable of the circuit is dependent on itself, i.e. its definition at any one time depends on its definition at an earlier moment.

In this general definition there is no limitation of the possible objects and variable characteristics which can have a causal connection in the shape of a 'loop-relation' (H. SCHMIDT). In fact, the organizational form of feedback is found at all levels of existence. The general theory of feedback is therefore valid for circuits of any objects and variables (circuits in machines with, for example, electrical, mechanical or hydraulic qualities, in animals and social groups; values, in animals and social groups; and psychophysical circuits of man's behaviour with the outside world).

In general theory a feedback system must be thought of as a circular system of at least two sub-systems (Fig. 1).

The systems are (mathematically) defined by the functional dependence of the output and input variables. The feedback circuit as a whole must be regarded as a system with at least one input and one output (in this the identically disappearing time-function $x(t) \equiv 0$ can be taken as a possible input, which is to say there is no input). If a circuit is examined with an input ($x$) and an output ($y$), then it can be divided into two sub-systems in such a way that its function is represented in the blockdiagram in Fig. 2. The input $x_o$ of system 1 is dependent not only on the input of $x$ of the whole circuit but also on the feed-

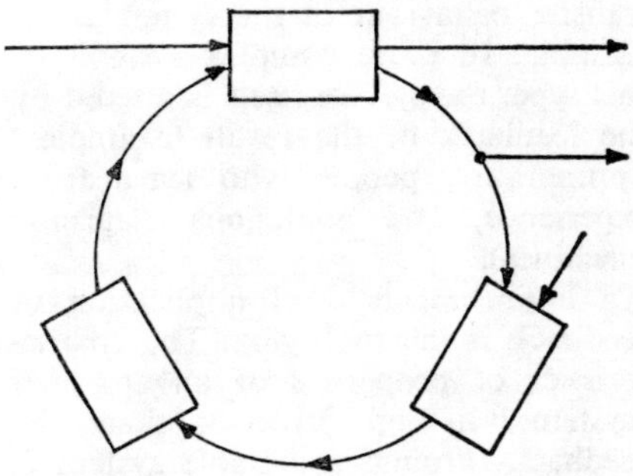

1 Feedback

back variable $x_r$ which depends on $y$ via system 2; $y$ is at the same time the output of system 1 and of the whole circuit. There is no general systemization of feedback systems: here only a few important types can be given.

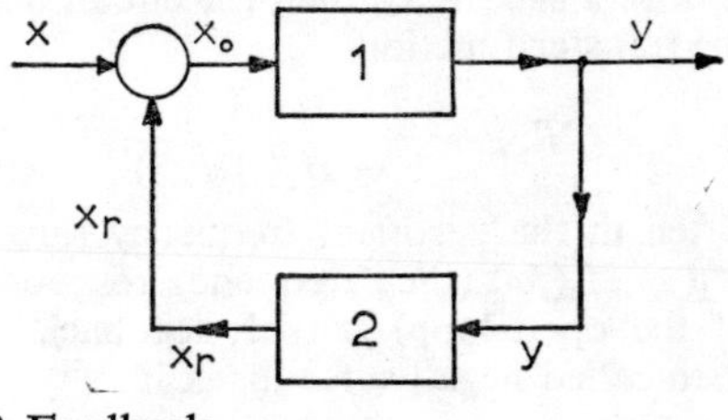


2 Feedback

Perhaps the most important class are systems with the structure of sensory motor loops. The input $x$ is given as the goal of the system. The output $y$ is the result of the operation executed by system 1. This is referred back via system 2 and compared with the goal given in the input. As a result of the comparison (variable $x_o$) the operation of system 1 is altered mainly in such a way that a better approximation of the result to the pre-given goal is achieved. The simplest systems of this type are *feedback control systems in which the transfer behaviour of the system is invariable. In more complex systems of this type, the system itself is altered by the feedback of the result (examples: optimalizers, people who learn from experience, and analogous *learning machines).

An important field of application of feedback is in amplifying. The characteristics of properties of an amplifier (system 1 in Fig. 2) can be altered by feedback through a suitable system 2, and adjusted to the technical task at hand.

The mathematical processes according to which feedback circuits can be treated are worked out most completely for linear systems. Often calculations are made with the transfer-function. If in Fig. 2 the two systems 1 and 2 have the transfer function $H_1(s)$ and $H_2(s)$ and if $x_o = x + x_r$, then the circuit has the transfer function

$$H(s) = \frac{H_1(s)}{1 - H_1(s)H_2(s)}.$$

Often in the pertinent frequency range $H_1(j\omega)H_2(j\omega)$ (the *frequency response of the open loop) is real; feedback is then called negative feedback if

$$H_1(j\omega)H_2(j\omega) < 0$$

i.e. $|H(j\omega)| < |H_1(j\omega)|$,

and positive feedback if

$$1 > H_1(j\omega)H_2(j\omega) > 0,$$

i.e. if $|H(j\omega)| > |H_1(j\omega)|$.

When there is stronger positive feedback, if $H_1(j\omega)H_2(j\omega) = 1$ or more precisely if $1 - H_1(s)H_2(s)$ has zeros with positive real parts, then the loop becomes unstable (cf. *stability), and it executes a self-excited oscillation independent of the input value. Oscillation generators are also an important class of feedback circuits.

Bode, H. W.: Network Analysis and Feedback Amplifier Design. New York 1946. Schmidt, H.: Bemerkungen zur Weiterentwicklung der allgemeinen Regelkreislehre. Grundlagenstudien Band 3, H. 3 (1962) pp. 75–84. Wiener, N.: The Human Use of Human Beings. Boston 1950.

**Feedback, absence of**

Rückwirkungsfreiheit

liberté d'action en retour

однонаправленность

*The characteristic of a transfer system of being able to exert an effect in one direction only.*

There are transfer systems with two variables $x$ and $y$, such as a simple lever or a passive electrical *four terminal network, which can exert an effect in both directions, $x \rightarrow y$ and $y \rightarrow x$. In these input and output can only be distinguished if they are connected to other systems in such a way that only one variable is excited from outside. Also, there is the class of transfer systems which have only one direction of effect, e.g. $x \rightarrow y$. Here, $y$ can have no effect on $x$. Such systems are called 'directional' systems. The characteristic of being directional is often called absence of feedback (although it must be admitted that this concept occurs in literature with varying and sometimes imprecise meanings).

A distinction is made between two types of directional systems: (1) systems with auxiliary energy, e.g. an amplifier; in these, the input controls the output (the energy of which comes from any similar energy reservoir), without the actual energy being transmitted. (2) Systems which do not have an amplifying effect, in which therefore the whole of the performance of the output comes from the input. (Examples: galvanometers and bimetallic thermometers.)

In a transfer system with more than two 'ports' (several inputs or several outputs) the transfer behaviour of each two 'ports' can in the same way be called directional or non-directional.

**Feedback control; closed loop control**
Regelung
réglage; régulation
регулирование
*See under* *Feedback control system

**Feedback control system; servomechanism; control loop**
Regelkreis; Regelsystem; geregeltes System
boucle de régulation
регулирующий контур; замкнутый контур регулирования

*A *feedback system which serves to make a variable independent of disturbing influences, so that it always has a pre-given value.*

1 To explain a feedback control system let us take a technical problem. Let us take a system in which several physical variables occur which are dependent on each other. Let one of the variables, the *output $x$, be causally dependent on the other variables, the *input variables $y, z_1, z_2, \ldots$: $x = x(y, z_1, z_2, \ldots)$. As it is used for a special purpose, $x$ should always have a certain pre-given value, the *index value or set point $x_k$. If the task of retaining this is solved by control, then the system is called the *controlled system*, $x$ the *controlled condition*, the value of $x$ the *actual value of the *controlled condition, and the deviation $x - x_k$ of the actual value $x$ from the index value $x_k$ the *deviation*.

2 All input variables apart from $y$, i.e. $z_1$, $z_2, \ldots$ can adopt any values $\zeta_1, \zeta_2, \ldots$ within a certain range. However, $x$ can have the index value $x_k$ if one bestows a suitable value $\eta$ to $y$ so that $x(\eta, \zeta_1, \zeta_2, \ldots) = x_k$. In order that this may be practicable, $y$ must be an accessible and adjustable value, and is called the *regulating variable. The remaining input variables $z_1$, and $z_2$ are not defined by making $x$ equal to $x_k$, but by being dependent on external causes; some are defined by the application of the system, some even are unknown. In connection with the task of making the deviation zero, their effect on $x$ is a disturbance, and they are therefore called disturbances or perturbances. The division of the input variables of the system into regulating variables and disturbances does not depend on the system as such but on the interaction of the system with other systems. Often many inputs are possible disturbances. Let this example serve as a demonstration: let the given system be a room and the output the room temperature. This is conditioned by several inputs, for example external air temperature, direction and speed of wind, radiation from the sun, number of people in the room, number of open windows and the output of the heating system. The last two variables can be called the regulating variables. In the manual control of the room temperature, the opening of windows is often taken as a regulating variable; in automatic control, the output of the heating system.

3 The task of making the deviation zero can be solved in two principally different ways, by *open-loop control and *closed loop control. To solve the problem by open-loop control the following must be known: the dependence of the controlled condition $x$ on all the input variables of the system, i.e. the function $x = x(y, z_1, z_2, \ldots)$ as well as the respective values of the disturbances. One can then produce a control device which measures the disturbances and alters the regulat-

ing variable dependent on the disturbances in such a way that the effect of any alterations of the disturbances on $x$ is removed. There is an open chain of effect in which the disturbances have an effect on $x$ either via $y$ or directly, see blockdiagram 1 which is drawn only for the perturbance $z$.

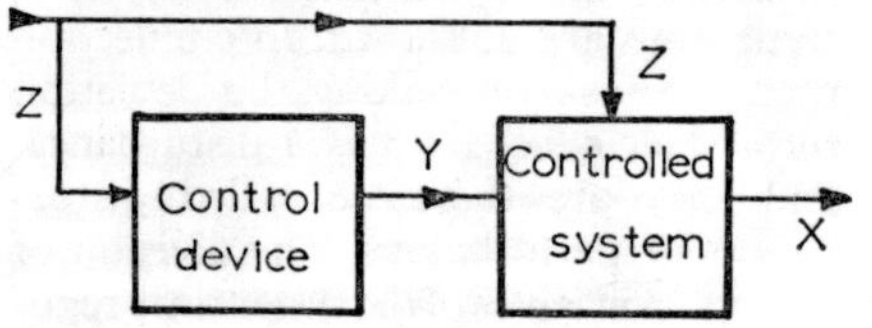


1 Open-loop control

The actual value of $x$ and hence the success of the control is not taken into account: this is clearly a defect. The possibility of applying open-loop control is further limited in that only rarely are all disturbances and their effect on $y$ precisely known. *Closed loop control (or feed-back control) avoids both these shortcomings: its basic task is to make the regulating variable dependent on the controlled condition. A second system, the controller with the input $x$ and the output $y$ is connected up with the

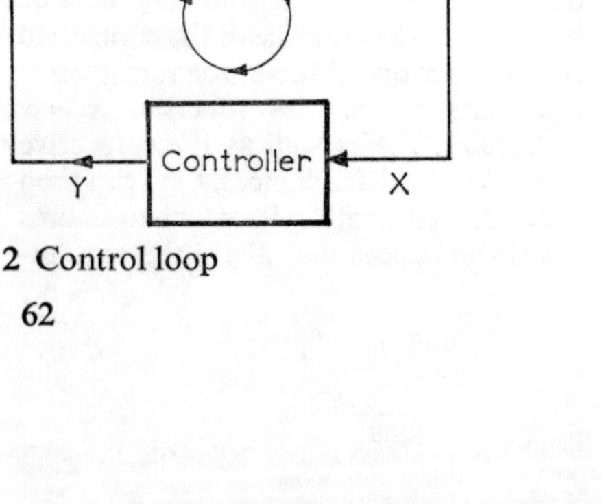


2 Control loop

controlled system which apart from the disturbances also has the input $y$ and the output $x$. The result is a cyclic system (see diagram 2), namely the feedback control system.

This system is a feedback system. Its form is not, as is the case with open-loop control, an open chain, but a closed circuit.

*Feedback is negative if, when $x$ experiences a positive deviation from the index value through the effect of disturbances, the regulating variable is altered by the regulator in such a way that it effects a decrease of $x$. It is characteristic that closed loop control only becomes effective if the regulating variable deviates measurably from the index value. Therefore the task of making the deviation zero, which is solved by open-loop control when known disturbances occur, is not solved exactly by closed loop control. But closed loop control does have the advantage of making the controlled condition largely independent of any disturbances.

4 The controller has various functions. It has a device for measuring the actual value $x$ of the controlled condition. It also has to produce (by comparison with the index value) a signal for the deviation $x_w$. In this the measured value of the controlled condition is compared with the index value; the control operation is not influenced by the actual deviation, but by the measured deviation. Errors or disturbances which affect the measuring instrument must be avoided, as their influence is not compensated for by closed loop control.

If the index value is constant, then no special element is needed for forming the deviation. In this case the control system is termed a regulator. Every feedback control system contains a correcting element, which is best regarded as part of the controller (the analysis of a feedback control system into elements with various functions, or the correspondence of its parts to these elements is often not possible). The correcting element alters the regulating variable $y$, a principal input of the controlled system, dependent on the deviation $x_w$. The system which has the input $x_w$ and the output $y$ can consist of corrective elements (apart from the correcting element mentioned above) of various types, which influence the time-cycle operation, e.g. reduce the deviations which occur or else increase the stability. Controllers are divided according to their time-cycle operation: (a) proportional controllers (P-controllers): $y$ is proportional to $x_w$; there occurs even in the stationary state an off-set error: (b) integral controllers (I-controllers) in which $y$ is proportional to the time-integral of $x_w$, or a combination of both (PI-controllers); in the stationary state $x_w$ becomes 0; (c) controllers in which $y$ is also dependent on the rate of change of $x_w$ (derivative controllers) (e.g. PID-controllers). The use of the differential-quotient of $x_w$ serves mainly to increase the *stability of the feedback control system.

5 The mathematical examination of feedback control systems is carried out according to the same methods used generally in *linear systems and feedback circuits, namely, not only by means of the differential equations of linear circuits, but also by means of *frequency response, *transfer function, *step response (cf. *stability).

6 The historic development of the practice and theory of feedback control systems took the following course, sketched briefly. The beginnings of closed loop control of machines can be found in the eighteenth century, e.g. windmills, steam engines; until the end of the nineteenth century the technique was limited, by and large, to this field. The first complete mathematical theory of feedback control systems was by J. C. MAXWELL in 1868 and J. WISCHNEGRADSKI in 1877. In the first decades of the twentieth century the application of closed loop control was extended to all fields of technology. Then everything which these many varied technical feedback systems had in common was compiled to form a general control technique (H. SCHMIDT). Then it was discovered that animals also have feedback control systems for the various physiological variables, and they have precisely the same structure as those produced technically (H. SCHMIDT, R. WAGNER); also, that all activities of man are in the form of a feedback control system (action circuit: A. GEHLEN, H. SCHMIDT).

7 Examples of technical, physiological and anthropological feedback:

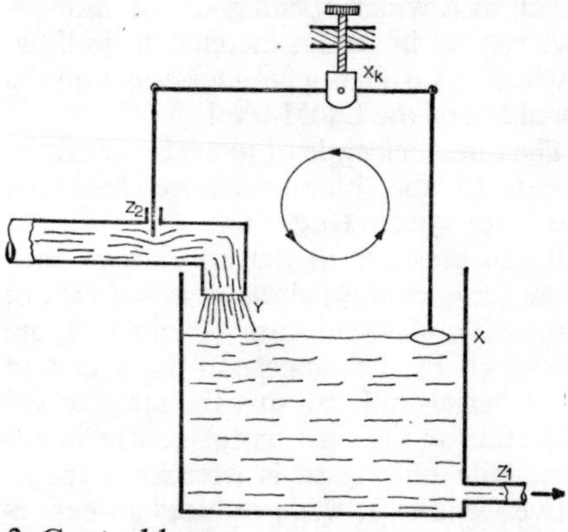


3 Control loop.

X level of liquid; $X_k$ index value proportional to the level of the bearing; Y volume of liquid flow per time unit; $Z_1$ varying consumption; $Z_2$ varying pressure of liquid.

In Fig. 3 a liquid-level feedback control system is represented. The controlled system consists of a container with an in-flow and out-flow. The controlled condition is the level of the liquid which is dependent on the volume of in-flow of the liquid (regulating value) and the consumption of the liquid (disturbance $Z_1$). The controller (P-controller) consists of a float as the measuring device, a lever-type coupling and a sliding shut-off valve in the in-flow pipe as a correcting element. The adjustment of the index value occurs by adjusting the height of the lever-bearing. The quantity of liquid flowing into the container (regulating variable) depends not only on the opening of the shut-off valve but also on the pressure of the liquid in front of it: this is a disturbance ($Z_2$) affecting the correcting element. The closed nature of the control loop is obvious: if the liquid-level sinks due to increased consumption, the float also sinks; this results, via the lever mechanism, in a wider opening of the shut-off valve and hence an increase in in-flow, which in turn has a counter-effect on the sinking of the liquid-level.

The same principle of interaction can be seen in the blood-pressure feedback control system (Fig. 4).

If the pressure in the aorta rises then the nerve-endings situated in the wall of the blood-vessel are excited more strongly by the increase in the stretch of the vessel-wall; by this the state of excitation in the vaso-motor centre in the medulla oblongata is decreased (negative feedback); this produces an expansion of the peripheral vessels, that is, a decrease in the resistance to the flow, and hence a decrease of the blood-pressure (cf. *biological regulation and *homeostasis).

All deliberate actions of man occur in the form of a loop. In its elementary shape, which is also the form of the execution of many movements in ani-

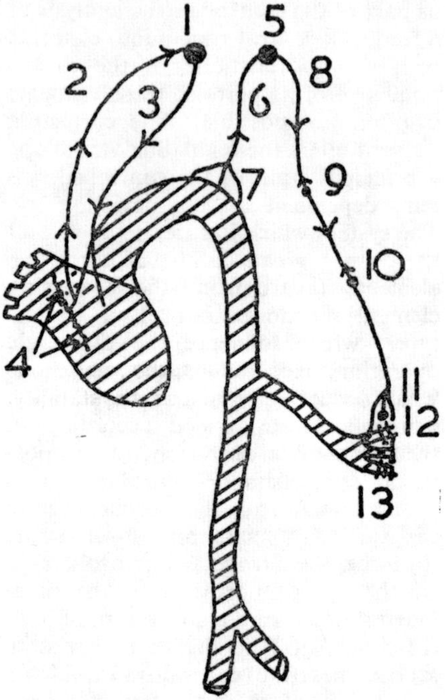


4 Blood pressure feedback control system.

1 cardio-inhibitory centre; 2 afferent nerve of the heart; 3 cardiac depressor nerve (X cranial nerve vagus); 4 stretch receptors; 5 highest nerve centre of the blood vessels (vaso-motor centre in the medulla oblongata); 6 nerve regulating blood pressure; 7 stretch receptors; 8 nerve path in spinal cord for control of blood vessels; 9 nerve cell in spinal cord for controlling blood vessels; 10 interconnecting nerve cell (sympathetic); 11 vessel nerve; 12 peripheral centres of the vessel nerves; 13 smooth muscle fibres in vessel wall.

mals, it is a simple feedback control system which is formed from elements of an inorganic, physiological and psychological nature. For example, if a craftsman is producing a certain object, he continually takes notice of the state of the material he is working with (measurement of the actual value of the controlled condition), compares it with the imagined final state (the index value) and according to the deviation corrects the movement of his hands and of the tool (function of the correcting element).

DIN 19226. Normblatt über Benennungen und Begriffe der Regelungstechnik, 1954 (Entwurf einer Neufassung Mai 1962). GEHLEN, A.: Der Mensch. Rowohlts deutsche Enzyklopädie, 4th edn. Bonn 1950. LEONHARD, A.: Die selbsttätige Regelung. Springer-Verlag, Berlin, Göttingen, Heidelberg 1957. OLDENBOURG, R. C.; SARTORIUS, H.: Dynamik selbsttätiger Regelungen. Band 1, R. Oldenbourg, München 1951. OPPELT, W.: Kleines Handbuch technischer Regelvorgänge. Verlag Chemie, Weinheim 1960. SCHMIDT, H.: Denkschrift zur Gründung eines Institues für Regelungstechnik. (1st edn. 1941). Grundlagenstudien aus Kybernetik und Geisteswissenschaft, Beiheft Bd. 2 (1961). SCHMIDT, H.: Die Entwicklung der Technik als Phase der Wandlung des Menschen. Z. VDI 96 (1954) pp. 118–22. SOLODOWNIKOW, W. W.: Grundlagen der selbsttätigen Regelung. R. Oldenbourg, München and Berlin 1959. WAGNER, R.: Probleme und Beispiele biologischer Regelung. Thieme, Stuttgart 1954.

**Feed-forward control**
Vorwärtsregelung
régulation par l'amont
прямое регулирование

*In general synonymous with *open-loop control.*

An expression used in amplification techniques to describe the influence of parameters occurring near the output of a block diagram. (Example: Alteration of the lower frequency amplification factor dependent on the amplitude of the demodulated high frequency in a radio receiver). In control techniques, feed-forward control is much the same as regulation through disturbance feed-forward.

**FEINSTEIN's theorem**
FEINSTEINscher Satz
théorème de FEINSTEIN
теорема Фейнштейна

FEINSTEIN's theorem states that with certain restrictions on a *channel one can find a sufficiently large number of distinguishable words which the channel correctly transmits.

If the channel is stationary, if it works without *anticipation and has a finite memory (cf. *memory of a channel) then for a sufficiently large $n$ and for as small an $\varepsilon > O$ as one wishes one can find a family $\{u_i\}$; $i = 1, 2, \ldots, N$ of distinguishable words, so that $N > 2^n (C-\varepsilon)$ is valid for their number. In this $C$ is the channel capacity. A family of words $\{u_i\}$ from the input alphabet $A$ is called distinguishable if a family $\{V_i\}$; $i = 1, 2, \ldots, N$ of sub-sets of the *message space $B^I$ exists at the output of the channel, so that these sub-sets contain no common words and the probability becomes

$$P_{ui}(V_i) = P\{y \in V_i \mid x = u_i\} > 1 - \varepsilon$$

GRELL, H. (ed.): Arbeiten zur Informationstheorie. I. Dtsch. Vlg. d. Wissenschaften, Berlin 1963. HENZE, E.: Einführung in die Informationstheorie. Beiheft 3, Elektronische Datenverarbeitung, 2nd Ed. 1965.

**Field of events**
*See* *Probability field

**Filter**
Filter
filtre
фильтр

*Apparatus for separating certain parts of a material or process.*

Whilst in chemical technology, for example, certain parts of a material are separated, as in the case of a solution (a liquid or a filtrate) from sediment (undissolved hard material), in electrical information-technology certain parts of a process are separated from each other. Different types of filter are: *frequency filter, time filter, *amplitude filter, *predictor, etc.

**Flow diagram; flow chart**
Flussdiagramm
organigramme
(детальная) блок—схема программы

*An overall schematic representation of a program in its essential features, independent of the computer.*

Before the *instructions of a *program are written down the flow chart must be used to ascertain the sequence of the steps of the program. These individual steps are written down in small boxes, whose shape is different for assignment, tests, comparisons and decisions; these boxes are normally rectangles, rhomboids, trapezia or ovals. The sequence, the 'flow' of the calculation, is ascertained by connecting these boxes by arrows. In this way it is easy to scan loops, jumps and branches. If the sequence of various program-steps is irrelevant, then they may be placed in the same box.

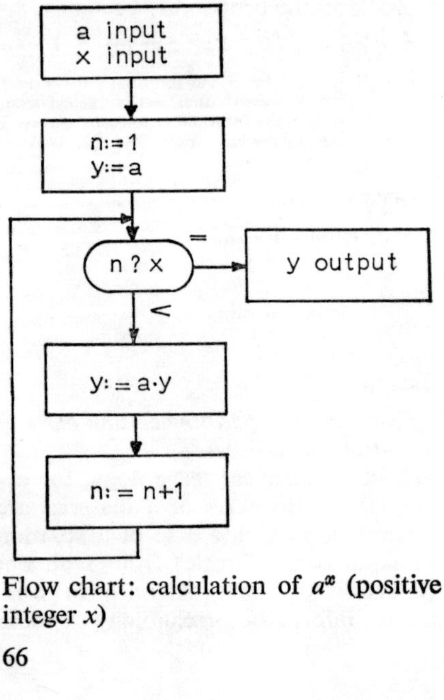

Flow chart: calculation of $a^x$ (positive integer $x$)

A rectangular box always has one input and one output, whereas a test-box can have one input and several outputs ('yes, no'; or 'equal, unequal, larger, smaller'). Value-assignment is often written in two ways, either by ZUSE's 'Result-arrow') (e.g. $b + c = > a$) or by the ALGOL symbol 'is replaced by' (e.g. $a: = b + c$). A comparison has either the form '*a* ?*b*' (answer e.g. 'equal') or '*a* equal *b*?' (answer e.g. 'yes') (see diagram).

GÜNTSCH, F. R.: Einführung in die Programmierung Digitaler Rechenautomaten. pp. 29–31, De Grayter, Berlin 1960.

**Focalized-diffused-excitation**
Konvergenz-Divergenz-Schaltung
circuit à convergence-divergence
—

*General method for the conduction of information in an organism based on lateral and temporal *inhibition and hence contrast-formation, as well as on the complicated networks within the sensory-organ system.*

The *specific afferent of a sensory-organ system is constructed in the sense of a focalized-diffused-excitation, whereby in the area of the sensory organs a local contrast-formation is made possible by inhibition, and in the area of higher centres the execution of mediating-processes which operate statistically are made possible by *facilitation. Excitations which are capable of contrast-formation and temporal mediation are the neuro-physiological pre-conditions for the occurrence of contrasts, and on the highest level, of abstraction. Focalized-diffused-excitation also permits an explanation for the fact that in the field of sensory physiology, a deterioration of the occurrence-probability of a certain event compared to the expectancy-probability of the stimulus can be observed when simple stimuli are being processed, yet when complex stimuli are being processed, an improvement in the behaviour-probability at the end of the central-nervous information processing can be achieved.

KEIDEL, W. D.: Grenzen der Übertragbarkeit der Regelungslehre auf biologische Probleme. Naturwiss. 48 (1961) pp. 264–76. MOUNTCASTLE, V. B.: Convergence and organizational principles in the nervous system. International Symposium on Principles of Sensory Communication. Boston 1959.

**Font standardization**
Zeichennormierung
normalization des caractères; standardization des caractères
стандартизация или нормирование образов

*The agreement of features of quality and shape for producing magnetic and optical scripts which will achieve an optimal accuracy in automatic recognition.*
In order to be able to use the simplest possible *character readers with a correspondingly low range of variation and to guarantee the best possible accuracy in recognition, certain type fonts are worked out and standardized. This means that generally accepted specifications are created for the manufacturers of both printers and character readers. The bodies responsible for font standardization are in the U.S.A. the X3–1 committee of the American Standards Association (ASA), in Germany the Arbeitskreis 2b of the Deutsche Normenausschuss (DNA), and in Britain the British Standards Institute (BSI).

**Forgetting**
Vergessen
oubli
забвение

*Decrease in the reproductability of a learned fact with the passage of time.*
The first systematic examination of forgetting is found in EBBINGHAUS's studies on memory (1885). He examined the reproductability of learned meaningless syllables, which decreases with the distance in time from the learning. The degree of forgetting at a certain point of time can be ascertained in different ways. In the *saving* method the test subject is asked to re-learn the already learned material. The number of times the material has to be offered in the re-learning in relation to the number of repetitions necessary in the original learning results in an evaluation of forgetting. The *reproduction* method consists of the proportion of individual stimuli (e.g. meaningless syllables) which is correctly reproduced from a learned repertory after a given length of time, while the *recognition* method requires the test subject to identify the learned stimuli in a larger repertory. Tests of this type result in the approximately linear dependence of the amount of forgetting on the logarithm of the period of time that has elapsed since learning. Some of the variables which clearly influence forgetting are: the amount of meaning in the material learned, the type of activity which follows the learning (sleep helps above all the retention of meaningless stimuli), and the attitude of the test-subject towards the material. If the material is repeatedly offered to the test-subjects after having already been learned successfully (overlearning) the subsequent process of forgetting is clearly slowed down.

HILGARD, E. R.: Theories of Learning. Appleton-Century Crofts, New York 1956. HOFSTÄTTER, P. R.: Psychologie. Fischer Lexikon 6, Frankfurt 1957.

**Formants**
Formant
formants
форманты; основные частоты (звука)

*Characteristic amplitude- (or energy-) distribution in the frequency-spectrum of a signal (especially in aural sounds).*

If an amplitude-distribution in the frequency-spectrum of a signal can be approximated by a function

$$g(\nu) = A_0/\sqrt{\sigma^2 + 4\pi^2(\nu - \nu_F)^2}$$

then it is said that this signal is monoformant. The formant itself can be characterized by the formant-frequency $\nu_F$ and the formant-width (half-value width) $W_F = (\sqrt{3}/\pi) \times \sigma$ ($\sigma$: the fade-constant of the signal). If a signal can be regarded as the overlap of several formants of different formant-frequency, then this is called poly-formant. In the vowel-spectrum two or three formants can normally be ascertained. The formant-frequencies can also be calculated from articulation data (position of articulatory organs) as the characteristic value of the mouth and throat cavity, which can be regarded as articulation-filters.

MEYER-EPPLER, W.: Grundlagen und Anwendungen der Informationstheorie. Springer-Verlag, Berlin, Göttingen, Heidelberg 1959. UNGEHEUER, G.: Elemente einer akustischen Theorie der Vokalartikulation. Springer-Verlag, Berlin, Göttingen, Heidelberg 1962.

**FORTRAN (formula translation) language**
FORTRAN
langage Fortran
фортран

*A problem-orientated *programming language for solving mathematical-technical and business problems.*

Fortran uses the usual arithmetical symbols and bracketings and permits the use of indices (according to special rules). Control statements replace certain *instructions and generate orders with regard to *loops (program-sections which are run through several times). The description of *input and *output of data is facilitated by special statements. For the translation of a program written in FORTRAN into machine-code many computers have *compilers available. Compilers demand (or permit) some machine-dependent commands (e.g. the reservation of a section of the *store for data) and the observation of certain rules when a program is being written.

**Four terminal network**
Vierpol; Zweitor
quadripole
четырёхполюсник

*Transmission device with one input and one output.*

The treatment of the electrical properties of a four terminal network is a subject of network theory. Characteristic values of a linear four terminal network are open circuit and short circuit independence and transfer function. A distinction is made between passive and active four terminal networks. The former are constructed only from energy storing and energy dissipative (passive) elements (resistance network, *filter). Active four terminal networks contain, in addition to passive elements, regulated energy sources, e.g. *amplifiers.

ARTUS, W.: Einführung in die elektrische Nachrichtentechnik. R. Oldenbourg, München 1957.

**FOURIER analysis**
*See* *Harmonic analysis

**FOURIER integral**
FOURIER-Integral
intégrale de FOURIER
интеграл Фурье

Method for the representation of any functions by integrals of the following type:

$$F(x) = \frac{1}{\sqrt{2\pi}} \int_{-\infty}^{+\infty} \{a(t)\cos tx + b(t)\sin tx\}\mathrm{d}t$$

the functions $a(t)$ and $b(t)$ are given by the following integrals:

$$a(t) = \frac{1}{\sqrt{2\pi}} \int_{-\infty}^{+\infty} f(x) \cos xt \, \mathrm{d}x$$

$$b(t) = \frac{1}{\sqrt{2\pi}} \int_{-\infty}^{+\infty} f(x) \sin tx \, \mathrm{d}x$$

The transformation of functions with the help of FOURIER integrals is useful in the calculation of control and information series. (cf. *FOURIER series).

**FOURIER series**
FOURIER-Reihe
série de FOURIER
ряд Фурье

Method of description of any functions with a finite period by series which are formed from the harmonic functions $\sin x$ and $\cos x$.
If the period has been normalized to $2\pi$ the following is general:

$$f(x) = a_0 + \sum_{n=1}^{\infty} (a_n \cos nx + b_n \sin nx)$$

The coefficients are defined by the relations:

$$a_0 = \frac{1}{2\pi} \int_{-\pi}^{+\pi} f(x) \, \mathrm{d}x$$

$$a_n = \frac{1}{\pi} \int_{-\pi}^{+\pi} f(x) \cos nx \, \mathrm{d}x$$

$$b_n = \frac{1}{\pi} \int_{-\pi}^{+\pi} f(x) \sin nx \, \mathrm{d}x$$

The development of a function into a FOURIER-series has great advantages, especially in the calculation of control-equations and of transfer-characteristics of information system.
(cf. *FOURIER integral).

**Freedom**
Freiheit
liberté
свобода

*Name for the logical impossibility of deducing *imperatives solely from observable facts or mathematical and logical statements.*

The assertion of freedom, independent of the conflict between determinism and indeterminism, is possible, as the determinist must deny the existence of imperatives. Anyone who acts practically, however, always behaves as if he were striving towards a goal on which he must therefore previously have decided. He must, therefore, first have the function of a *captain.
It is impossible to give an objective standard definition of freedom, as the greater number of alternatives there are to choose between in any situation, the greater the freedom is. As however, some decision has normally to be made between several questions in any situation, this offers several free choices which cannot simply be added up, but must be

weighted (the choice of a career is more important than the choice of a hat!). This weighting itself is a subjective evaluation.

FRANK, H.: Über die wissenschaftliche und die ideologische Komponente im Mass der Freiheit. Zeitschrift für Philos. Forschung Band XVI (1962).

**Frequency**
Häufigkeit
fréquence
частота

By the absolute frequency of an event $E_i$ is understood the number $N_i$ which shows how often this event has occurred during a statistical experiment.
By the relative frequency of the event $E_i$ is understood the number $h_i$ which expresses $N_i$ relative to $N$, the total number of all the events which have occurred. For a possible number of events $u$ the following is valid: $h_i = \frac{N_i}{N}$ when $i = 1,2,\ldots,u$, with $N = N_1 + \ldots + N_u$. The following is always valid: $h_1 + h_2 + \ldots + h_u = 1$.
Example:

$$\begin{array}{llll} E_1 & n_1 = 5 & h_1 = 0,5 & \\ E_2 & n_2 = 2 & h_2 = 0,2 & u = 3 \\ E_3 & n_3 = 3 & h_3 = 0,3 & N = 10. \end{array}$$

**Frequency filter**
Frequenzfilter
filtre de fréquence
частотный фильтр

*A *filter which sifts certain frequencies or frequency-ranges of the spectrum of a time varying process.*
Special filters are: low-pass, high-pass, band-pass, band-filter, frequency-blocker, frequency switch.
The job of a low-pass filter is to let through oscillations in the frequency-range $0 \leqslant \omega \leqslant \omega_g$ with as little attenuation as possible (pass band), whereas in the complementary range $\omega_g \leqslant \omega \leqslant \infty$ (stop band) the oscillations are let through with as high an attenuation as possible—i.e. not let through ($\omega_g$ = cut off frequency). A high-pass filter has the opposite task, i.e. to block as strongly as possible in the range below $\omega_g$ and to let through as much as possible in the range above $\omega_g$. Band-pass and band-filter should attenuate weakly in the frequency range $\omega_{g1} \leqslant \omega \leqslant \omega_{g2}$ and block outside this range. The frequency-blocker has the opposite task to that of the band-pass. Whereas the filters mentioned above are *four terminal networks, the frequency-switch is a six terminal network, i.e. a switch with one input and two outputs. It is either a combination of a low-pass and a high-pass, or of a band-pass and frequency-blocker. Band-pass and band-filter have the same task, but differ in construction. Whereas the band-filter contains magnetically loosely coupled inductancies as its essential component, the band-pass and the other frequency-filters mentioned contain no loosely coupled inductancies.

CAUER, W.: Theorie der linearen Wechselstromschaltungen. 2nd edn. Akademie-Verlag, Berlin 1954.

**Frequency range**
Frequenzband
gamme de fréquence
полоса частот; диапазон частот; частотная полоса

In information - transmission - systems only those *oscillations are normally transmitted and processed whose frequencies lie within the frequency range 300 c/s–3400 c/s. In this case the information-transmission-system has a range of 3100 c/s.

**Frequency response; harmonic response**
Frequenzgang
réponse harmonique
частотная характеристика

*Distinguishes the dynamic behaviour of a *linear system by giving the relationship of the output to the input with regard to its magnitude and phase, if the input changes sinusoidally with time.*

For a linear system with the input $x$ and the output $y$ the following differential equation with constant coefficients $a_i$ and $b_k$ may be valid:

$$a_0\frac{d^ny}{dt^n} + a_1\frac{d^{n-1}y}{dt^{n-1}} + \ldots + a_{n1}\frac{dy}{dt} + a_ny =$$

$$= b_0\frac{d^mx}{dt^m} + b_1\frac{d^{m-1}x}{dt^{m-1}} + \ldots + b_{m1}\frac{dx}{dt} + b_mx$$

The system is excited at the input with a harmonic oscillation $x = x_0e^{j\omega t}$; then one obtains at the output in a stationary state (i.e. when the initial oscillations have died down) an oscillation of the same frequency but of different amplitude and phase: $y = y_0e^{j(\omega t+\varphi)}$. Their ratio

$$\frac{y}{x} = \frac{y_0e^{j(\omega t+\varphi)}}{x_0e^{jwt}} = \frac{y_0}{x_0}e^{j\varphi} = Ae^{j\varphi} = F(\omega)$$

is called the frequency-response of the system. It is a complex number whose modulus $A$ is equal to the ratio of the amplitudes and whose argument $\varphi$ is equal to the difference between the phases of the input and output oscillations. $A$ and $\varphi$ are functions of the frequency $\omega$. Log $A$, which depends on the frequency, is called the (logarithmic) gain or attenuation and the argument $\varphi$ the phase-shift.

The frequency response is determined from the differential-equation by inserting the equations for $x$ and $y$. One then has

$$a_0y_0(j\omega)^ne^{j(\omega t+\varphi)} + \ldots + a_ny_0e^{j(\omega t+\varphi)} =$$

$$= b_0x_0(j\omega)^me^{j\omega t} + \ldots + b_mx_0e^{j\omega t}$$

and from this, after division by $x_0e^{j\omega t}$:

$$F(\omega)[a_0(j\omega)^n + \ldots + a_n] = b_0(j\omega)^m +$$

$$+ \ldots + b_m;$$

The frequency response is therefore:

$$F(\omega) = \frac{b_0(j\omega)^m + b_1(j\omega)^{m-1} + \ldots + b_m}{a_0(j\omega)^n + a_1(j\omega)^{n-1} + \ldots + a_n}.$$

The differential equation of a system can therefore be stated if its physical construction is known; on the other hand, the frequency response can be found simply by measurement. Frequency response completely describes, in the same way as the differential equation, the transfer characteristics of the system. If the input-function is not a stationary oscillation, but any time-function, then this can be represented as a sum (or integral) of stationary harmonic oscillations of differing frequency (cf. *FOURIER series and *FOURIER integral). According to the principle of superposition (cf. *linear system) the output function is equal to the sum of the oscillations which would appear as a result of the individual input oscillations. Frequency response may also be regarded as a special case of a *transfer function.

Leonhard, A.: Die selbsttätige Regelung. Springer-Verlag, Berlin, Göttingen, Heidelberg 1957. Oldenbourg, R. C.; Sartorius, H.: Dynamik selbsttätiger Regelungen. Band 1. R. Oldenbourg, München 1951. Oppelt, W.: Kleines Handbuch technischer Regelvorgänge. Verlag Chemie, Weinheim 1960. Solodownikow, W. W.: Grundlagen der selbsttätigen Regelung. R. Oldenbourg, München 1959.

# G

**GABOR information-cell**
GABORsche Informationszellen
cellules (informatives) de GABOR
информационные ячейки Габора

*Quanta (finite magnitude) of the time-frequency-representation of a signal.*

The introduction of quanta is based on the uncertainty $\Delta\nu$ in frequency-measurement with a finite integration-time $\Delta t$. The following is valid: $\Delta\nu \approx 1/\Delta t$. Each range represents a *logon of the localization range $\Delta\nu\Delta t$. To this is assigned a numerical value which gives the analysis-result for this range. The finite set of numerical values in a two-dimensional time-frequency-representation, which represents a signal, is its GABOR-matrix.

MEYER-EPPLER, W.: Grundlagen und Anwendungen der Informationstheorie. Springer-Verlag, Berlin, Göttingen, Heidelberg 1959.

**Gate**
Tor
conditionneur; circuit de porte
схема совпадений

*A *logical circuit corresponding to *conjunction.*

A signal-input is used as a controlling input which is able to switch one or more inputs through to the output. By this, the original bivalence of the signals is extended: even a non-bivalent input signal can be switched by a gate by means of a binary drive pulse. A gate of this sort corresponds to an electronic switch.

ZEMANEK, H.: Logische Algebra und Theorie der Schaltnetzwerke. In: Steinbuch, K. (ed.): Taschenbuch der Nachrichtenverarbeitung. Springer-Verlag, Berlin, Göttingen, Heidelberg 1962.

**Generalization**
Generalisierung
généralization
генерализация

*Generalization exists if an organism reacts to the stimulus $S'$ with a probability other than nil by a reaction $R$, which was originally conditioned to the stimulus $S$ which stands in a similarity-relation to $S'$.*

If one carries out a classical or instrumental *conditioning which results in a connection of the stimulus-state $S_i$ with a reaction of the class $R_i$, there results a conditional probability $p(R_i/S_i)$. If one now offers to the organism concerned another stimulus-state $S_i'$, which is similar to $S_i$ and to which no other reaction-class $R_i$ is conditioned, then $R_i$ occurs with the probability $p(R_i/S_i') = \eta p(R_i/S_i)$. The numerical total of the 'generalization-gradient', $\eta$, always lies between 0 and 1, and is, for a certain value of $S$ and a set value of $S'$, equal for every $p$. In the *learning theories of ESTES, BUSH and MOSTELLER $\eta$ can be interpreted as the quotient of BOREL's measure of the set of stimulus-elements $\mu(S \cap S')$ contained in $S$ and $S'$ over the measure of the set of stimulus-elements $\mu(S')$ which constitutes $S'$. It is therefore a measure of the relative similarity of two stimulus-states. Corresponding to the described stimulus-generalization, there is also a reaction-generalization, in which a reaction $R_i$ of an organism is substituted by a similar behaviour $R_i'$.

LUCE, R. D.: Developments in Mathematical Psychology. Glencoe, Illinois 1960. HILGARD, E. R.: Theories of Learning. Appleton-Century Crofts, New York 1956.

**German technical phonetic script**
TLD (Technische Lautschrift des Deutschen)
écriture phonétique (technique) allemande

---

*An encoding of German sounds by the normal alphabet used in connection with the possibilities of speech-recognizing machines (phonetograph) and of speech-producing machines *(vocoders). This script can also be easily manipulated by humans.*

The guiding principle behind TLD is to obtain by the use of the already extant letter repertory a transfer of language to script which will permit one: (1) to write correctly the correct pronunciation of German (using as the norm SIEBS's 'stage-German', or standard German) by the simplest possible rules without understanding the content, and conversely (2) to read correctly whatever has been written correctly. Present orthography (i.e. according to DUDEN) does not satisfy these demands: e.g. *mahlen* is pronounced identically to *malen* (compare English 'bow' and 'bough'). This means that an unambiguous reversible relation has to be produced between sounds (or sound sequences) and letters (or letter sequences). This is most simply achieved by allotting one single letter to each sound (e.g. C to *sch*, X to *ch* and Q to *-ng-*) and using these consistently: e.g. never using V for F, QU for K, Y for Ü; and also always using either capitals *or* small letters; and conversely by allotting one single sound to each letter used (e.g. KS instead of *x*, TS instead of *z*) which must also be used consistently (so that voiced and unvoiced *s*, and open and closed *o* and *ö* can always be distinguished from each other in script. The last-mentioned requisite, however, does not apply in TLD to the differentiation between very fine phonetic differences (so that the open or closed pronunciation of *i*, *ü* and *u* is not differentiated, nor the difference between front and back *ch*, or between *i* and *j*). The letters X, C, Q, V, Y, Z and J which, as a result of the above requisites and compromise, become vacant are allotted the sounds *ch*, *sch*, *ng*, open *o*, open *ö*, voiced *s* and dead *e*. Long vowels are shown by a double vowel, and a glottal stop by '. All other characters retain their former meaning. So *Sprachschwingung* is encoded as 'CPRAAXCWIQUQ', and *Fördersorgen* and 'FYRDJRZVRGJN'. As, in contrast to automatic *speech recognition, a phonetically perfect automatic production of speech is neither technically feasible in the foreseeable future nor of any great practical value, 'simplified' TLD does not entirely fulfil the conditions of the second part of the principles mentioned at the beginning; this means that it uses E instead of J, S instead of Z, Ö instead of V (except before Ö). In fact, with only a minute increase in the percentage of ambiguities, Ö could be replaced by E, Ü by I, Ä by E, G by K, B by P and D by T, although there are admittedly no texts written in this simplified phonetic script. The average information per letter (sound) in full TLD is: $H(Z) = 4{\cdot}5$ bit (against 4·2 bit in orthography with radical use of small letters[1]); the average specified information when the preceding letter (sound) is known is: $H(Z) = 3{\cdot}4$ bit and when two preceding letters are known: $H_{xy}(Z) = 2{\cdot}5$ bit. The transcription of an orthographical text into TLD considerably shortens the

[1]All German nouns, whether proper or common, are normally written with a capital initial letter (translator's footnote).

former (i.e. in German, the number of sounds spoken is on average less than the number of orthographical letters).

ALSLEBEN, K.; et al.: Sprache und Schrift im Zeitalter der Kybernetik. Schnelle, Quickborn 1963,
STEINBUCH, K.: Automat und Mensch. Springer-Verlag, Berlin, Göttingen, Heidelberg, 2nd edn. 1963.

**Gestalt psychology**
Gestaltpsychologie
psychologie de la forme
гештальтпсихология

A movement in psychology which has been important since KOHLER in showing the unity of psychic life. The basic idea is that the parts of a shape only have meaning by the fact that they belong to a whole, i.e. a shape cannot be split up into its elements without losing the meaning which it possessed as a whole. Consequently the concept *form* in the sense of an integrated whole, contradicts the old-fashioned interpretation according to which perception was a mosaic-like combination of isolated sensations. A tune is more than the notes of which it consists: it continues even if one transposes all its notes. A form is more than the sum-total of its elements. This concept is valid for every whole which is integrated not only in space but also in time. Behaviour can be thought of as a Gestalt (configuration), i.e. as a mental whole which transcends the mere combination of its elements.

Gestalt psychology is no abstract theory. It is founded on many experiments. Above all, it can easily be proved that a Gestalt is to a certain degree independent of its elements: a circle which is broken at one point is still regarded as a circle.

**Grammar**
Grammatik
grammaire
грамматика

*Description of the structure of a *language.* A distinction must be made between the following two types of grammar: (1) prescriptive grammar, which indicates the correct use of a language to those who are unsure of it; and (2) scientific-descriptive grammar, which renders explicit to members of a speech-community all features of the phonetic, graphetic, formal and material aspects of a language of which they are unconscious. Grammar (1) is not completely explicit nor does it need to be, as it is directed at the intelligent reader who, while reading, applies his ability to correlate and to arrange facts independently. Grammar (2) has to try to make more explicit the facts given in the language and in grammar (1), and the ability necessary for interpretation in their total interrelationship. This is best achieved by the formulation of a formalized grammar. The theory of formalized grammars requires: (1) the statement of an explicit scheme of rules and notations and a specification of the conditions which must be fulfilled by a given set of rules within this framework in order to be regarded as the grammar of a language; (2) the statement of how such a grammar produces an explicit enumeration of sentences with the appropriate structure-description.

The interpretation of these statements must not demand any special linguistic ability on the part of the user, because it is precisely this which is to be characterized. A grammar satisfies these demands if, on the basis of the statements, a program for an automaton for the production or analysis of linguistic expressions can be written without any difficulty, or if the structure of the grammar can be transferred directly into an automaton-structure. An automaton of this sort is called a linguistic automaton. The form of the rules which are to be permitted for grammar-description often determines a limitation of the representable sets of linguistic expressions and their structure-description. A distinction must be made *inter alia* between the following grammar-types in accordance with their increasing force of expression: (1) finite state-grammar; (2) context-free constituent-structure grammar; (3) transformational grammar. Most present-day formalized grammars are of type (2) which does not yet allow an adequate description of the language-structure; this is even more true of type (1). The theory of grammar has close connections with the theory of automata, inasmuch as both grammar and automaton are formulated in terms of the characterization of expression-sets. In this respect the following automata-conceptions correspond to the three types of grammar mentioned above: (1) finite *automaton (and analogue: cf. *MARKOFF-source); (2) push-down automaton or push-down programming system; (3) *TURING machine.

CHOMSKY, N.: Syntactic Structures. Mouton, s'Gravenhage, 1957. CHOMSKY, N.: On the Notion 'Rule of Grammar' in: Jakobsen, R. (ed.): Structure of Language and its Mathematical Aspects. American Mathematical Society, Providence, 1961. CHOMSKY, N.: Explanatory Models in Linguistics. In: Nagel, E. et al. (ed.): Logic, Methodology and Philosophy of Science. Stanford Univ. Press 1962. CHOMSKY, N. and MILLER, G. A.: Introduction to the Formal Analysis of Natural Languages. CHOMSKY, N.: Formal Properties of Grammars (in Handbook of Mathematical Psychology, Vol. II, Ed. LUCE, R. D., BUSH, R. R., GALANTER, E. J. Wiley, New York, 1963. S. GINSBURG: The Theory of context-free Languages. SCHNELLE, H.: Programmieren linguistischer Automaten. In: Steinbuch K.; Wagner, S. W. (eds.): Neuere Ergebnisse der Kybernetik. R. Oldenbourg, München 1963.

**Graph**
Graph
graphe
граф

*Either a graphic means of representation used in science, or a topologic structure.* A graph as a means of representation is given by the following data:

A 1 a set $M$ of elements $\{m_1, m_2, m_3, \ldots m_N\}$

A 2 a relation $R$ in $M$, i.e. a sub-set of the pair-sets of $M$ ($R \leqslant M \times M$). In certain circumstances several relations are given in $M$.

B 1 a representation of the elements of $M$ as vertices or nodes (i.e. seen to be relatively closed elements of a representation-system, e.g. letters, circles or points).

B 2 a representation of the element-pairs of $R$ as directed or undirected edges (i.e. the connections between the nodes, such as continuous, broken or dotted lines with or without direction-indications, e.g. by arrows).

The statements A 1 and A 2 alone define an abstract graph which is identical to a structure in the sense of mathematical structure-theory. A graph, as a topological structure, can be obtained if one replaces the statements B 1 and B 2 by the following:

C 1 an interpretation of the elements of $M$ as points in a topological space

C 2 an interpretation of the elements of $R$ as arcs between the points of a topological space fixed under C 1.

KÖNIG, D.: Theorie der Graphen. Chelsea, New York 1950. BERGE, C.: Théorie des Graphes et ses applications. Dunod, Paris 1958. SCHNELLE, H.: Zeichensysteme zur wissenschaftlichen Darstellung. Verlag Stuttgart-Bad Cannstatt 1962.

**Group coding**
Gruppenverfahren
procédé des groupes; méthode des groupes

---

A process to represent the *characters $A_i$ of an *alphabet $i$ by the characters $A_j$ of an alphabet $j$; in this process a group of characters of the alphabet $j$ corresponds to every character of the alphabet $i$. The location of the characters $j$ and their meaning is arranged by a set of instructions (cf. *code).
If $l$ different characters exist in the alphabet $j$ then groups of $n$ such characters can represent a total of $k = l^n$ characters of the alphabet $i$. So for example, with the Arabic numbers (0, 1, . . . 9) $l = 10$, and with $n = 3$ the 1000 different numbers from 0 to 999 can be represented.
This means:

$$1703 = 1 \times 10^3 + 7 \times 10^2 + 0 \times 10^1 + 3 \times 10^0$$
$$abcd = a \times 10^3 + b \times 10^2 + c \times 10^1 + d \times 10^0$$

ZEMANEK, H.: Elementare Informationstheorie. Oldenbourg, München, Wien, 1959.

**Group dynamics; psychology of groups**
Gruppendynamik
psychologie des groupes
групповая динамика

*Results of research in psychology which are concerned with behaviour in groups of people.*
A group exists if at least two people are in *communication with each other and thus influence each other's behaviour. Every group has certain performance advantages over an individual. The combination of strength of several individuals which is often necessary for simple physical tasks (e.g. lifting of heavy loads) needs a controlled co-ordination of both movement and strength, and hence the communication which constitutes a group. In jobs for which a certain correct solution has to be found, a similar performance-advantage of a group over an individual results from the expected adjustment errors. However, this presupposes an efficient communication within the group and the recognition of each correct partial-solution of one member of the group by all the remaining members. Moreover, groups can create an expectation in which standards are established for a correct pattern of behaviour in situations for which there is no real objective criterion for the judgement of behaviour. A special kind of group-standard is shown by stereotypes, that is, ideas about people or groups (of people or other sets of data) are found to be almost identical in all members of the group; sometimes these stereotypes deviate widely from the reality described in them. If groups exist for any length of time, structures develop within them in which the preferences and the frequency of communication of any two members are reflected. Apart from this, certain group-members take on certain functions within the groups, which are called *roles*. The study of groups reveals a set of interesting conformities which can in part be passed on to larger groups (e.g. races and nations).

HOFSTÄTTER, P. R.: Gruppendynamik der modernen Physik. Rowohlts deutsche Enzycloped. 38 Rowohlt, Hamburg 1957.

**Growth regulation**
Wachstumsregulation
régulation de la croissance
регулирование роста

*The total of all effects and mechanisms by which metabolic growth of a living organism is held within norms and proportions which are characteristic for that type.*

Obviously external factors (such as lack of nutrition or decreased $O_2$-partial pressure) can have an inhibitory effect on growth. But the organism does not react passively even to these factors: for example, reserves of fat are mobilized as sources of energy in the event of lack of nourishment. However, by far the most important are the internal growth mechanisms. Their end result is often expressed in the allometric law of growth, which states that the relative growth in mass of two components of the same organism are proportional to each other. Moreover, the complicated phenomena of embryology and organic morphogenesis (at present one of the most important unsolved problems in biology) depend on this regulation. The concept of a *field of events plays an important role, but details remain unexplained. Generally, the excessive growth of one part of the organism is called hypertrophy. Associative phenomena (i.e. those which belong to the whole aggregate rather than to the individual cell) have been shown for growth and for the differentiation of tissue cells. The influences which lead to the division of cells should be of primary importance. Even the bio-chemical processes of a cell are related to each other by several mechanisms. So in bacteria, for example, it is found that the available quantity of substrate largely dictates both the production and the effective strength of ferments (enzymes). In addition to this, growth of the whole organism in Metazoa is also regulated by hormones, of which the somatotropin of the hypophysis and the thyroid hormone are the most well known, but by no means the only ones (cf. *endocrine system). Fairly soon a state is reached in which active mass-turnover occurs, but no more mass growth worthy of mention (steady state). Closely related to normal growth are the neo-plastic symptoms of cancer, which can be regarded as unregulated growth, *regeneration and the healing of wounds.

BERTALANFFY, L. von: Theoretische Biologie. Band II, 2nd edn. Francke, Bern 1951. KÜHN, A.: Vorlesungen über Entwicklungsphysiologie. Springer-Verlag, Berlin, Göttingen, Heidelberg 1955. WADDINGTON, C. H.: The Nature of Life. George Allen and Unwin, London 1961 and Atheneum, New York 1962.

# H

**HAMMING distance**
HAMMING-Distanz
distance de HAMMING
расстояние Хемминга

*The number of differently marked (i.e. by 1 or 0) binary-locations of two code-words.*

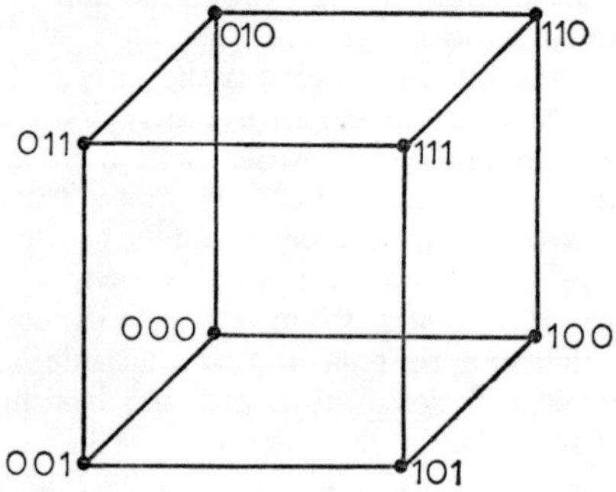


The concept *distance*—used in connection with codes—results from a spacial interpretation, as the result of which the code-words of a binary-code with $n$ locations are allotted to the corners of an $n$-dimensional information-space. Then the HAMMING distance between two code-words corresponds to the minimum distance (measured by the number of connective edges) between the corners of the information-space which were allotted to the code-words. A HAMMING distance $d$ represents a (dimensionless) measurement for the surety of a binary-code against disturbances. For *error-detection the following is valid: $f_E = d - 1$, in which $f_E$ = the number of detectible errors in the binary characters in a code-word. For *error-correction of binary characters the following is valid:

$$f_K = \frac{d}{2} - 1 \text{ when } d \text{ is even}$$

$$f_K = \frac{d-1}{2} \text{ when } d \text{ is uneven}$$

$f_K$ is the number of corrigible errors in binary characters in a code-word. If desired, the following simultaneous combinations are possible when, for example, $d = 5$:

(1) 0 error-correction and up to 4 error-detection
(2) 1 error-correction and 2 or 3 error-detection
(3) 1 or 2 error-correction and 0 error-detection.


HAMMING, R. W.: Error Detecting and Error Correcting Codes. Bell System Tech. Journ. 29 (April 1950) No. 2, 147–60. STEINBUCH, K. (ed.): Taschenbuch der Nachrichtenverarbeitung. Springer-Verlag, Berlin, Göttingen, Heidelberg 1962.


**Harmonic analysis; FOURIER analysis**
Harmonische Analyse;
FOURIERanalyse
analyse harmonique; analyse de FOURIER
гармонический анализ (анализ Фурье)

Process for the analysis of a periodic time-function $s(t)$ (cf. *oscillation) with a period $T$ into its fundamental

$$A_o \sin(\omega_o t + \varphi_o)$$

(= 1st harmonic) and into its higher harmonics $A_i \sin(i\omega_o t + \varphi_i)$ with $i$ = 2, 3, 4, . . . etc. (2nd, 3rd, harmonic). For carrying out harmonic analysis there exist arithmetical, graphical and experimental methods (cf. *spectrum). Non-periodic time-functions can be examined with the help of periodographic analysis of their spectrum.


MEYER-EPPLER, W.: Experimentelle Schwingungsanalyse. Ergebn. d. exakt. Naturw., 23 (1950), pp. 53–126.

**Harmonic response**
*See* *Frequency response

**Hedony**
Hedonie
hédonie; tonus affectif
——
*A quantitative measurement calculated from observations in the environment of an animal or of an artefact; its increase represents the approach of the animal to its goal.*
In *learning machines or other aim-orientated systems, some measurement for goal-proximity is essential, a measurement which will control the operation. SELFRIDGE called this measure *hedony* because of its analogy to the wish-function of an animal. As a synonym, WIENER suggested the concept *affective tone*.

SELFRIDGE, O. G.: Pattern recognition and learning. In: Cherry, C. (ed.): Information Theory. Butterworth, London 1956. WIENER, N.: Kybernetik. Econ, Düsseldorf 1963. ANDREW, A.M.: Learning machines. In: Mechanization of Thought Processes. H.M.S.O., London 1959.

**Heuristics**
Heuristik
heuristique
эвристика
*Rules which lead to new knowledge.*
Problems given to *computers in connection with the investigation of artificial *intelligence are usually well-defined, i.e. there are methods, the use of which enables one to ascertain whether a solution proposed by a computer is acceptable. In principle, such problems can normally be solved by finding from amongst all the possible solutions one which is acceptable. In practice, however, the number of possible solutions is so large that rules must be given by which the search is limited to solutions which are likely to be acceptable. These rules do not prove the acceptability of a solution, they merely direct the search. The set of these rules is called *heuristics*.

MINSKY, M. L.: Some methods of artificial intelligence and heuristic programming. In: Mechanization of Thought Processes. H.M.S.O. London, 1959.— MINSKY, M. L.: Steps towards artificial intelligence, Proc. I.R.E., Vol. 49, (1961) pt. 8.

**Hierarchical principle**
Hierarchieprinzip
principe de hierarchie
иерархический принцип
*Selective principle for keeping higher central-nervous levels free of detailed information.*
The hierarchical principle is a fundamental principle in the information-selection of an organism, and hence decisive for the performance of the sensorium. Essentially identical with the *reafferent principle, which occurs primarily in the motor half of the central-nervous function, the function of the hierarchical principle is to keep the higher central-nervous levels free of subordinate routine-jobs.

HOLST, E. von; MITTELSTAEDT, H.: Das Reafferenzprinzip (Wechselwirkungen zwischen Zentralnervensystem und Peripherie). Naturwiss. 37 (1951) pp. 464–76. KEIDEL, W. D.: Beispiele und Probleme einer kybernetischen Physiologie des ZNS und der Sinne. In: Bericht über den 23. Kongress der Deutsch. Ges. für Psych., Verlag für Psychologie (Hogrefe), Göttingen 1963, pp. 103–23.

**Hierarchization**
Superierung; Superzeichenbildung; BIRKHOFFscher Übergang
hierarchization
——
*The ability of compressing details into a whole, or of recognizing what is intrinsic by one example.*
In psychology (i.e. *narrowness of consciousness*) it is accepted that the contents of two separate perceptions (i.e.

musical notes) cannot enter the *consciousness (i.e. enter the *short-term memory) as such but only simultaneously by becoming parts of a graduated whole (e.g. a chord) from which they can be extracted again only after subsequent analysis. (The whole which is actually appercieved (cf. *apperception) is therefore more than the quantity of its components: the principle of supersummativity of Gestalt psychology.) In the theory of characters the graduated whole is called a *super-character, the synthesis of this super-character is called *hierarchization by complex formations.*

Moreover, it is also accepted in psychology (*ability of invariant formation*) that objectively different stimuli, which in principle could also be distinguishable subjectively, are not distinguished when equal attentiveness is shown to each note, so for example the notes of the chord C-G and the chord D-A are not distinguished—all that is perceived is the super-character *perfect fifth* (principle of transposition of Gestalt, cf. *Gestalt psychology). In character theory the combination of *equivalent* characters of a class, which is in turn a super-character, is called *hierarchization by class-formation.*

Generally, and abstracting from human perception, any defined spatial-temporal arrangement of characters in a character-repertory is called a super-character of a graduated repertory. In the same way every defined sub-set of the characters of a repertory are called the super-characters of a higher repertory. The act of construction of the super-character is called hierarchization or BIRKHOFF's transfer, the act of analysis of the super-character into its formative sub-characters or the act of specifying the sub-characters which represents the super-character at that moment is called MOLE's transfer.

The repertories of super-characters do not form any clear hierarchy, i.e. the direction of hierarchization is not clearly defined. For example, verse can be classified according to a rhythmical scheme or a rhyme scheme.

FRANK, H.: Kybernetische Grundlagen der Pädagogik. Pt. III. Agis, Baden-Baden 1962.

**Homeostasis**
Homeostase
homéostasie
гомеостазис

*A condition in which the important internal variables of a living organism are kept constant within physiological limits despite disturbing influences. A form of *biological regulation.*

Living organisms possess many mechanisms for maintaining specific internal conditions. If, for example, the body-temperature of higher animals is increased by exertion or by a change of outside temperature, the blood vessels on the surface of the skin expand, perspiration starts and metabolism is slowed down; these devices cause a cooling-off of the body. On the other hand, when the body becomes cold, mechanisms are put into action which cause a rise in temperature. The constant value of internal variables which can be observed in a healthy animal are only maintained by the continual activity of compensatory mechanisms; they are examples of the physiological application of *feedback.

CANNON, W. B.: The Wisdom of the Body. Norton, New York 1932.

**Homeostat**
Homeostat
homéostat
гомеостат

*A machine built by ASHBY which demonstrates the principle of *ultrastability.*
The homeostat actually carried out consists of four similar units, but in principle any number is possible. Each unit contains a potentiometer and gives an output signal dependent on the slide-position of the potentiometer. A series of inputs are led to the unit; these inputs are connected to coils whose magnetic fields influence a magnet linked to the slider of the potentiometer and thereby shift the slider. The positions of the slider represent variables which must accept values within given limits. Only certain connection-patterns permit a suitable regulation. Those unsuitable for this are modified by random-wired step-switches, so that the system finally possesses a connection-pattern which permits a satisfactory regulation of all variables. If the homeostat is altered manually, for example by a change of the connections to a coil or by mechanical coupling of sliders, it will once more alter its connection-pattern until a satisfactory regulation of the variables is possible.

ASHBY, W. R.: Design for a Brain. Chapman and Hall, London (2nd edn.) 1960.

**HUFFMAN's tree**
HUFFMANbaum
arbre de HUFFMAN
дерево Хуффмана

*A graphic representation of certain (so-called redundancy-saving) binary codes (cf. *encoding) which are optimal for a certain probability-distribution (cf. *field-of-events).*
In the theory of *graphs a 'tree' is understood to be a set of points which are connected in pairs by an arc in such a way that:
1 no arc ends at the initial starting point, (the root-point)
2 no arcs start at $u \geq 2$ points (so-called branch-points)
3 one arrow ends at every point except the root-point.
A binary HUFFMAN tree is a tree in which either no arrows or two arrows begin at every point.
The $u$ signs $Z_i$ of a binary repertory which has to be encoded are written at the $u$ branch-points. The two arrows of every other point of a tree which lead away are marked by the binary-code elements 0 and 1. The path from the root-point to a sign $Z_i$ can be then denoted by a binary sequence, e.g. 00101. This is the encoding of the sign by (in this example) $l_i = 5$ bits. The average length of the binary-sequence (or its expectancy-value) used for encoding is $H_C = \sum_{i=1}^{u} p_i . l_i$ bits, in the event of $p_i$ being the relative probability of $z_i$. $H_C \geq H$ is always valid; $H$ represents the average *information of the character $z_i$. $H_C = H$ is valid if and when the relative probabilities of the characters $h_i = 2^{-l_i}$. In this case the code represented by the HUFFMAN's tree is HUFFMAN's optimal code.
If the relative probabilities of the characters are not altogether negative whole powers of 2, then $H_C > H$. The distribution of the $u$ characters to $u$ branch-points, for which $H_C$ adopts the smallest value when the given frequency-distribution is $(h_1, h_2, \ldots, h_u)$, and also when the HUFFMAN tree is varied within the repertory of trees with $u$ branch-points, represents the HUFFMAN optimal-code in a general sense. The HUFFMAN optimal code can therefore always be represented by a HUFFMAN tree. This is also true for less economical codes, e.g. that of FANO, not however for that of SHANNON (cf. *encoding).

HUFFMAN, D.: A Method for the Construction of Minimum-Redundancy Codes. Proc. IRE, 40 (1952) pp. 1098–1101. FRANK, H.: Grundlagenprobleme der Informationsästhetik; Mathematischer Teil. J. Hess, Waiblingen 1959. FRANK, H.: Kybernetische Grundlagen der Pädagogik; Mathematischer Teil. Agis. Baden-Baden 1962.

# I

**Icon**
Ikon
icon
икон

*A certain type of character with *meaning (representative character, a character for . . .).*

Consciousness is attributed to the source of icons (icons are therefore designations), or, what is the same thing, sociocultural signs, not real indices. Designations are divided into symbols and icons; whereas a symbol's meaning is allotted to it by agreement (which may be motivated in some way), which means that a symbol encodes (cf. *encoding) its meaning and fulfils an essentially communicative function, an icon represents its meaning (to which it is similar) without necessarily having to fulfil a communicative function. Examples: portraits, caricatures, program theme-music.

**Ideogram**
Ideogramm
idéogramme
идеограмма

*Sign used to communicate a concept independently of the spoken word.*

*Ideograms are used for *communication without recourse to a natural language. To achieve this, every concept is allocated an unambiguous sign, an ideogram (e.g. in traffic signs a Z meaning a double bend, two crossed lines meaning a junction). In contrast to this, the names of concepts in most natural languages are represented by phonetic symbols.

The use of ideograms is characteristic of formalized *languages in mathematics and logic. Ideograms appear only at a primitive level in natural languages.

**Imperative**
Imperativ
impératif
императив

*A message which does not describe a state, but which demands, permits or forbids its realization, is contained in an imperative, which is made valid by the pragmatic *semiotic aspect of signs.*

In principle, imperatives cannot be deduced solely from facts (or statements) but only from other imperatives, sometimes with the additional use of statements. The methods used to justify (not prove) the obligation (not truth) of imperatives form the content of normative or imperative logic. Systems consisting solely of imperatives are called normative ideologies. Just as statement systems (such as non-Euclid geometry) contain unprovable basic-statements (axioms), normative systems contain unjustifiable basic imperatives (postulates), from which may be deduced a decision on the obligation of the other imperatives of the system (*pilot decisions*, cf. *pilot), which however must themselves be posited by a *free* original decision (captain decision, cf. *captain). (*Freedom* in this context means non-deductability in the sense of imperative logic; it is therefore connected with the extentialistic concept of freedom, not with that of indeterminism.)

FREY, G.: Idee einer Wissenschaftslogik. Philosophia Naturalis IV No. 4 (1957) pp. 434–91. FRANK, H.: Über die wissenschaftliche und die ideologische Komponente im Mass der Freiheit. Zeitschrift f. Philosoph. Forschung Band XVI (1962).

**Implication**
Implikation
implication
импликация

*Binary logical connective with the symbol* $\supset$ *or* $\rightarrow$; *so implication corresponds to the connection of statements by 'if . . . then'; i.e. the truth-value of the deduction 'from . . . follows . . .' is examined.*
Truth-table:

| | | | | |
|---|---|---|---|---|
| $a$ | $T$ | $T$ | $F$ | $F$ |
| $b$ | $T$ | $F$ | $T$ | $F$ |
| $a \supset b$ | $T$ | $F$ | $T$ | $T$ |

The formula connecting implication with *negation and *disjunction (cf. *BOOLEAN algebra) is as follows:

$$a \supset b = \bar{a} \vee b.$$

**Inclusive OR**
*See* *Disjunction (inclusive)

**Index register**
Indexregister
registre index
индексный регистр; регистр адресов

*A special *register of a *computer.*
Index registers are to be found in the *control unit of a computer, or work in conjunction with it. Their length is mostly equal to the length of the address section of an *instruction. They assist *address modification or counting. Their content can be set, altered, compared to other values, stored or transferred to other registers of the computer by (mainly very fast) instructions. Negative values in the index registers are as a rule represented by complements. Computers usually have several index registers. Their use greatly facilitates the organization of the execution of a program.

**Index value; set point; control value**
Sollwert
valeur de consigne; valeur à atteindre
требуемая величина; предписанное значение; номинальная величина; заданное значение регулируемой или измеряемой величины; установленная величина

*A fixed pre-given value which must be achieved by a physical variable (cf. *actual value, *controlled condition) by means of *feedback control (closed loop control) (cf. *feedback control systems, especially section* 4).

OPPELT, W.: Kleines Handbuch technischer Regelvorgänge. Verlag Chemie, Weinheim 1956.

**Indirect addressing**
Adressensubstitution
substitution d'adresse
переадресация

*The automatic alteration of the address section of an *instruction.*
It is sometimes of advantage if the *address in an *instruction does not give the location of the *operand, but a location in the *store in which the actual address is to be found. This fact must be specially marked in the instruction. The address-section of such a marked instruction is replaced by a completely different address before execution. Both the old and the new address may have been modified before use (cf. *address

modification). The new address may again be supplied with a substitution flag, in other words, be replaced by yet a further address. This gives rise to the danger of infinite loops.

**Information**
Information
information
информация

*A logarithmic measure of the improbability of a *message or a character in a given situation, or of the occurrence of an event.*

Let a finite *field $Z$ of messages or characters define a given situation. Let $z_k$ be one of these characters and $p_k$ its probability. Then four characteristics of the information $Inf(z_k)$ are necessary, without which the measurement of information is insufficient:

1 the information is a function of $p_k$, but not also of $p_l$, $k \neq l$;
2 this function always depends on $p_k$, in which $0 < p_k \leq 1$;
3 the information of a double-event, whose one partial result $z_k$ (probability $p_k$) stems from the field $Z$, but whose other partial result $x_i$ (probability $p_i$) stems from the second field $X$ which is independent of $Z$, is equal to the sum of the information of the partial results.
4 the information of $z_k$ is then equal to the information-unit '1 bit' if $p_k = 0{\cdot}5$.

A simple mathematical argument shows that the only measurement which satisfies these four conditions is as follows:

$$I(z_k) = \log_2 1/p_k.$$

Sometimes, (especially in Russian literature) 'Information' is used to designate not 'information' but the expectancy-value of information, namely:

$$H(Z) = \sum_{k=1}^{n} p_k \log_2 1/p_k$$

When used in psychology and the arts it is, however, preferable to give the expression $H(Z)$ the designation 'average information' of the field $Z$, or, in so far as the information-carrying event is not yet at hand, the *'uncertainty' of the field $Z$. The designations *entropy and *negative entropy are widely used for $H(Z)$, although this is rather controversial, as $H(Z)$ does not possess a real physical dimension like entropy.

If the observed probability-fields $X$ and $Z$ are dependent on each other, then the conditional information is:

$$Ix_i(z_k) = \log_2 1/px_i(z_k) = \log_2 1/p_i(z_k)$$

or put another way:

$$I(z_k \mid x_i) = \log_2 1/p(z_k \mid x_i) = \log_2 1/p(2_k)$$

if $px_i(z_k) \equiv p(z_k \mid x_i)$ is the conditional probability of $z_k$ in $Z$ given the event $x_i$ in $X$.

Information is only one of the measurable aspects of a message and its relation to the latter (with which it is not synonymous) is much the same as that of mass to material. The type of message and its value can be understood as little as can be understood the chemical composition of gold or lead from knowing their mass. However, informationless messages are, in principle, valueless. Subjective information (cf. *information, subjective) is the name given to the information of an event in a field, whereby instead of the probability-vector $\{p_1, \ldots, p_u\}$ of this field, a subjective probability-vector $\{p_1^{(s)}, \ldots, p_u^{(s)}\}$ dependent on the receiver is collated to events and forms the basis of information-calculation.

The statistical aspect of the syntactical *semiotic aspect of characters is measured by information. The same measurement can however be applied to the field of *meanings (whose probability-vector does not need to be identical with that of the field of characters of synonyms and homonyms). By this an attempt is made to grasp also the statistical aspect of the semantic semiotic aspect of characters by semantic information. The extended definition of semantic information of CARNAP and BAR-HILLEL uses another method.

SHANNON, C. E.: A mathematical theory of communication. Bell System Technical Journal 27 (1948). GRELL, H. (ed.): Arbeiten zur Informationstheorie. I, II. Dtsch. Vlg. d. Wissenschaften, Berlin 1957. ZEMANEK, H.: Elementare Informationstheorie. R. Oldenbourg, München 1959. MEYER EPPLER, W.: Grundlagen und Anwendungen der Informationstheorie. Springer-Verlag, Berlin, Göttingen, Heidelberg 1959. JAGLOM, A. M. and I. M.: Wahrscheinlichkeit und Information. Dtsch. Vlg. d. Wissenschaften, Berlin 1960. FRANK, H.: Kybernetische Grundlagen der Pädagogik. Part 2. Agis, Baden-Baden 1962. BERGER, E. R.; PILOTY, H.: Erläuterungen zu den in der Informationstheorie verwendeten Begriffen der mathematischen Statistik. NTZ Heft 1 (1963).

**Information, aesthetical**
Information, ästhetische
information esthétique
эстетическая информация

There are essentially two processes for the production of aesthetical information: (1) *negative-entropy processes which aim for a subjective yield of statistical arrangement of characters. They dominate the synthetic phase of aesthetic perception and also the conception-phase of aesthetic production, in which the concept of the work of art which is to be created is planned by the artist without considering questions of detail. (2) Entropy processes, i.e. processes for increasing statistical information. These create innovation and originality in the production of works of art by the individual configuration of the work, i.e. by a deviation from the artistic norm. In the analytical phase of aesthetic perception, entropy processes occur as processes of special interpretation of works of art.

GUNZENHÄUSER, R.: Ästhetisches Mass und ästhetische Information. Schnelle, Quickborn bei Hamburg 1962.

**Information, semantical**
Information, semantische
information sémantique
семантическая информация

*The semantic information of a sentence in a given language-system is often understood as the class of all sentences of this system which follow from this one sentence; it is however better defined as the class of all the content elements which follow from it; sometimes even as a measure of this class. In order to avoid misunderstandings, 'semantic information content' should be used for the first concept, and 'amount of semantic information' for the second.*

The problem of the semantic information content of a sentence goes beyond the framework of statistical *information theory and can therefore only be treated within that of semantic information theory. Within the framework of a given language system, the class of all sentences (perhaps only of all synthetic sentences) which are logically implied by this sentence are often taken as an 'explicatum'. Logically true sentences then have minimum content (perhaps even nil), logically false sentences have maximum content, and synthetic sentences a content between the two. In order to assign some measure to this concept, it is best to first define it as a class of all content elements (weakest synthetic sentences, negations of state descriptions) which follow from the given sentence. In assigning this measure, conflicting adequacy conditions are often stipulated. It is sometimes stipulated as a condition of the additivity of the amount of information of a *conjunction (i.e. as a condition for $\mathrm{Inf}(A \;\&\; B) = \mathrm{Inf}(A) + \mathrm{Inf}(B)$) that $A$ and $B$ are content-disjunct, sometimes however that they are inductively independent of each other. The best method of treating this situation is to accept the existence of two measures and then to explicate them in different ways. Thus the amount of additive semantic information under content disjunctness is called the content measure (Cont), and the amount of additive semantic information under inductive independence is called the information measure (Inf). Both are measures of improbability or, in the psychological sense, surprise. If now a probability measure ($m$) of the sentences of the language system is defined, then $\mathrm{Cont}(A)$ can be defined as $1 - m(A)$ and $\mathrm{Inf}(A)$ as $-\log_2 m(A)$. Cont then varies between 0 and 1, and Inf between 0 and $\infty$, whereby the extreme values are always accepted by the tautologies and contradictions. Conditional measures can be introduced in the usual manner. The theorems

$$\mathrm{Inf}_B(A) = \log_2 m(B) - \log_2 m(A \;\&\; B)$$

and

$$\mathrm{Cont}_B(A) = m(B) - m(A \;\&\; B)$$

are the best ways of reproducing the relationship between these two measures. By analogy to statistical information theory more complicated functions can be introduced. The most interesting are no doubt semantic analogies of entropy and of *transinformation.

The language-systems for which these concepts were defined do not go beyond the so-called applied first-order predicate calculus. Attempts to extend this range are in progress.

BAR-HILLEL, Y.; CARNAP, R.: Semantische Information. Brit. J. Phil. Sci., 4 (1953) pp. 147–57.

**Information, subjective**
Information, subjektive
information subjective
субъективная информация

In *communication between a transmitter and a receiver, the *information of a *message from the transmitter is only equal to the information which the receiver obtains from this message if the finite scheme (cf. *repertory, *probability distribution of these characters) of the transmitter is identical to the finite scheme of the receiver (reciprocal process).

If the repertories or probability distributions of the transmitter and receiver are different, i.e. if the received information of a message is not the same as the transmitted (objective) information, then one talks of subjective information on the side of the receiver (the subject). This concept is important in human communication, as the finite schemes of two people are, generally speaking, never identical, especially in learning-processes (vocabulary, frequency of words used, modes of behaviour, transition to various super-sign repertories). The objective and subjective information of a message can also be different if the receiver has some foreknowledge of the message, i.e. if the message is stored partially or completely in the *memory (cf. mechanical *memory).

CUBE, F. von: Grundsätzliche Probleme bei der Anwendung der Shannonschen Formel auf Wahrnehmungstheorie und Lerntheorie. Grundlagenstudien aus Kybernetik und Geisteswissenschaft, Band 1 (1960).

**Information, transmitted**
*See* *Transinformation

**Information content**
Entscheidungsgehalt
content d'information
объем информации

*Concept of mathematical information theory and the theory of encoding.*

The information content of a possible character or event from a *field $X$ of the order $u(X)$ is defined to

$$I_0(X) = \log_2 u(X).$$

The expression $H(X) \leq I_0(X)$ is always valid if $H(X)$ is the average *information (or *entropy) of the field $X$. Equality only occurs if all events in the field have the same probability, $1/u(X)$.

BERGER, E. R.; PILOTY, H.: Erläuterungen zu den in der Informationstheorie verwendeten Begriffen der mathematischen Statistik. NTZ Heft 1, 1963, pp. 49–52.

**Information processing**
Nachrichtenverarbeitung
traitement de l'information
переработка или обработка информации

*A scientific discipline concerned with the theory and technique of the processing of messages.*

Information processing includes recognition, processes and arrangements which serve the transmission of *messages according to rational rules. This transmission can be achieved by electrical, mechanical, optical or other processes. Information processing also includes the aids used in the preparation of the transmission and for showing its result. The form of the signals which are to be transmitted (electrical, mechanical or optical) is irrelevant (STEINBUCH). The data which occur within a problem are similarly messages in the above sense. This means that data processing is a part of information processing.

Fringe areas of information processing are, amongst other things, automation theory (cf. *automaton, *computer), *learning machines, *intelligence (artificial), *pattern recognition and automatic *translation.

STEINBUCH, K.: Nachrichtenverarbeitung. Elektron. Rechenanlagen Band I Nr. 1 (1959) pp. 17–19.
STEINBUCH, K. (ed.): Taschenbuch der Nachrichtenverarbeitung. Springer-Verlag, Berlin, Göttingen, Heidelberg 1962.

**Information psychology**
Informationspsychologie; kybernetische Psychologie
psychologie informationnelle
информационная психология

*A general term for all attempts to apply concepts and models of *cybernetics and especially of *information theory to the interpretation and partly even to the quantitative representation of psychological phenomena.*

As is the case with every empirical science, psychology uses models, and inherent in its terminology is a system of conceptual models. This means that for many phenomena several equally valid psychological interpretations are possible, which differ only in their choice of an underlying model, and hence several explanations can be put forward to account for the same phenomena, i.e. various theories may be isomorphic to each other. (Similarly, in mathematics the same fact can be represented purely geometrically, or in the terminology of analytical geometry.) Secondly, the formation of psychological models involves the abstraction of essential features of the subject to be represented. As however an objective criterion of essential features independent of the selected model does not exist, several equally valid psychological interpretations are possible, which are distinguished by the difference between their models, and more particularly in terms of their respective definitions of what is 'essential'. (Similarly, physics has conceptual models of rigid bodies and elastic bodies which abstract from the essential property of deformation or at least of plasticity.) By resorting to model theory, information psychology tries to justify the use of originally technical concepts such as *information, *encoding, *channel, storage, control, etc. In at least three essentially different experimental psychological fields the measure of information has proved itself. Firstly, it has shown that the *transinformation transmitted by absolute judgement adopts a maximum value (cf. *channel capacity) which is almost independent of the range of the *field of stimuli and even almost independent of their position within a linear stimulus-continuum. For example, without complete hearing ability an unconfused *recognition of more than five sounds which are different only in frequency is not possible, regardless of where the sounds lie in the sonic range of pitch. The maximum transinformation in pitch-perception is approx. $\log_2 5$ bit (POLLAK), in the perception of degree of sweetness or salinity approx. $\log_2 3$ bit (BEEBE-CENTER, ROGERS and O'CONNEL), and in the interpolation of index positions between two scale marks approx. $\log_2 8$ bit (GARNER and HAKE; McGILL). It is assumed that 5 or 3 or 8 stimuli are available for absolute judgements, and that they are optimally distributed over the stimulus-continuum (ATTNEAVE). Secondly, various experiments resulted in a linear relationship between reaction times (MERKEL; HYMAN; MORIN, FORRIN and ARCHER) or perception times (HOWES and SOLOMON; MILLER, BRUNER and POSTMAN) and the average information content, (cf. *short-term memory).

Thirdly, the measure of surprise value (FRANK) deduced from the information measure has been found of value both for the quantitative interpretation of the experimental results, and for the prediction of the statistical influence of examples ('example behaviour') on free patterns of behaviour and finally even within *informational aesthetics founded on psychology (cf. *maximum effect). Close agreement between theory and empirical findings were frequently achieved by reference to the theory of redundancy-saving binary *encoding.

In contrast to the terminology of information theory, that of control-theory (cf. *feedback control system) has until now had only a basic meaning for information psychology. Radical behaviourism had tried to limit psychology to an analysis of the stimulus-reaction-transmission properties of the system 'man', which was understood as a *linear system; in this, *introspection was not used and the concept of feedback played no part, although quantitative statements were desired. On the other hand, 'comprehensive psychology', orientated to the arts, considered quantitative statements as inessential, and introspective methods as a fundamental tenet. Reactions to stimuli, in contrast to spontaneous, planned actions, then become less important. With goal-orientated action, a constant feedback of information, i.e. a feedback control system, was presupposed. Information psychology adopts as an attempt to synthesize these two assessments both the ideas of feedback control and the methods of introspection, as well as the demand for quantitative experimental results.

ATTNEAVE, F.: Applications of Information Theory to Psychology. Henry Holt & Co., New York 1959. FRANK, H.: Kybernetische Grundlagen der Pädagogik.—Eine Einführung in die Informationspsychologie. Agis, Baden-Baden 1962. FRANK, H.: Informationspsychologie und Nachrichtentechnik. In: Wiener, N.; Schadé, J. P. (eds.): Nerve, Brain and Memory Models. Elsevier, Amsterdam 1963. FRANK, H.: The psychological link of a statistical feedback mechanism explained by means of information theory. In: Hughes, G. M. (ed.): Homeostasis and Feedback Mechanism. Sym. Soc. Exp. Biol. Cambridge Univ. Press, 18 (1964). LANGER, D.: Informationstheorie und Psychologie. Hogrefe, Göttingen 1962. LUCE, R. D.: The Theory of Selective Information and some of its Behavioral Applications. In: Luce, R. D. (ed.): Developments in Mathematical Psychology. The Free Press, Glencoe (Illinois/USA) 1960. ROHRACHER, H.: Regelprozesse im psychischen Geschehen. Sitzungsberichte der Österreichischen Akademie der Wissenschaften, 23bm No. 4, pp. 3–21.

**Information retrieval**
Informationserschliessung
redécouverte d'information
воспроизведение информации

*Concept for systematic methods for the controlled search for information in an automatic archive.*

*By automatic archive* one understands a data-processing machine which is specially constructed and organized for information retrieval. Its essential components are (besides input and output mechanisms) a *store (tape-store, drum- or plate-store, punch-cards, photographic stores) and comparison-units. *Arithmetic units are not usually necessary. In information retrieval information is understood as the encoded statements on the factual content of documents (publications of all types, patents, legal briefs, medical reports, criminal records, store-cards, personal documents, etc.). In this the way in which information is arranged and represented is essential. There is a distinction between (*a*) document-systems where the information is arranged by documents (reference index, bibliographies, library catalogues, lists of suppliers (arranged by authors)) and (*b*) descriptor systems where information is arranged by descriptor (subject-index, punch-card index, and lists of suppliers (arranged by items)).

The system of searching normally consists of the comparison of the whole *content* of the automatic archive with the search instructions, and of writing out all the store contents which correspond to the search instruction.

Both classified systems and non-classified systems can form the basis of the processing of information in automatic archives. In the former case, it is assumed that there exists a *machine-sympathetic* classification-system, i.e. the classification characteristics should be as easily encodable as possible. In the latter case, one assumes the existence of a finite descriptor-list, in which all descriptors are considered as information elements on the same level independent of each other.

**Information theory**
Informationstheorie
théorie de l'information
теория информации

*The mathematical theory of information.* After preparatory assessments which were made at the latest after HARTLEY (1928), C. E. SHANNON founded information theory in 1948 by the introduction of the *bit as the unit of a statistical measure of information, by the definition of channel capacity and by formulating SHANNON's fundamental theorems. These state that independent of the disturbance of a channel and of the type of *messages given off by a *source, these messages can be transmitted without error by suitable *encoding with a speed $H$ (bit/unit time) if $H$ is the information given off from a source per unit time, if $C$ is the capacity of the channel, and if $H < C$. SHANNON transferred this theorem to include channels for non-digital *signals. Further developments and refinements of the basic theorem have been made by McMILLAN, FEINSTEIN, CHINTCHIN, ZAREGRADSKI, etc.

SHANNON, C. E.: A mathematical theory of communication. Bell System Technical Journal 27 (1948). SHANNON, C. E.: Communication in the presence of noise. Proc. IRE, Vol. 37, Pt. 1 (1949) pp. 10–21. GRELL, H. (ed.): Arbeiten zur Informationstheorie, I, II. Dtsch. Vlg. d. Wissenschaften, Berlin 1957. ZEMANEK, H.: Elementare Informationstheorie. R. Oldenbourg, Wien and München 1959. JAGLOM, A. M. and I. M.: Wahrscheinlichkeit und Information. Dtsch. Vlg. d. Wissenschaften, Berlin 1960.

**Informational aesthetics**
Informationsästhetik
esthétique informationnelle
информационная эстетика

*The attempt to apply methods of *cybernetics and especially of *information theory and *information psychology to aesthetic problems, in which no attempts are made to set or justify aesthetic values.*
Informational aesthetics is a fringe activity of the informational sciences. As every science, it has a descriptive and a theoretical stage.

In the descriptive stage statistical methods and *algorithms are applied to works of art, which are understood as complexes of *characters and *supercharacters, for example, by determining the content or the speed of the offer of information, by ascertaining the informational exploitation of the work of art by various signs, whose conspicuousness-values and surprise-value are calculated at various places or at various times (cf. *maximum-effect), and also other statistical values such as dispersion, etc., (cf. *mathematical analysis of music, *mathematical analysis of language). (W. FUCKS, M. BENSE). Descriptive informational aesthetics can also measure those factors of a work of art, with whose value the subjective pleasure in a work of art grows in a group of test-subjects, and by a suitable assessment of this factor a *measure of aesthetics can be sought, which will allow a forecast of the average evaluation of a work of art in a society for which the test-subjects are representative (BIRKHOFF). Descriptive informational aesthetics can in principle be precise and incontestable as long as one avoids the question: 'In how far are its forecasts aesthetically relevant?'

On the other hand theoretical information aesthetics, like every theory, refers to a more or less adequate model, and is therefore contestable, as soon as it transfers statements from the model to reality, that is, wishes to explain symptoms of aesthetic realization, perception and judgement by man. An assessment of theoretical informational aesthetics was first tried by A. MOLES. MOLES put theoretical informational aesthetics on the basis of *information psychology by stressing that the flow of information of a transient work of art should not be much greater than the capacity of a *short-term memory, so that it can still be perceptible, but not much smaller lest it appear boring or banal. This claim was later intensified by the concept of *hierarchization and extended to non-transient works of art (FRANK). From this, an informational aesthetic explanation was found for the deterioration of the music of ancient Greece after the transition to purely instrumental music (GOUBEAU). GUNZENHÄUSER tried to express BIRKHOFF's measure of aesthetics by the theory of aesthetics. ALSLEBEN tried to transfer the theories of informational aesthetics to new fields (cf. *informational typography). To the two principles of descriptive informational aesthetics (works of art must (1) be regarded as *messages, to whose source *consciousness is attributed and (2) be expressed by mathematical methods) two further demands are added in theoretical informational aesthetics, namely:

(3) The mathematical characteristics of a work of art gained in this way must be related to the statements achieved by information psychology on the psychological parameters of man which affect his aesthetic realization or perception.

(4) From here one must seek the necessary conditions which a work of art must fulfil in order to be considered as beautiful in a given society; the fulfilment or non-fulfilment of these conditions must be ascertainable by an algorithm, in other words, aesthetic judgement must be programmable. However, the programming of aesthetic realization is not a generally accepted principle of informational aesthetics, as it is difficult to reconcile such a demand with the first principle (we are not accustomed to ascribing *consciousness to an *automaton).

FUCKS, W.: Gibt es mathematische Gesetze in Sprache und Musik? Umschau Heft 2 (1957). MOLES, A. A.: Théorie de l'Information et Perception esthétique. Flammarion, Paris 1958. BENSE, M.: Aesthetica II–IV. Agis, Baden-Baden 1956/60. FRANK, H.: Grundlagenprobleme der Informationsästhetik und erste Anwendung auf die mime pure. J. Hess, Waiblingen 1959. GOUBEAU, J.: Ein informationsästhetischer Ansatz zur Deutung der griechischen Musikgeschichte. Grundlagenstudien Band 1, Heft 5 (1960) pp. 129–36. GUNZENHÄUSER, R.: Ästhetisches Mass und ästhetische Information. Schnelle, Quickborn bei Hamburg 1962. ALSLEBEN, K.: Ästhetische Redundanz. Schnelle, Quickborn bei Hamburg 1962. FRANK, H.: Kybernetische Analysen. Schnelle, Quickborn 1964.

**Informational approximation**
informationelle Approximation
approximation informationnelle
информационная аппроксимация

In probability learning it has been shown in experiments that man is, in general, capable of ascertaining the objective probabilities of a transmitter if the *repertory of the transmitter is not too large (some 4 to 6 characters). When the repertory is larger, deviations occur, both in forecast experiments and in assessment experiments. This fact gives rise to the thesis that even after a learning process has been finished, a difference can exist between objective and subjective probabilities. This means that *probability learning, i.e. the exact comprehension of objectively given probabilities, must be distinguished from informational approximation (difference of objective probabilities).

**Informational didactics**
Informationsdidaktik
didactique informationnelle
информационная дидактика

In traditional didactics, quantitative methods are rarely used. A frequent point of view is that, in principle, quantitative statements cannot be made because of the difference of the contents which have to be learned, and of the subjectivity of the association of ideas and meanings. Informational didactics based on *cybernetics, which in this context is defined as the science of possible intervention in the learning processes of man, achieves quantitative statements (or more precisely, information-theoretical statements) in the following way: firstly, the *messages (in the general sense) which are to be transmitted are examined for their measurable structures (objective and subjective information content, possibilities of redundancy production, etc.), then the regularities (conformities) resulting in the structural field are described in the form of a theorem (cf. *informational theory of learning), and finally the theorems gained in this way are transferred by allotting them to the real processes of learning and teaching. From the point of view of the theory of information, the essential task of didactics is the production of subjective redundancy for the person learning (cf. *didactics (mechanical), *memory (mechanical) and *super-characters).

**Informational sciences**
Informationswissenschaft; geisteswissenschaftliche Kybernetik
informational sciences
sciences informationnelles

——

*One of the three main areas of *cybernetics which comprises, amongst other things, information theory, mathematical theory of language, information psychology and informational aesthetics. The extension of informational sciences in the realm of techniques (in the general sense of the word) is called cybernetical social science. The technical part of cybernetical pedagogics is one of the most important parts of it.*

FRANK, H. (ed.): Automatische Nachrichtenverarbeitung (Introduction). S. Fischer, Frankfurt/M. 1964.

**Informational theory of learning**
Redundanztheorie des Lernens
théorie informationnelle de l'apprentissage

——

The various processes of learning can be described from the point of view of the pupil as processes of the decrease of information or—with the concept of *redundancy—as processes of a subjective increase of redundancy, in which this redundancy may be produced in various ways: by the learning of probabilities, by mechanical memory and by the formation of super characters.
In the informational theory of learning, a transmitter with the finite scheme $(Z_i, p_i)$ and a self-organizing receiver with the finite scheme $(Z_i, w_i)$ are postulated, in which the receiver must possess the following features:
1 within a finite period of time the subjective probabilities $w_i$ tend to the objective probabilities $p_i$ of the transmitter,
2 the receiver must have a *short-term memory and a long-term memory, each with a constant capacity for information-recording,
3 the receiver must be able to form *super-characters.

The learning processes of the receiver can now be described by the following three processes with increasing redundancy: (*a*) *probability learning and *informational approximation; (*b*) mechanical memory (cf. *memory, mechanical); (*c*) processes of *redundancy at super-character level and *redundancy by steps.
Not only processes of learning but also processes of perception, of thinking, of social relations (cf. *group entropy) and of aesthetic realization can be included under the concept of redundancy. There are therefore various redundancy theories according to the field they concern.

**Informational typography**
Informationstypographie
typographie de l'information
информационная типография

*The practice of arranging printed matter by applying knowledge gained from information theory and Gestalt psychology.*
Informational typography falls in the

general sphere of a practical theory of representation: it makes a clear distinction between the following:

1 the intention of the transmitter in relation to the receiver, as well as the selection of the receiver.
2 The object of representation, the context projected as a representative *model, also called the *referent.
3 the means of representation, all consciously produced *characters
4 the presentation of the model; operations and characters which achieve the desired presentation of the model.

Different means of representation in informational typography are: (*a*) script characters and numerical characters; (*b*) diagrams; photographic illustrations; sketches; (*c*) typographic signals; all practicable stimulus patterns (cf. *stimulus, psychological) which are not characters in the sense of (*a*) or (*b*); (*d*) typographical characters, typographical signals or combinations of these signals which possess *meaning. Different kinds of type, size of type, spacing, interspacing, paper, spatial distributions in a book, etc., therefore produce typographical signals which are used in informational typography as characters to enable a shorter means of expressing the text or a quicker rendering of the message contained in it, and to represent additional relationships between propositions or statements. The system of characters to be used is worked out and agreed on by the author and the typographer. Informational typography is based especially on research in *information theory, *learning theory and psychology of perception (cf. *Gestalt psychology, *perception) by FRANK, GUNZENHÄUSER, METZGER, MOLES.

ALSLEBEN, K.: Ästhetische Redundanz Schnelle, Quickborn bei Hamburg 1962. ALSLEBEN, K. et al.: Sprache und Schrift im Zeitalter der Kybernetik. Schnelle, Quickborn bei Hamburg 1963. ALSLEBEN, K.: Probleme bei der Verwendung von Sichtfeldern. In: FRANK (Edit): Lehrmaschinen in kybernetischer und pädagogischer Sicht. Vol. II Klett, Oldenburg, Stuttgart, München 1964.

**Inhibition, lateral**
Hemmung, laterale
inhibition latérale
торможение

*The effect of certain interconnecting relays in sensory-organ systems of organisms, which helps contrast-formation.* The *specific afferent leaving the *receptors and leading to the projection-cortex is interconnected in such a way that via collateral connections in neighbouring synergistic *synapses, a weak excitation has an augmenting effect on the strong neighbour-excitation, and a strong one has a repressive effect on the weak neighbour-excitation. A local contrast-formation system of this type increases the local excitation-gradient in contrast to the stimulus-strength gradient. In general, the predominant principle in an organism is that in the information-conduction system of the sensory organs an excitation array is always accompanied by a state of lateral inhibition. Lateral inhibition is used mainly for contrast-formation in the space-sensory organ, the eye: in the auditory organ, the ear, it is only used in the higher central-nervous layers. In the former, a lateral inhibition of on-elements, and, in addition, a lateral activation of off-elements is essential for contrast-formation.

HARTLINE, H. K.: Inhibition of visual receptors by illuminating in the limulus eye. Fed. Proc. 8 (1949) p. 69. HARTLINE, H. K.; RATLIFF, F.; MILLER, W. H.: Inhibitory interactions in the retina and its significance in vision. In: Florey, E. (ed.): Nervous Inhibition. Pergamon Press, Oxford, London, New York, Paris 1961, pp. 241–84. REICHARDT, W.; MACGINITIE, G.: Zur Theorie der lateralen Inhibition. Kybernetik 1 (1962) pp. 155–65.

**Inhibition, temporal**
Hemmung, zeitliche
inhibition temporelle
торможение

*The suppression of post-phase excitations in parallel information-circuits made possible by certain interconnecting relays in the sensory-organ system.*

Two parallel information channels within the specific afferent running from the *receptor to the cortex are co-ordinated with each other in such a way that the one with strong excitation (or, after *encoding, with a faster action-potential sequence and also a shorter latency) blocks both channels via an inhibition-relay neuron, although the first signal of the faster action-potential sequence can still pass; the remaining signals, above all those in the more weakly excited channel, are completely suppressed.

In the acoustic sensory-organ system temporal inhibition is used, for example, to suppress the separation of two sound stimuli in one *moment where the time difference is used for a spatial interpretation of the stimulus, namely the direction of the sound-source.

SCHNEIDER, M.: In: Rein, H.; Schneider, M.: Einführung in die Physiologie des Menschen. 11th edn. Springer-Verlag, Berlin, Göttingen, Heidelberg 1960, p. 550. KEIDEL, W. D.: Grenzen der Übertragbarkeit der Regelungslehre auf biologische Probleme. Naturwiss. 48 (1961) pp. 264–76.

**Input** (I)
Eingabe
grandeur d'entrée; entrée
ввод; вводное устройство; устройство ввода данных

*Concept from electronic data processing.*

The input of data and instructions into program-controlled *computers and data-processing machines can normally be done by hand, i.e. by using a keyboard, a process which, because of its slowness, can only be used in exceptional cases (correcting or checking). A quicker input of information which is free of errors can be achieved by the use of so-called input media, i.e. intermediate carriers of information on which information is recorded with the help of external machines. For this purpose the following are suitable: (*a*) punch-cards with an input speed of approx. 800 cards per minute (*b*) punched tape with an average speed of 500 characters per second (*c*) magnetic-tape machines with a speed of up to 60,000 characters per second (*d*) other special apparatus such as automatic *pattern recognition machines for a certain sign *repertory, *magnetic ink font readers, or machines for the recognition of accoustic signs. At present the machines listed under (*a*) to (*c*) are those normally used. They record the information 'off line', i.e. independently of the working of the computer, as long as the calculating unit itself is busy with other tasks. Magnetic tape machines require a very complicated and expensive installation, so that at present they are only used in larger computers. The input of punch-cards has been adopted by the manufacturers of office machines (e.g. the HOLLERITH system) and enables the easy exchange of information cards.

KNÖDEL, W.: Programmieren von Ziffernrechenanlagen. Springer-Verlag, Wien 1961.

**Input** (II)
Eingang
entrée
вход

*Place in a mechanism at which its surroundings exert a direct effect; also this effect itself.*

One must differentiate between energetic and informational effect, and often one uses *input* to describe only the latter, i.e. the data entering the mechanism. It must however be observed that *information is always associated with energy. See also *input (I).

COUFFIGNAL, L.: Kybernetische Grundbegriffe. Agis, Baden-Baden 1962. OPPELT, W.: Kleines Handbuch technischer Regelvorgänge. Verlag Chemie, Weinheim 1956.

**Input quantity; input signal; input value**
Eingangsgrösse
grandeur d'entrée; valeur d'entrée
входная величина

*A value which quantitively denotes the input (II), i.e. the direct effect of surroundings on a mechanism.*
The semantics or pattern of *information must be represented by one or more input signals, in order to be able to be transmitted to the *input(I) of a mechanism (cf. L. COUFFIGNAL). One tries to solve the problem of fitting the input value to the semantics by increasing the number or the exactitude of the input value. Because of the exchange between quantity and quality, the representation of the semantics of information can be achieved only approximately by input value.

COUFFIGNAL, L.: Kybernetische Grundbegriffe. Agis, Baden-Baden 1962. OPPELT, W.: Kleines Handbuch technischer Regelvorgänge. Verlag Chemie, Weinheim 1956.

**Instantaneous value**
*See* *Actual value

**Instruction**
Befehl
instruction
команда

*Instruction to a (digital) computer.*
Automatic *computers can develop long series of calculation and control operations without human assistance. (cf. *program.) The instructions are inserted before the program is executed in a form which is comprehensible to the computer (e.g. coded in *binary numbers) and then summoned in sequence by the *control unit of the computer. By *instruction* one understands a single order for the execution of the operation. This order leads to a command for an arithmetical, logical or organizatory *operation.
An instruction consists of an operational section which gives—in code—what is to be done (add, change sign, etc.) and an address section which shows where the number to which this operation is to be applied is to be found in the internal *store of the machine.
There are basic differences in instructions: (*a*) calculation instructions (add, subtract, find the square, change sign, etc.); (*b*) instructions which clear the arithmetic unit or certain locations, i.e. set them to zero; (*c*) instructions for shifting and rounding of numbers; (*d*) store and transfer instructions which transfer the information from the store to the arithmetic unit and from the arithmetic unit back to the store; (*e*) comparison instructions which compare the content of two storage locations with each other and retain or reject the result; (*f*) jump-instructions which interrupt the regular flow of the program. Specified jump instructions alter the program organization dependent on certain mathematical or logical circumstances such as comparisons, etc.; (*g*) instructions for the index and marker sections of the machine, which facilitates the indirect addressing and organization of the program; (*h*) instructions for the input and output of information; (*i*) instructions for equip-

ment fitted as auxiliaries to the computer (line printers, magnetic drums, etc.).

Knödel, W.: Programmieren von Ziffernrechenanlagen. Springer-Verlag, Wien 1961.

**Instruction, conditional**
Befehl, bedingter
instruction conditionnée
условная команда

In contrast to an unconditional instruction, an instruction or order for an operation which can only be executed when certain conditions are fulfilled. The most well-known is the conditional jump instruction which is used, for example, in leaving loops dependent on whether an iteration process has resulted in the predetermined accuracy, or alternatively after a preset number of iterations.

**Instruction code**
Befehlscode
code d'instructions
код команд; код команды

*Arrangement on the one hand of instructions, and on the other hand of numerical or alpha-numerical characters, which can be read directly by a specified data-processing unit (i.e. without translation).*

Speiser, A. P.: Digitale Rechenanlagen. Springer-Verlag, Berlin, Göttingen, Heidelberg 1961.

**Intelligence**
Intelligenz
intelligence
интеллигенция

*The factor which participates in the materialization of the most varied psychic performances.*

The concept of intelligence in psychology is based on the observation that tests which comprise any performances show positive correlations with each other (cf. *correlation coefficient). The various definitions of the general psychic feature which is manifested in these positive correlations show intelligence to be the ability 'to act purposefully, to think sensibly, and to effectively come to terms with one's environment' (WECHSLER). Various authors stress the ability to learn and the ability to readjust (successful behaviour in new situations) as the main indications of intelligence. As a theoretical concept, intelligence cannot be directly defined empirically, it is inferred by registrable 'intellectual performances'. The measurable level of comparable intellectual performances during childhood and adolescence rises at first, only to fall off again slowly. This fall-off begins even before the age of 20. The development of multiple factor-analysis has shown that intelligence cannot be understood as a one-dimensional ability. Various methods of measuring the level of intellectual performance are shown by intercorrelation matrices, from which result several statistically independent factors of intelligence. The most important of these can be interpreted as mastery of language, word fluency, arithmetical ability, spatial ability, speed of comprehension, memory, decisive thinking (THURSTONE). The importance of the individual factors for the occurrence of certain types of performance shifts with age.

Wechsler, D.: Die Messung der Intelligenz Erwachsener. Bern, Stuttgart 1956.

**Intelligence, artificial**
Intelligenz, künstliche
intelligence artificielle
искусственная интеллигенция

*A general term for all types of intelligent behaviour which are to be regarded as programmable.*

Whilst self-organizing systems (cf. *self-organization) in the main realize the possibilities of adopting a certain form of organization by *communication with their environment, artificial intelligence comprises the next highest functions such as actual *learning, the solving of problems, inductive inference, etc. Characteristic of this is a heuristic section (cf. *heuristics) which from the program or machine gives instructions whose aim is an improvement of activity: this presupposes the storage of residual experience values and the ability to adjust. Recognizable examples of artificial intelligence are *programs for *computers, which may have as their goal the proving of geometrical theorems or algebraic expressions, or finding grammatical rules.

MINSKY, M.: Steps toward artificial intelligence. Proc. IRE 49 (1961) pp. 8–30.

**Intelligence quotient**
Intelligenzquotient
quotient intellectuel
степень интеллекта

*The measured value of the intelligence of a person; it is assessed from performance in psychological tests, and permits a comparison of the intellectual capability of a given person with a reference group defined by in terms of age, sex, occupation, etc.*

A child who is still at an age where intelligence is still growing can be set a series of tasks which demand intellectual performance. The level of performance shown in the execution of this assignment will correspond to the average performance of a certain age-group which is then called the mental age ($MA$) of the child examined. The ratio of mental age ($MA$) and chronological age ($CA$) of the child multiplied by 100 is then its intelligence quotient (I.Q.). This definition: $\text{I.Q.} = 100\frac{MA}{CA}$ cannot be used with adults, as here there is no increase in the level of performance with increasing age. According to WECHSLER, I.Q. is therefore usually defined in such a way that the average level of performance of a certain age-group is set at 100. The unit of the I.Q. is obtained by depicting the registered levels of performance of each age-group in certain tasks as a normal distribution, whose average 50 per cent range is limited by two values which are defined as I.Q. = 90 and I.Q. = 110. I.Q. is thus a measured value which is defined by a frequency distribution, and hence not a real quotient.

WECHSLER, D.: Die Messung der Intelligenz Erwachsener. Bern, Stuttgart 1956.

**Intelligibility**
Verständlichkeit
intelligibilité
понятность; процент внятно воспринятых слов

*A subjective measure to characterize an information transmission system.*

Let $S_1$ denote the number of syllables offered via an information transmission system to several receivers, and $S_2$ the average number of syllables correctly understood by the receivers. Then the syllable-intelligibility $B_s$ is defined by $B_s = \frac{S_2}{S_1} \times 100\ (\%)$. The word-intelligibility $B_w$ and the sentence-intelligibility $B_t$ are defined in the same way, if words and sentences are offered instead of syllables.

The relation $B_t \geqslant B_w \geqslant B_s$ exists between the sentence-intelligibility $B_t$, the word-intelligibility $B_w$ and the syllable-intelligibility $B_s$.

MEYER-EPPLER, W.: Grundlagen und Anwendungen der Informationstheorie. Springer-Verlag, Berlin, Göttingen, Heidelberg 1959.

**Interaction**
*See* *Reciprocal action

**Interneuron**
Zwischenneuron
neurone intermédiaire
промежуточный нейрон

*An interconnecting element (co-ordination element) in information conduction paths of organisms.*

Information conduction paths in organisms, such as the specific afferent between the *receptor and the projection cortex area are always constructed like a *focalized-diffused-excitation. These are reached by a complicated network of a large number of parallel chains of neurons with collateral connections and interneurons. The *inhibition necessary for contrast formation is possible in this way and is in fact proven in the area of the spinal cord.

ECCLES, J. C.; PATT, P.; KOKETSU, K.: Cholinergic and inhibitory synapses in a pathway from motoraxon collaterals to motoneurons. J. Physiol. 126 (1952) pp. 524–62. PESSARD, A.: The role of neuronal networks in sensory communications within the brain. New York, London: MIT-Press and J. Wiley, 1961. WALL, P. D.: The transmission systems for skin sensation. In: Rosenblith, W. (ed.): Sensory communication. New York, London: MIT-Press and J. Wiley, 1961.

**Introspection**
Introspektion; reversive Selbstbeobachtung
introspection
интроспекция; самонаблюдение

*The observation of one's own conscious processes (thinking, feeling, wishing) in such a way that these are disturbed by the observation.*

While consciousness accompanies all conscious processes without modifying them in any way, and is as such merely of interest to philosophy as a 'consciousness-immanent self-observation' (ROHRACHER), it is possible to make contents of the consciousness, e.g. a nascent feeling, the subject of further deliberation before it disappears from the consciousness (i.e. before the end of *duration). This deliberation (or introspection) is, however, itself a conscious process which needs time during which nothing except this deliberation can enter the consciousness (the *short-term memory). Also this deliberation itself can lead to further reflection. This process of 'reversive self-observation' or introspection does not occur simultaneously with the perceptual event, but rather follows it (before the duration is over); it exerts an influence upon subsequent actions. Since the natural sequence of conscious processes is changed by introspection, and since these processes can therefore never be recognized faultlessly by introspection, the behaviourist school of psychology rejected introspection as an analytical tool in favour of a more objective analysis using only functional dependencies between reactions and stimuli. Since, however, this results in a great deal of information being lost by conscious processes, and as it is indisputable that the *transinformation gained from conscious processes by introspection is not zero (even in physics it has been known since HEISENBERG that every observation disturbs the observed, on which, however, information may be gained from the observation, even if it is finite information), information psychology admits introspection as a method.

ROHRACHER, H.: Einführung in die Psychologie. Urban & Schwarzenberg, Wien (Innsbruck, 7th edn.) 1960.

**Invariancy**
Invarianz
invariabilité
инвариантность

A mathematical value or property is called invariant (or more precisely, invariant to a transformation $T$) if it remains unaltered by $T$. Such a value is called *an invariant* and the characteristic *invariance*.

**Jump instruction**
Sprungbefehl
saut; instruction de saut
команда условного или безусловного перехода

*A special *instruction in the *program of a *computer.*

A distinction is made between conditional and unconditional jump instructions. The unconditional jump instruction of the form '$B_{m+k}$: jump to $B_m$' results in the instruction sequence $B_m$, $B_{m+1}, \ldots B_{m+k-1}$ being carried out over and over again (cf. *loop). The conditional jump instruction of the form '$B_{m+k}$: jump to $B_m$ if a certain condition is fulfilled, otherwise go to $B_{m+k+1}$' enables the interruption of the repetition of the instructions sequence $B_m, B_{m+1}, \ldots B_{m+k-1}$ (cf. *instruction, conditional).

RUTISHAUSER, H.; SPEISER, A. P.; STIEFEL, E.: Programmgesteuerte digitale Rechengeräte. Birkhäuser, Basel and Stuttgart 1951.

# L

**Language**
Sprache
langage
язык

*A decisive basic structure in human patterns of existence and behaviour.*

Almost all activities of human beings, especially of intelligent ones, are influenced by language and often accompanied by linguistic expression. Language can be regarded under the four aspects of human behaviour: the generally human aspect, the sociological aspect, the individual aspect, and the aspect connected to situation. In certain respects the following three areas of language can be distinguished:

1 the central nucleus: every-day speech;
2 variants and modifications of every-day speech: the two extremes of (*a*) poetic language and the language of cults, and (*b*) scientific or specialist language;
3 formalized, mathematically constructed languages (which are not regarded by linguisticians as languages in the full sense of the word).

If a language is used to discuss another language, then the latter is called the *object language, the former a meta language. In principle, any language from one of the above areas can be used to describe the language in either of the others. But it remains open as to how much of the area to be described can be depicted. Scientifically, only a specialized linguistics language or a correspondingly formalized language is suitable for use as a meta language. In any description using this, an attempt is made to emphasize the essential nucleus of the language form, and to regard stylistic and individual details of situation-conditioned speech as variations of this nucleus. From a scientific viewpoint, language is shown to be a connected system of linguistic elements which exerts an effect in nearly every sphere of human experience and in communication between people of a language community. The system is therefore recognizable in its effects, i.e. the specific linguistic structure of experience, which is different from language to language, and the oral or written expression of communication. Linguistic description often begins with the latter, the phonetic or the written aspect, *syntax in its broad sense (cf. *semiotics). During the process of comprehension, the phonetic or written substrata, the language-*signals, are allocated a complex of other perceptions and experiences of a linguistic or non-linguistic nature (either stored or perceived at that moment), i.e. an interpretation of the language-signal which is more or less the one generally accepted in that language community. The unit of language-signal and its proper interpretation is called the *character or sign. The description of the relationships which exist between the linguistic interpretations belongs to the theory of meaning, whereas the description of the reciprocal effect between language and experience belongs to the theory of reference. These two aspects are sub-aspects of *semantics. On the other hand, the syntactical and meaning aspect can be combined to form the aspect of language-structure, i.e. of *grammar. The reciprocal relationship between language and actions of individuals and communities is described in the pragmatic aspect or the aspect relating to effect.

Weisgerber, L.: Von den Kräften der deutschen Sprache. I, II. Schwann, Düsseldorf 1962. Weisgerber, L.: Die vier Stufen in der Erforschung der Sprache. Schwann, Düsseldorf 1963. Bar-Hillel, Y.: Language and Information: Selected Essays in their Theory and Application. Addison-Wesley, Reading. Mass. and Jerusalem Science Press, Jerusalem 1964, Bierwisch, M.: Grammatik des deutschen Verbs. Studia Grammatica II, Akademie-Verlag, Berlin 1963. Chomsky, N.: Syntactic Structures. Mouton, s'Gravenhage 1957. Chomsky, N.: Aspects of the Theory of Syntax, The MIT Press, Cambridge, Mass, 1965.

**Language, object**

*See* *Object language

**Language translation** (Mechanical)
Sprachübersetzung, automatische
traduction automatique
машинный перевод; автоматический перевод

*The translation of texts of one language (source language) into texts of another language (target language) by automatic data-processing machines.*

It is obvious that a process of automatic language translation is the better, the greater the number of morphological-syntactical and content elements of the pertinent language structure (cf. *language, *grammar, *mathematical language analysis) of a text which can be unambiguously ascertained by an automatic process and can be transferred into and realized in a foreign language. As the grammars of natural languages explicitly formulate only a fraction of the actual regularity of the languages, automatic translations comparable to those done by humans can only be achieved in the distant future (if at all) after intensive linguistic research and development of new and general processes and descriptive methods of formal language analysis. The present processes of lexical translation (the automatic use of a bilingual dictionary) and of morphological and syntactical analysis and translation (e.g. Russian-English) have produced results of only a very low quality, and the value of these rough renderings of the informational content of an original text is debatable.

Natl. Phys. Lab.: 1961 Intern. Conf. on Machine Translation of Languages and Applied Language Analysis I, II. H.M.S.O., London 1962. BAR-HILLEL, Y.: The present status of automatic translation of languages, In: Alt, F. L. (ed.): Advances in Computers I. pp. 91–183. Academic Press, New York 1960. EDMUNSDON, H. P. (ed.): Machine Translation. Prentice Hall, Englewood Cliffs N.J. 1961. OETTINGER, A. G.: Automatic. (Transference, Translation, Remittance, Shunting) In: Brouwer, R. A. (ed.): On Translation. Harvard Univ. Press, Cambridge Mass. 1959. OETTINGER, A. G.: Automatic Language Translation. Harvard Univ. Press, Cambridge Mass. 1960.

**Languages, formalized**
Sprachen, formalisierte
langages formales
формальный язык

*A calculus in which the expressions are given a meaning by means of an interpretation.*

To construct a formalized language a known language is needed in which it can be described. This *meta language must be separated from the *object language, i.e. the represented language. If this difference is not observed, paradoxes occur. As the meta language used does not generally have the necessary degree of exactness one is at first confined to those expressions with which the manipulation of symbols can be clearly described. By these means of expression, the formal part of the language (calculus or formal system) is established free of any meaning as *play* with symbols. This is the task of *syntax. The calculus then obtains by *semantics an interpretation by allotting the figures meaning. This demands a meta language which is more comprehensive than that necessary for the construction of syntax.

The theory of formalized languages contributes greatly to the development of mathematical philosophy and influences the development of problem-orientated *programming languages, as well as of a general theory of language.

CARNAP, R.: Einführung in die symbolische Logik. Springer, Wien 1954. CHURCH, A.: Introduction to Mathematical Logic. Princeton University Press 1956.

**Learning**
Lernen
apprentissage
обучение; учение

*Acquisition of skills or knowledge in men or animals. Also used for similar phenomena in automata (cf. *learning machines)*

The concept *learning* is applied to a variety of symptoms which control all information recording and storage in an organism. In general, learning causes an alteration in behaviour which is manifested in an *adaptation to its surroundings. Habituation is the simplest manifestation of learning. (The organism reacts more weakly to similar stimuli which are repeated again and again). ASHBY proved that habituation is a natural feature of very complex systems (not necessarily living systems). It is thought that the mechanism of learning is based on, amongst other things, the alteration of the character of the synaptic connections between *neurons. HEBB summoned neural reverberation for short-term storage, which leads to synaptic long-term facilitation.

THORPE, W. H.: Learning and Instinct in Animals. Methuen, London 1956. HEBB, D. O.: Organization of Behaviour. Reprinted Science Edition, New York 1961. ASHBY, W. R.: The Mechanism of Habituation. In: Mechanization of Thought Processes. H.M.S.O. London 1959.

**Learning machines**
Lernende Automaten
automates d'apprentissage
обучающиеся автоматы

*An *automaton which improves its efficiency as a result of its experience. This happens either with the help of a teacher or by reciprocal action with its surroundings.*

To be considered as a learning machine, an automaton must filter a great part of the information which it has recorded and use it to alter its behaviour. So the mere storage of information and the complete surrender of this stored information cannot be regarded as evidence of learning: tape-recorders cannot learn. The above definition applies to some extremely simple pieces of apparatus: for example, self-optimizing (cf. *optimize) regulators, a learning matrix and UTTLEY's conditional probability computer. According to PASK, an automaton is not a learning machine until it changes itself in such a way that it can be described at different times by differing variables.

ANDREW, A. M.: Learning Machines. In: Mechanization of Thought Processes. H.M.S.O. London 1959.

**Learning matrix**
Lernmatrix
matrice à apprendre
матрица обучения

*Matrix-shaped circuit-structure for the reconstruction of simple learning processes (cf. *learning machines).*

A learning matrix is a matrix-shaped structure of rows and columns at the intersections of which are connective-elements (see diagram). Functionally there is a difference between the learning-phase and the testing-phase.

In the learning-phase characteristics $\{E\}$ are interpolated to meanings $B$ by the following method; (1) a set of characteristics (encoded by *binary or *analogue electrical *signals) is introduced component by component into the columns of the learning matrix; (2) at the same time, the meaning (also as a signal) which is to be interpolated selects a line of the learning matrix; and (3) the characteristics are stored by setting the connective elements of the selected line. Examples of the connective elements are adjustable resistances, magnetic cores or *transfluxors.

In the testing-phase, either the meaning which was interpolated into an offered set of characteristics during the learning-phase is given by an extreme-value circuit according to certain similarity-criteria (e.g. *HAMMING distance) (if no meaning was interpolated to the offered characteristics, then the meaning of those characteristics is given which is most similar to the offered set), or the set of characteristics interpolated and stored during the learning phase is ascertained by the giving of a meaning. Learning matrices can be linked to form chains.

STEINBUCH, K.: Die Lernmatrix. Kybernetik 1, H. 1 (1961) pp. 36–45. STEINBUCH, K.; PISKE, U.: Learning Matrices and their Applications.: IEEE Transactions on Electronic Computers, Dec. 1963 (with full bibliography on learning matrices).

**Learning theories; learning models**
Lerntheorien; Lernmodelle
théories de l'apprentissage
теории обучения

*Theories which explain learning-processes which are considered as given if the probability of the occurrence of a class of modes of behaviour changes (as a result of previous experience) when there is a situation of a certain kind.*

A series of learning theories is based on the contiguity of GUTHRIE, according to which associative connections are built up between spatially or temporally connected *stimuli or *reactions. According to ESTES an organism takes a random sample $X$ from the set of

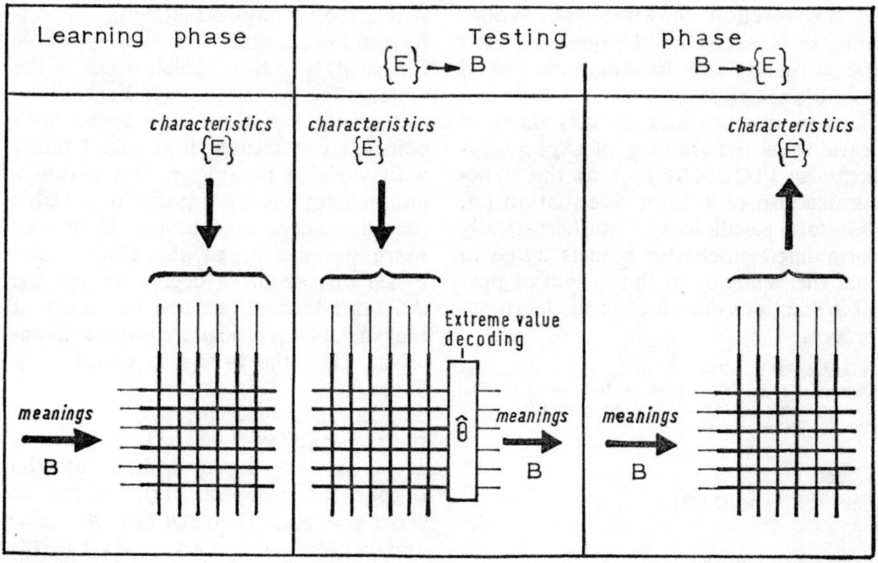


'Conditional connectives' are formed when {E} and B are inserted

The 'most similar' meaning B results after the input of {E}

{E} follows the input of B

Learning matrix

stimuli *S* during *perception. The *probability of a reaction *A* is equal to the quotient from the BOREL measured value of the stimulus elements contained in *X*, which are conditioned to *A* and the measured value of the whole random sample set *X*. With every reaction there follows a conditioning of all elements in *X* to this reaction. A later stochastic learning model (BUSH and MOSTELLER, 1951) can be traced back to similar assumptions. The vector *P* of the probabilities of all reactions possible in a situation is changed in a learning event by vector-multiplication with a stochastic matrix *T*. The *T* to be used must fulfil a series of formal conditions and is dependent on the reaction in question and the consequence (e.g. reward-punishment). The learning-process can then be represented as a *MARKOV chain of stochastic vectors.

In the widely recognized theory of HULL a behaviour strength is given to each stimulus-reaction connection. It is a negatively accelerated exponential function of a number of preceding strengthenings by reward or knowledge of success after the occurrence of the same connection. From behaviour-strength and other variables there results a net reaction potential, on which various measurable aspects of the reaction are stochastically dependent.

LUCE attributes *v* values to the possible reactions. In a learning-event the *v*

of the reaction shown alters. Probability of a reaction is the quotient from the pertinent $v$ and the sum of the $v$ of all possible reactions.
Further theories and models describe learning as the training of expectancy-attitudes (TOLMAN) or as the structuralization of a stimulus-situation (cf. *Gestalt psychology). Mathematically formulated stochastic models agree in that the *entropy of the system of possible reactions decreases in the learning-process.

HILGARD, E. R.: Theories of Learning. Appleton-Century Crofts, New York 1956. LUCE, R. D.: Developments in Mathematical Psychology. Glencoe, Illinois 1960.

**Limen**
*See* *Threshold (II)

**Liminal difference**
*See* *Differential threshold

**Linear system; linear transfer system**
Übertragungsglied, lineares

——

линейное передаточное (трансляционное) звено

A system can be used as a linear system if it has the following structure: a variable which occurs at a certain point of the system, the input, can be given any value or sequence of values. The alteration of this input variable is transferred in a continuous causal relationship to another point of the system where the output variable of the system changes as the effect of the given cause. It is also possible for a linear system to have several input variables and/or several output variables; then the output variables are dependent on the input variables in a similar way.
The mathematical definition of a linear system can be achieved, as in fact can that of any physical system, by differential equations for the variable (physical) quantities which occur in the system. The system is called linear if the differential equations are linear with constant coefficients. It is called linear with variable parameters if the differential equations are linear with variable time-dependent coefficients. If one or more parameters of the system and hence one or more coefficients of the differential equations are functions of the variable physical quantities themselves, then the system is called non-linear.
The linearity of a linear system is expressed as follows: let the time function $x(t)$ as the input induce at the output the response $y(t)$, written in short $y = y(x)$. Then $y(n\,x) = n \times y(x)$ and $y(x_1 + x_2) = y(x_1) + y(x_2)$ (principle of superposition). Most linear systems are not exactly linear; on the other hand, the theory of linear differential equations with constant coefficients is particularly simple and clear, so that one uses wherever possible the linear approximation of the exact equations. The error which is made by this idealization is insignificant in many cases, and in many other cases it can be ignored at least for small alterations of the variables.
The behaviour of a linear system can be described mathematically in several ways; the usual definitions are achieved by differential equation, *frequency response, *transfer function, and *step response.

GILLE, J. C.; PELEGRIN, M.; DECAULNE, P.: Lehrgang der Regelungstechnik. Band 1, R. Oldenbourg, München und Berlin 1960. OLDENBOURG, R. C.; SARTORIUS, H.: Dynamik selbsttätiger Regelungen. Band 1, R. Oldenbourg, München 1951. SOLODOWNIKOW, W. W.: Grundlagen der selbsttätigen Regelung. R. Oldenbourg, München and Berlin 1959.

**Locus**
Ortskurve
——
кривая геометрического места (точек); кривая концов вектора; круговая диаграмма; местная кривая

*The representation of complex-valued functions of electrical communication theory in graphical form dependent on the real frequency.*
An example of such a function is the impedance-function of a two-terminal network. For any chosen real frequency $\omega$ (cf. *oscillation) there results a complex value of impedance. If one inserts for every real $\omega$ the complex impedance value point for point into a rectangular system of co-ordinates (real part = abscissa; imaginary part = ordinate), then one obtains the locus of the impedance.

WUNSCH, G.; Theorie und Anwendung linearer Netzwerke. Part 1. Geest & Portig, Leipzig 1961.

**Logic**
Logik
logique
логика

*Doctrine of decisive thinking when all psychological details are abstracted.*
A distinction is made between formal logic, which to a large extent goes back to ARISTOTLE, and which examines only the structure of the correct decision independently of its content, and the transcendental logic of KANT and the ontologic or metaphysical logic of HEGEL and more recently G. GÜNTHER. The algebraization of formal logic by LEIBNITZ, BOOLE, SCHRÖDER, FREGE, RUSSELL and WHITEHEAD is called *mathematical logic.

HILBERT, D.; ACKERMANN, W.: Grundzüge der theoretischen Logik. 4th edn. Springer-Verlag, Berlin, Göttingen, Heidelberg 1959.

**Logic, mathematical**
Logistik
logique mathématique
логистика

*The modern algebraic form of formal *logic.*
The elementary component of mathematical logic is propositional calculus. Propositions are designated by letters (proposition-variables), just as numbers are in numerical algebra. For the usual bivalent logic, each proposition-variable can adopt only one of two possible *truth values*; true or false. Through **propositional functions* (also called logical functions, connectives, or operators); cf. *conjunction, *implication, *disjunction, *negation) there results from one or more propositions a new one whose truth value depends in a certain way on the truth value of the *atomio statement*. Propositional calculus is of interest to cybernetics because switching algebra develops physical models of it.
Whilst propositional calculus abstracts from the logical structure of theorems, this structure is taken into account in the higher branches of mathematical logic (predicate calculus, set logic, modal calculus, etc.).
In all these calculations, time is irrelevant; only the extension of mathematical logic to the theory of *TURING machines deals with the dimension of time as well.

**Logical circuits**
logische Schaltungen
circuits logiques
логическая схема

*Technical realizations of the functions of logical algebra, operator elements in contrast to store elements.*
Bivalent-logical *Boolean algebra states

that with two logical variables 16 functions are possible, of which ten functions are true functions of two variables. To realize them mechanically, the digital principles of information technology are used predominantly, in which two different current levels or the states 'current/no current' are allotted to the two states of the variables. In principle, there exist the possibilities of static and dynamic techniques. Whereas with the former only alterations of the variables result in alterations of the state of the network, in dynamic techniques only the existence or the lack of *pulses is decisive. The functions are evaluated only at discrete times given by a clock generator. Correspondingly there are the older realizations by *relay, and the more modern form and therefore the form used almost exclusively nowadays, of bistable circuits. The main field of application of logical circuits is in information processing systems, above all digital *computers in which the *control unit and the *arithmetic unit consist of many logical circuits. With a single propositional function (cf. *SHEFFER's stroke, or *nor-function) as a basis, one could overcome every imaginable task by means of various combinations; in practice, however, for reasons of economy use is made of *conjunction, *disjunction, *negation, *equivalence and *non-equivalence. In modern solid-state techniques logical circuits are constructed from diode and transistor circuits, and a construction from *magnetic cores has even been attempted. Diodes are exceptional in that their circuits are cheaper and simpler, but normally after two stages they require signal amplification and regeneration, nor do they allow negation of a function or of a variable. Transistor circuits on the other hand can reproduce the function, with amplification and negation, in one stage, but are more expensive and more liable to disturbance. Integrated circuitry will overcome these difficulties.

In principle the processes of even large logical circuits are regarded as simultaneous. The introduction of a defined *transit time leads to the storage of previous activity and thereby to sequential circuits.

STEINBUCH, K. (ed.): Taschenbuch der Nachrichtenverarbeitung. Springer-Verlag, Berlin, Göttingen, Heidelberg 1962.

**Logical connective; logical operator**
Verknüpfung, logische
fonction logique
логическая связь

*The allotment of a truth value (T 'true' or F 'false') to one or two propositional variables (unary or binary connective) with the value repertory T and F (cf. *semantics).*

Together with logical connectives, propositional variables form a *Boolean algebra, i.e. a formalized language. The *syntax of this language enables the automatic execution of certain logical proofs (cf. *theorem proving program). In *programming languages the following logical connectives are generally used:
(*a*) *negation (unary); (*b*) *conjunction; (*c*) *disjunction; (*d*) *implication; (*e*) *equivalence, *non-equivalence; (the connectives (*b*) to (*e*) are binary; the order corresponds to the rule of precedence with regard to processing when several logical connectives occur in the same expression). All binary logical connectives, as well as negation, can be expressed solely in terms of a *nor-function or *SHEFFER's stroke.

HILBERT, D.; ACKERMANN, W.: Grundzüge der theoretischen Logik. 3rd edn. Springer-Verlag, Berlin,

Göttingen, Heidelberg 1949. LORENZEN, P.: Formale Logik. W. de Gruyter & Co., Berlin 1958.

**Logical value of occupancy**
logischer Stellenwert
valeur logique
——

*Concept in cybernetical logic gained from the generalization and formalization of values of traditional propositional logic.*
This generalization refers to the application of the principle of permanence with regard to the rules of construction for functors, as well as to polyvalence; formalization refers to the abstraction of classical truth values to mere levels which are interpreted in cybernetical logic as degrees of reflection. Generalized value of occupancy logic of polyvalent logic contains classical propositional logic as a sub-system with the logical positions 1 and 2; the logical position 3 would be a so-called 'foreign' value in this system.
The purpose of the concept is the construction of a logic which can describe the change of digital and analogue structure in the neural system of man, and can therefore become the basis of a cybernetical technique which simulates subjectivity.

**Logon**
Logon
logon
логон
*Concept in the *theory of information.*
On the basis of the theory of information, physical signals can be quantized. If one ignores the quantization of amplitude-values and limits oneself to the range of time (and where possible of frequency) then the resultant quanta are called logons. The total number of quanta of this type is called logon content (cf. *GABOR information-cell).

MEYER-EPPLER, W.: Grundlagen und Anwendungen der Informationstheorie, Springer-Verlag, Berlin, Göttingen, Heidelberg 1959.

**Loop**
Programmschleife
boucle
*Concept in programming techniques of *computers.*
A loop is a sequence of instructions $I_m, I_{m+1} \ldots I_{m+i}, I_{m+k}$ in which the instruction $I_{m+k}$ is a *jump-instruction and leads back to the instruction $I_m$. The loop is left by a conditional instruction (cf. *instruction, conditional): this can also be the instruction $I_{m+k}$.

# M

**Machine code, machine language**
Maschinensprache
langage machine
машинный язык; язык машины
*Form of representation of data and *instructions in which they can be directly processed by a data-processing machine.*
Machine code is the term used, especially with digital *computers, for the *repertory of instructions which are encoded by the *code used in the computer for number representation (instruction lists in machine code).
Instructions which are not expressed in machine code are not—or are incorrectly—interpreted by the computer.

To simplify the programming, *programming languages (pseudo-codes) are frequently used, which before they are carried out must be translated by the computer with the help of a translator (cf. *assembler, *compiler) in the machine code of the computer in question.

KNÖDEL, W.: Programmieren von Ziffernrechenanlagen. Springer-Verlag, Wien 1961.

**McMILLAN's theorem**
McMILLANscher Satz
théorème de McMILLAN
теорема Макмиллана

McMillan's theorem shows that for stationary sources (cf. *source, stationary) the *random variable

$$f_n(x) = -\frac{1}{n}\log q(K_n),$$

in which $q(K_n)$ is the *probability of a word of $n$ letters of the *alphabet of the source $[A, q]$, converges in the mean to an invariant function (cf. *invariance) $h(x)(h(Tx) = h(x))$, which for ergodic sources (cf. *source, ergodic) almost certainly agrees with the *entropy of the source. From this follows the convergence in probability: i.e. for as small a $\varepsilon$, $\delta > 0$ as required and for a sufficiently large

$$n: P\{| f_n(x) - H | < \varepsilon\} > 1 - \delta,$$

i.e. one can for a sufficiently large $n$ divide all $n$-membered words $K_n$ of the source into two classes in such a way that some are distributed asymptotically with the uniform distribution $q(K_n) \approx 2^{-n(\mathrm{H}+2)}$, and that together all the other words have a probability as small as required.

GRELL, H. (ed.): Arbeiten zur Informationstheorie I. Dtsch. Vlg. d. Wissenschaften, Berlin 1957. HENZE, E.; Einführung in die Informationstheorie. Beiheft 3, Elektronische Datenverarbeitung (2nd edit. 1965).

**Magnetic core**
Ferritkern
ferrite; tore magnétique
ферритовый сердечник; ферромагнитный сердечник

*A ring-shaped element of ferro-magnetic material.*

Magnetic cores are made of ferro-magnetic material. They possess 2 distinctive temporal stable magnetic states: positive and negative remanence $\pm B_r$, to which the binary numbers 1 and 0 are assigned. The magnetic state of a magnetic core is changed by means of a current-pulse in a wire leading through the magnetic core. The read-out process can either destroy or retain the stored information.

Magnetic cores are used predominantly in *core stores as store-elements for binary information, and also for switching in *logical circuits.

SPEISER, A. P.: Digitale Rechenanlagen. Springer-Verlag, Berlin, Göttingen, Heidelberg 1961.

**Magnetic disc store**
Magnetplattenspeicher
mémoire à disques
запоминающее устройство на магнитном диске; магнитный накопительный диск

*A store for large quantities of information in data-processing systems with several circular discs which rotate around the same vertical spindle.*

The discs are spaced from each other by a few centimetres. The *magnetic head (usually several heads) moves past the discs in a vertical direction by means of compressed air, turns in between two discs and can now either read or write data. Compressed air issuing from the head keeps the distance between the head and the discs constant. The *address is established by giving the disc, the track (concentric circles) and

the sector. Motors, amplifiers and tracking devices are all part of magnetic disc stores.
*Capacity: $10^7$–$10^9$ bits; average *access time: 0·05–0·5 s.

SPEISER, A. P.: Digitale Rechenanlagen. pp. 355–7. Springer-Verlag, Berlin, Göttingen, Heidelberg 1961.
WINCKEL, F.: Technik der Magnetspeicher. pp. 296–298. Springer-Verlag, Berlin, Göttingen, Heidelberg 1960.

**Magnetic drum store; drum store**
Magnettrommelspeicher
tambour; mémoire à tambour
запоминающее устройство на магнитном барабане; магнитный накопительный барабан

*A cylinder rotating around a vertical axis; it has a magnetizable surface and, in data-processing systems, serves as a store.*
A firm hollow cylinder, in which the drum rotates, has at least one *magnetic head for every track (= drum range), which, in contrast to that in the *magnetic tape store, does not touch the surface. *Clock tracks determine the writing and reading time as well as the address. Motors, writing and reading amplifiers and tracking device are also parts of a drum store. *Capacity: approx. 500,000 bits; average *access time: 5–10 ms.

SPEISER, A. P.: Digitale Rechenanlagen. pp. 332–55. Springer-Verlag, Berlin, Göttingen, Heidelberg 1961.
WINCKEL, F.: Technik der Magnetspeicher. pp. 285–296. Springer-Verlag, Berlin Göttingen, Heidelberg 1960.

**Magnetic head**
Magnetkopf
tête magnétique
магнитная головка

*A small electro-magnet of a special shape for writing and reading on magnetic layers (coatings).*
A magnetic head is a type of horseshoe magnet of Mu-metal with a very small air gap. The gaps are only millionths of a millimetre in size. Opposite the gap the core carries a coil. If an electric current flows through this coil, then a magnetic field results in the Mu-metal which depends on the current for direction and strength. This results in a magnetic field across the gap. By a non-magnetic body (a mica plate) in the air-gap, the field is deflected to the space in front of the gap. Any magnetic material (e.g. magnetic tape) is magnetized at this point.
If an alternating current flows through the coil, then a corresponding alternating field results in the magnetic head, and the material in front of the gap is re-magnetized to the periodicity of the current. If the material moves past the gap, then the individual instantaneous values of the magnetic field, which are different in direction and strength, lead to a corresponding magnetization of various areas of the material. By this the variations of the current are stored magnetically. There are also magnetic heads which make use of the Hall effect. If the magnetized material is now moved past the magnetic head, then the magnetic alternating field in the coil of the magnetic head which has arisen in the area of the air-gap induces a corresponding electrical alternating voltage. In this way the stored information can be read.

SPEISER, A. P.: Digitale Rechenanlagen. Springer-Verlag, Berlin Göttingen, Heidelberg 1961.

**Magnetic ink font**
Magnetschrift
écriture magnétique
магнитная запись

*Script written in a magnetizable colour to enable a simple and sure automatic *pattern recognition.*

*Mostly specially shaped script-signs which are produced with a magnetizable colour (e.g. by the addition of iron oxide to the inks); they enable an especially easy scanning and accurate recognition.*
Very common is the E 13-B script of the American Bankers Association (ABA) standardized in 1959. If this script is scanned by a one-track *magnetic head then every character produces its own characteristic current pattern which can be recognized using one of the familiar correlation processes (cf. *correlation function).
BULL's CMC-7 script must also be mentioned; here the individual numbers are represented by a vertical hatching with two wider spacings. One advantage of a magnetic ink font is that dirtying the paper has practically no effect on pattern recognition. A disadvantage is that it is essential to have special printing machines which must be able to satisfy the most stringent demands of accuracy.

**Magnetic tape store; tape store**
Magnetbandspeicher
mémoire à bande magnétique
накопитель на магнитной ленте; запоминающее устройство на магнитной ленте

*A store for larger quantities of binary encoded data in data-processing systems on the principle of tape-recorders.*
A tape device consists of a mechanical drive, tracking device and amplifiers as well as *magnetic heads (writing, reading and erase heads). The tape (plastic carrier with a magnetic coating), usually 1000 metres long with interchangeable spools, or 100 metres long in cassettes, is drawn across the heads with a slight pressure. The different speeds of the tape and the capstans during operation are compensated by photo-electrically or pneumatically controlled buffer bands. The clock track is erased with the information tracks and written again. Storage *capacity: 50–100 million bits; average *access time: approx. 100 s.; read/write speed: 2·5–3·5 m/s.

SPEISER, A. P.: Digitale Rechenanlagen, pp. 380–4. Springer-Verlag, Berlin, Göttingen, Heidelberg 1961.
WINCKEL, F.: Technik der Magnetspeicher, pp. 301–306. Springer-Verlag, Berlin, Göttingen, Heidelberg 1960.

**Management games**
Unternehmensspiele
jeu d'entreprise

Management games are models for economic and managerial theories on the basis of the mathematical theory of games. In the simpler games, the results can be calculated manually; more complicated games are programmed for and calculated by electronic computers. Management games are action models of economic markets. The supply side consists of model factories working in competition. For every business are collected the data which are normally necessary to plan for the future. They are fed into the models as parameters. The demand side is formed by clients whose marketing or purchasing behaviour follows certain model ideas. Also, the market is subject to random influences.
In management games the various firms have a series of decisions to make on the basis of their individual situations, decisions which correspond to a definite *works policy*. The various managements are in competition with each other. The model serves to allot numerical values to the decisions taken; by the use of computers, the results of the management of every factory can be produced in a very short while; this result is for a period which can stretch over months or years. Further decisions are then possible on the basis of these new results.

BLEICHER, K.: Unternehmensspiele. Simulationsmodelle für unternehmerische Entscheidungen. Verlag für Unternehmensführung, Baden-Baden 1961. MUNZ, M.: Unternehmensspiele und betriebswirtschaftliche Theorie. BULL-Informationen 27 (1963).

## MARKOV chain

MARKOFFsche Kette
chaîne de MARKOFF
цепь Маркова

A MARKOV chain is a *stochastic process $\{X_t, t \in T\}$ with countable states $i, j, k, \ldots$ in which for every pair of parameter values $\tau < t \in T$ the distribution of $X_t$ is determined by that of $X_\tau$, and data on 'past' states $X_\vartheta$, $\vartheta < \tau$ do not alter this distribution.

A MARKOV chain fulfills the MARKOV condition, that is, it is valid for every $n$, $t_j \in T$ and any states

$i_j, t > t_1 > t_2 > \ldots > t_n$:

$$P\{X_t = k \mid X_{t1} = i_1, X_{t2} = i_2, \ldots, X_{tn} = i_n\} = P\{X_t = k \mid X_{t1} = i_1\}.$$

The conditional probabilities

$$P_{ik}(\tau, t) = P\{X_t = k \mid X_\tau = i\}$$

are called the transfer probabilities. It follows that

$$0 \leq P_{ik}(\tau, t) \leq 1, \sum_k P_{ik}(\tau, t) \leq 1,$$

in which summation is over all states $k$ and

$$\lim_{t \to \tau} P_{ik}(\tau, t) = \delta_{ik} = \begin{Bmatrix} 1 \\ 0 \end{Bmatrix} \text{ for } \begin{Bmatrix} i = k \\ i \neq k \end{Bmatrix}.$$

If the set of all states is non-enumerable, then one talks of a MARKOV process. If a parameter set $T$ is also discrete, e.g. equal to the set of all non-negative integers, then one talks of a discrete MARKOV chain. If the transfer probabilities are only dependent on the difference $t - \tau$, then the process is called a MARKOV chain with stationary transfer probabilities. If $T$ is still discrete here, then one writes $P_{ik}(t, t + 1) = p_{ik}$ and calls $p_{ik}$ the elementary transfer probabilities and $(p_{ik})$ the transfer matrix (in the non-stationary case correspondingly for $t = \tau + 1$ in the case of discrete $T$). A MARKOV chain is defined clearly by giving its transfer probabilities and the initial distribution $q_i = P\{X_0 = i\}$.

BHARUCHA-REID, A. T.: Elements of the Theory of Markov-Processes and their Applications. McGraw Hill, New York 1960. KEMENY, J. G.; SNELL, J. L.: Finite Markov Chains. Van Nostrand Co., Princeton, N.Y. 1960.

## MARKOV source

MARKOFFsche Quelle
source markovienne
источник Маркова

A MARKOV source is a discrete stationary *MARKOV chain, i.e. a stochastic sequence of states to whose state-transfers characters of an *alphabet are allocated with the interpretation that these are realized according to the realization of the transfers. So the MARKOV source produces in the sequence of the state-transfers a stochastic character sequence. It is therefore an important example of a source of information. In the same way as MARKOV chains, MARKOV sources can be represented as *graphs (or equivalent matrices or lists of transfers), by introducing the characters as arcs.

Similar to the concept of a MARKOV source is the concept of the non-deterministic finite *automaton, and the concept (equivalent to the latter) of finite state *grammar. The essential difference is that in the last mentioned, some transfers from each state to other states are impossible, and some possible. The system contains no reference to the *probability of the choice of one of the possible transfers. On the other hand, all transfers are in principle possible in a MARKOV source, albeit sometimes with a probability of 0.

SHANNON, C. E.: The Mathematical Theory of Communication. Univ. of Illinois Press, Urbana 1949. MEYER-EPPLER, W.: Grundlagen und Anwendungen der Informationstheorie, Springer, Berlin 1959.

**Matching**
Anpassung
adaptation
приспосабливание

*Adjustment of the signal generator or signal receiver to the optimal function-property in connection with energy transmission.*

In physics, e.g. the power transfer from an electrical-generator to a consumer has its maximum value if the resistance of the consumer $R$ is equal to the internal resistance of the generator, i.e. $R = R_i$.

High frequency cables are matched to each other or to socket-connections if they all have the same wave impedance. In physics and physiology one often uses the term 'matching' for all processes in which the optimal function property with regard to the flow of information can be produced by adjusting the signal-generator or receiver (cf. *accommodation). In physics, for example, a curved projection screen to counteract the effects of optical faults of the projecting lens. In physiology, for example, the alteration of the position or refraction of the eye-lens to create a sharp picture in the retina.

Matching processes in connection with optimal recognition of stimulus differences are called *adaptation.

**Mathematical analysis of language**
Sprachanalyse, mathematische
analyse mathématique du langage
математический анализ языка

*The examination of the formal *structure of languages by mathematical methods.*

As language, especially written language, can be regarded as a set of elements, mathematical concept formations can be used (especially those of mathematical statistics on the one hand and of algebra and calculation theory on the other) to describe the structural dependencies of the linguistic units (letters, phonemes, syllables, word, word-classes, special forms, sentences, etc., etc.).

Mathematical analysis of language is used in the following fields:

1 The treatment of natural and artificial languages as a means of communication within *information theory, e.g. redundancy tests, optimal languages.
2 To ascertain characteristics and regularities of languages and language groups, 'la langue', e.g. automatic *language translation and the degree of relationship between languages.
3 The examination and characterization of the individual language of an author ('la parole'), e.g. in questions of authenticity, problems of chronological sequence.

FUCKS, W.: Mathematische Analyse von Sprachelementen, Sprachstil und Sprachen. Arbeitsgemeinschaft für Forschung des Landes Nordrhein-Westfalen, Heft 34a, Westdtsch. Verlag, Köln and Opladen 1953. FUCKS, W.: Die math. Gesetze der Bildung von Sprachelementen aus ihren Bestandteilen. NTF 3, 7 (1956). HERDAN, G.: Language as Choice and Chance. P. Noordhoff, N.V. Groningen 1956. MEYER-EPPLER, W.: Grundlagen und Anwendungen der Informationstheorie. Springer-Verlag, Berlin, Göttingen, Heidelberg 1959. BAR-HILLEL, Y.: Some recent results in theoretical linguistics. In: Nagel, E. et al. (ed.): Logic, Methodology and Philosophy, Stanford University Press, Stanford 1962.

**Mathematical analysis of music**
Musikanalyse, mathematische
analyse mathématique musicale
математический анализ музыки

*The examination of musical structures by mathematical methods.*

Just as is the case with language (cf. *mathematical analysis of language), music can be regarded as a set of elements (pitch and length of notes, intervals, etc.). On this assumption, mathematical concept formation can easily be applied to music and musical works.

The mathematical analysis of music strives for:

1 The characterization of musical works with the help of mathematical methods (e.g. statistics, theory of groups).
2 The detection of regularities to describe the development of the history of music.
3 The solution of special problems, such as questions of authenticity, dependencies, etc.

FUCKS, W.: Mathematische Analyse der Formalstruktur von Musik. Forschungsberichte des Wirtschafts- und Verkehresministeriums Nordrhein-Westfalen. No. 357 (1958). FUCKS, W.: Mathematische Analyse formaler Strukturen von Musik. Arbeitsgemeinschaft für Forschung des Landes Nordrhein-Westfalen, Westdeutscher Verlag, Köln, Opladen 1963. MOLES, A. A.: Informationstheorie der Musik. NTF 3 (1956) p. 47.

**Mathematical group dynamics**
Gruppendynamik, mathematische
dynamique des groupes; théorie mathématique de la dynamique des groupes
групповая динамика (матем)

*A concept for the description of the behaviour of at least two persons who have some well-defined effect upon each other.* In this case it is often, though not always, accepted that the number of members of a group is not too great, in order that typical mass-effects may be excluded. Moreover, it is much simpler to carry out experiments with small groups. Thus mathematical group dynamics includes branches of sociology and psychology. The interpretation which is to-day most widely accepted, and which goes back to K. LEWIN's field theory, states that the group as a whole forms a unit which contains more than just the sum of its parts. To give a simple example, it should be remembered that the feeling of belonging to a group has a decisive effect on the performances of an athlete in any competitive situation. There is also the point of view, perhaps not an altogether incorrect one, that a sufficiently broad knowledge of the individual can explain the behaviour of the group (F. J. ALLPORT). N. RASHEVSKY used this principle for describing the characteristics of the *central nervous system.

The mathematical treatment of the phenomena mentioned can be called mathematical group dynamics. The first step towards this is the quantitative measurement and comprehension of the effects; then models and equations corresponding to them are constructed. Even to-day one can talk of mathematical sociology which, even if it has not yet been completely developed, does possess a considerable range. For example, imitative behaviour and the conditions which contribute to the formation of the characteristics of leadership have been examined mathematically. Here it is only necessary to mention RASHEVSKY's treatment of imitative behaviour. If each member of a group has the choice between two modes of conduct $A$ and $B$, it is assumed that the probability in favour of $A$ is increased in an individual $x_1$, according to a certain law, if $x_1$ notices the same behaviour $A$ on the part of another member of the group. The same applies for $B$. The mathematical formulation of this fact then gives some information on the behaviour of the whole group in respect of the two alternatives $A$ and $B$.

LEWIN's original application of mathematical concepts has, justifiably, been sharply criticized (I. D. LONDON); yet there is no doubt that the methods and

results of mathematics can be of great use even in the social sciences.
Finally it should be noted that until now mathematical group dynamics has not been directly associated with *cybernetics. It is, however, clear that typical cybernetical concepts such as *organization, *feedback and *control (of the total activity of a group) are of decisive importance for group dynamics.

CARTWRIGHT, D.; ZANDER, A. (ed.): Group Dynamics; Research and Theory. Row, Peterson & Co., Evanston, Illinois and Elmsford, New York 1960, 1961, 1962. BONNER, H.: Group Dynamics; Principles and Applications. The Ronald Press Co., New York 1959. RASHEVSKY, N.: Mathematical Biology of Social Behavior. Univ. of Chicago Press, 2nd edn. 1959.

## Matrix store
Speichermatrix
mémoire matricielle
матричный накопитель

*A matrix arrangement of store elements, mainly as a *magnetic core store.*

At the points of intersection of the row and column wires the (mainly binary) store elements, e.g. magnetic cores or tunnel diodes, are arranged. A *bit is recorded by the store element when simultaneously across corresponding row and column wires a current $I$ is imposed. The circuit is such that no alteration of the condition of the store is effected by the current $I$ in the row or the column alone.
Signal reading occurs simultaneously for a whole row, which is selected with double amplitude ($2I$), in which the information occurs in the columns (i.e. parallel reading) or by selecting a single element (in practice the writing of a binary zero) in which the information is transmitted on a special reading wire (serial reading). A distinction is made between a destructive and a non-destructive reading of the store contents.

SPEISER, A. P.: Digitale Rechenanlagen. Springer-Verlag, Berlin, Göttingen, Heidelberg 1961.

## Maximum effect
Maximumeffekt
phénomène du maximum
эффект максимума

*Total of the psychological effects of the mathematical fact that the contribution of a *character to the expectancy-value of the *information of a *field of events is maximal if the character has the probability* $1/e$ *(some* 36·79 *per cent).*

If a (comprehensive) *message is to be built up from $N$ characters in such a way that the message is exploited for the largest possible transfer of information by the sign $z_1$, in which the probabilities of the *field of the signs is to be made equal to their relative *frequencies within the message, then if $h_1 = 1/e$, the information transferred by $z_1$, i.e. $N \times h_1 \times \log_2 1/h_1 = N \times A_1$, is maximal; ($A_1$ = 'informational exploitation' of the message in favour of $z_1$, or the 'average compactness' of the information of the message transferred by $z_1$). This follows directly by zero-ing the function $h \times \log_2 1/h$ with respect to $h$, and by solving the equation which thus arises with respect to $h$ (extreme-value definition). If one defines as the 'conspicuousness' $a_i$ of the character $z_i$ the relationship of the information $N \times A_i$ transferred by this character to the total information $N \times H$ of the message, or, which is the same thing, the relation of the exploitation-value to the *uncertainty $a_i = A_i/H$, then no character in the message is more conspicuous than $z_i$ if $z_i$ has the relative frequency $1/e$ (i.e. with 'maximal stress'). For constant $H$ the conspicuousness has its maximum at $h = 1/e$ if the function $a(h)$ is defined at this point (when $H < 0{\cdot}949$ this is no longer the case), otherwise for the largest $h < 1/e$ for which the function is still defined. This mathematical fact was originally used (1958, FRANK) for an information-psychological interpretation of an empiric statement made by BIRKHOFF, according to which 8/23 of the syllables of onomatopoeic verses could contain the onomatopoeic vowel without it being used 'superfluously'. A similar maximal stress (i.e. a frequency of the most conspicuous at 37 per cent) was also shown by examples of other kinds of art. Later the function $s(h)$ of the relative frequencies (which were estimated by unpractised test-subjects as $s_i$) of characters with the true relative frequency $h_i$ was interpreted as the conspicuous-function $a(h)$, which could be confirmed by the fact that characters with a greater frequency but a smaller conspicuousness than a comparison character were evaluated on an average less often than the latter. (This effect, as well as equating $s_i$ with $a_i$, is quickly counteracted by practice in frequency-guessing.) A stochastic theory on the selection of the contents of the *short-term memory which enter the *memory (the former records approx. 16 bit/sec., the latter only 0·4 to 0·8 bit/sec.) demands a maximal stress for whatever is to be passed into the memory. In the meantime, results of experiments to make a character of a prescribed repertory as conspicuous as possible within a message which otherwise could be freely shaped, have shown that a frequency in the region of 37 per cent was the most usual choice of test-subjects who were not familiar with maximum effect.

FRANK, H.: Sur un théorème d'esthétique informationnelle. Revue d'Esthétique, XI, 3/4 (1958), pp. 62–6. FRANK, H.: Über das Intelligenzproblem in der Informationspsychologie. Grundlagenstudien Band 1, No. 3 (1960) pp. 85–96. FRANK, H.: Zum Problem des vorbewussten Gedächtnisses. Grundlagenstudien Band 2, No. 1 (1961) pp. 17–24. FRANK, H.: Kybernetische Analysen. Schnelle, Quickborn 1964.

## MAXWELL's demon

MAXWELLscher Dämon
démon de MAXWELL
демон Максвелла

*An imaginary being which operates a small door in a dividing wall in a space filled with gas. It seems to be possible to create a difference in temperature between the two compartments by a suitable operation of this door.*

In the event of MAXWELL's demon only opening the door if a fast gas molecule approaches from the left-hand compartment, or a slow molecule from the right-hand one, he will cause a rise in temperature in the right-hand compartment in comparison with the left-hand compartment. This corresponds to a decrease of *entropy and clearly contradicts the 2nd principle of thermodynamics.

BRILLOUIN solved this contradiction by pointing out that MAXWELL'S demon could only receive the *information necessary for the suitable operation of the door at the cost of an increase in entropy. Consequently, negative entropy and information can be converted into each other.

BRILLOUIN, L.: Maxwell's Demon cannot operate. Journal of Applied Physics, Vol. 22, pt. 334 (1951).

## Meaning

Bedeutung
signification
значение

*That which is designated by a *sign by means of its semantic sign-function.*

If a sign is a representation-sign (i.e. a sign for . . .) then its referent is meaning. It can be co-ordinated to the sign by means of similarity to the sign (onomatopoeic words, pictures)—such representation-signs are called icons—or by a conventional encoding of meanings (these representation-signs are called symbols), or finally, in the event of the representation-sign not being a sociological or cultural sign but a real-sign, by the restriction of meaning and sign by the same method.

**Measure of aesthetics**
ästhetisches Mass
mesure esthétique
эстетическая мера

In a mathematical theory of aesthetic perception (on the basis of the mathematical-psychological aesthetics of H. v. HELMHOLTZ and G. FECHNER), G. D. BIRKHOFF developed around 1930 a theory of aesthetic form. He divides aesthetic objects into classes which are comparable in respect of their aesthetic value; in addition he examines various aesthetic factors of such classes (polygon shapes, networks, vase shapes, form of simple lyrics and musical compositions) and defines the relative *meaning of these invariables by allocating them certain numerical values as factors. This allows him the formation of a measure of aesthetics and also simple numerical comparisons of the objects of a class of works of art.
BIRKHOFF defines as a measure of aesthetics an expression with the form

$$M = O : C$$

($O$: the mathematical measure for classification content and structure-properties; $C$: mathematical measure for *complexity or syntactical construction.)
Starting from BIRKHOFF's theory a new bridge can be constructed to newer mathematical and cybernetical theories (cf. *informational aesthetics) which permit, with the help of auxiliary information-theoretical means, quantitative examinations of aesthetic processes of production and perception (as in the theory of texts, in pantomime, music, etc.). These auxiliary means supported BIRKHOFF's theory.

FRANK, H.: Informationsästhetik. Diss. Stuttgart, 1959. MOLES, A. A.: Théorie de l'information et perception esthétique. Flammarion, Paris 1959. BIRKHOFF, G. D.: A Mathematical Theory of Aesthetics. The Rice Institute Pamphlet, V. 19, pp. 189–324 (1932).

**Membrane**
Membran
membrane
мембрана; диафрагма; перегородка; перепонка

*A flexible partition between two regions of space, differentiating them, and which can be crossed by elements.*
In physiology there are several important membranes (cell membranes, etc.). In the nerve-membrane nerve-impulses arise via complicated feedback effects (cf. *feedback). The active behaviour of nerve-membrane is an important subject of cybernetic research.
In information theory *membrane* denotes an n-dimensional surface which subdivides an n-dimensional space into two areas, and which under certain conditions is porous for elements from both areas.
*Membrane* is applied above all to cell boundaries across which exchange occurs, e.g. a political frontier is a membrane in the social sphere; a radio station has the effect of a membrane in the cultural sphere.

WIESER, W.: Organismen, Maschinen, Strukturen. S. Fischer, Frankfurt/M. 1959.

**Memory**
Gedächtnis
mémoire
память

Every living organism is shaped by experiences in the past, as has been confirmed by many observations. A distinction must be made between memory and habit. Memory is the registration and the retention of facts for possible future use which may be expressed by recognition or recollection. Registration, retention and recollection are clearly synonymous and correspond to the function of, for example, a dictating machine; even recognition can be achieved by technical equipment.

PENFIELD's experiences show that memory contains subdivisions: during surgical operations he caused past situations to be recalled in the consciousness of the patient by local electrical stimulation. Injuries of certain types (corpus mamillaris, hippocampus, ammonite, cingulum) can result in lapses in recollection, e.g. KORSAKOFF's psychosis, although this is not so much a question of the destruction of the storage system as of defects in a release mechanism.

However, memory does not work purely mechanically; it is selective, it reflects the whole personality of the subject, it is a whole, it produces patterns dependent on variable criteria, whereas a mechanical system registers without distinction.

**Memory, mechanical**
Speicherung, mechanische
mémorisation mécanique
механическое накопление

If a receiver has to store the information of a given text in its repertory of characters (i.e. to learn by heart) then this means for the receiver a successive reduction of the subjective *information of this text. At each repetition of the text, in which the information is first recorded in the *short-term memory and then flows to a smaller section of the long-term memory, the subjective information is reduced by the amount of this already stored section. The reduction of information (cf. *informational theory of learning) is completed dependent on the number of repetitions, according to a geometrical sequence. A stored text (or a text learned by heart) has the subjective information 'zero' for the receiver (or the learner). Mechanical memory in the above sense must not be confused with storage by mechanical means (cf. *punch-cards, *punched tape).

CUBE, F. von: Grundlagenstudien aus Kybernetik und Geisteswissenschaft 1960/1961.

**Memory of a channel**
Gedächtnis eines Kanals
mémoire d'un canal
,память' канала

A *channel $[A, q_x, B]$ has a memory of length $m = 1, 2, \ldots$ if the probability $p_x(y_k = b)$, $b \in B$, $k$ fixed is dependent only on the input letters $x_k$, $x_{k-1}$, $x_{k-2}$, $x_{k-m}$ (and, in the event of the channel working with *anticipation, on letters placed after $x_k$). If $m = 0$ then this is a channel without a memory.

GRELL, H. (ed.): Arbeiten zur Informationstheorie. I. Dtsch. Vlg. d. Wissenschaften, Berlin 1957. HENZE, E.: Einführung in die Informationstheorie. Beiheft 3, Elektronische Datenverarbeitung 2nd edit. 1965.

**Message**
Nachricht
message
сообщение

*Colloquially: a general term for instructions, assent, communication or other characters, including for example pictures and tunes. In the theory of information the term is used more precisely for any combination of characters or states used in the transmission of information.*

There is no logical difference between a message and *characters (signs), merely a stylistic one: a message is itself a character which can build up from an arrangement of relatively complex characters. For example, one would call a sentence a message, but not normally a word; in other words, only relatively important *super-characters are as a rule called messages. (Message can also include the character as well as the *signal.) The main purpose of a message is to influence the behaviour of a receiver, and especially to motivate it to an indirect *realization (pragmatic, *semiotic aspect) or to convey certain facts (for example the goal) to it (semantic semiotic aspect), which is, of course, necessary for indirect realization. However, characters without *meaning or *imperative, e.g. a sonata, are also regarded as messages. The message is the function of the physical signal, namely to refer the receiver to something else, e.g. the origin or the meaning of the signal (cf. *referent). The receiver is either consciousness or an equivalent system. A message can, but does not have to, contain information. On the other hand, everything which contains information is a message.
Information theory understands a message as a series or sequence of events in the sense of probability theory. More precisely, a message is an infinite sequence $\mathfrak{x} = \{x_i\}$ of characters $x_i$ of an *alphabet $A$.

COUFFIGNAL, L.: Kybernetische Grundbegriffe. Agis. Baden-Baden 1962. NTG-Empfehlung No. 0102, NTZ 1963, No. 1, pp. 46–9.

**Message space; sample space**
Nachrichtenraum; Nachrichtenmenge
espace informationel
——

The information space $A^{I}$ of a *source or of a *channel with the *alphabet $A$ is the space of all infinite sequences $x = \{\ldots, x_{-1}, x_o, x_1, x_2, \ldots\}$ of letters of this alphabet.

HENZE, E.: Einführung in die Informationstheorie. Beiheft 3, Elektronische Datenverarbeitung 2nd edit. 1965.

**Meta language**
Metasprache
metalangage
метаязык

*A language in which another language is described.*
If a language $S_1$ is discussed in a language $S_2$ then $S_1$ is called the *object-language and $S_2$ the meta language. For example, in learning a foreign language, the mother tongue is normally the meta language and the foreign language the object language. The differentiation of these two languages is important in formalized languages (*See* *languages, *formalized).

**Minimax strategy; Minimax process**
Minimaxverfahren
règle du minimax
стратегия минимакса

*A strategy which accepts that the greatest use is made of any situation by everyone who is concerned in the situation.*
Before a decision is taken, the consequences (gain or loss) of all the alternatives are examined. These consequences can depend on the decision of a partner or on other influences. If an *algorithm is known for the content of a decision, there results a decision-tree; (if no algorithm is known then a *model can replace the description of a situation):

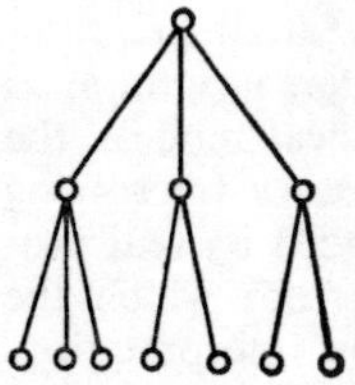

Initial situation for *A*

Initial situation for partner *B* or other influence

Situations resulting from the partner decision

It is supposed that the partner will select from the alternatives in the pertinent initial situation the one which is of the greatest benefit to him. For *A* the decision $x_0$ with the benefit $f(x_0)$ from the alternatives $x$, is therefore the most favourable; it selects the minimum from the maxima $f(x, y_0)$ (which are dependent on the output situation $x$) of the decisions $y$ with the benefit $f(x, y)$. That is, the decision $x_0$ with the benefit

$$f(x_0) = \underset{x}{\text{Min}} \; \underset{y}{\text{Max}} \; f(x,y).$$

The decision of the partner can depend on other influences. In this case the tree must be extended correspondingly. This does not necessarily mean that an end of the process has been achieved in every case, or not always with a realizable effort, as in the game of chess. The practical application of minimax strategy demands a break after a realizable finite number of steps, which may have to be achieved by suppositions in a model.

If instead of the benefit one examines the risk, then the considerations regarding maximum and minimum must be changed round. The information regarding a situation or the consequences of a decision can be either 'complete' (as in games with a definite result) or 'incomplete' (as the reaction of partners in business life). In the latter case, statistical aids (cf. *decision theory) are called upon.

Because of the pessimism which lies in the assumption that every participant will find the most favourable way, minimax strategy is often exposed to criticism.

NEUMANN, J. von; MORGENSTERN, O.: Spieltheorie und wirtschaftliches Verhalten. Physica, Würzburg 1961.

**Model**
Modell
modèle
модель

*A representation (in the most general mathematical sense of the word) of objects of research. Models (which are not always distinguishable from characters) play an important role in *heuristics and especially in pragma-logic (cybernetical heuristics).*

In order to be able to grasp the enormous variety of phenomena in an empirical area of research (physics, geology, physiology, psychology), the inessential features must be rejected, as the human consciousness (cf. *short-term memory) is only capable of keeping a limited amount of information present (cf. *duration) at any one time. The abstraction process (cf. *hierarchization) is shown clearly in the paradigm of the algebraic solution of problems. If one has to find the age of a father who is three times as old as his son who in turn is 24 years younger than the father, then only one number is to be found. Therefore, the father-son relationship and even the fact that the numbers mentioned refer to different ages is inessential. Algebra, by abstracting all these inessentials, represents the number being sought by the character $x$, and the fact from which an evaluation of $x$ will be decided by the equation: $x = 3(x - 24)$. By this the information content is considerably reduced, which means that the problem can be easily scanned and solved without any trouble. This representation is not perceivably unambiguous (isomorphic) but merely unambiguous (homomorphic); for the following quite different problem is shown as a representation by the same equation: How many houses has a village A which has three times as many houses as village B which in turn has 24 houses less than village A? In principle, all models can be understood as homomorphic diagrams of subjects or of subject-areas, and arise by ignoring the inessential: 'Their use can be compared to throwing away useless luggage' (SCHOPENHAUER). The process of rejecting and abstracting is, however, not sufficient heuristically, rather the invariant gained by abstracting (e.g. the concept) must be represented by a concrete content of consciousness or object of perception, namely by the image which results from the perception-process (in the example given: by the word which encodes the concept). Otherwise the above-mentioned invariant would 'completely escape the consciousness and would not serve it for the thought operations intended by it'.

Three essentially different levels of representation can now be distinguished: the physical, the visual and the abstract. In accordance with this a distinction is made between physical models (actually perceptible), perceptual models (imaginable), and conceptual models (verbal, linguistic).

Examples of abstract models are words and sentences, also algebraic expressions. Examples of visual models are building plans, switching diagrams, F. KLEIN's model of non-Euclid geometry, etc. Physical models are, for example, the models of aeroplanes in a wind-tunnel, mechanical models of conditioned reflexes, and *analogue computers or other *computers programmed for simulation. In physical models, the thought processes necessary for solving a problem can be replaced by real processes on the model, from which the solution is obtained by interpretation. For example, a differential equation can be solved by an analogue computer which has been properly programmed, as one of the graphs produced by it on a screen is interpreted as a solution.

Physical models of brain and consciousness processes are characteristic of *cybernetics. Just as anatomy has long recognized the arm of a handle as a model arm, engineering-cybernetics is concerned with 'thinking-devices' as a model of the processes of the brain or of the consciousness. Ideological arguments about cybernetics are based partially on the primitive confusion of the model with the original on which it is based, hence such protests as 'A machine cannot think', but partly because a model (by its very definition) does not represent the 'inessential'; yet often there is no objective criterion for the 'essential' of a process. (Is awareness an essential part of thinking?).

EICHHORN, G.: Zur Theorie der heuristischen Denkmethoden. Grundlagenstudien aus Kybernetik und Geisteswissenschaft. Band 2, Heft 1 (1961). EICHHORN, G.: Der Beitrag der Pragmalogik zur Theorie der Lehrmaschinen. In: Frank, H. (ed.): Lehrmaschinen in kybernetischer und pädagogischer Sicht. Klett and R. Oldenbourg, Stuttgart and München 1963. FRANK, H.: Informationspsychologie und Nachrichtentechnik. In: Wiener, N.; Schadé, J. P. (eds.): Nerve, Brain and Memory Models. Elsevier Publ. Co., Amsterdam 1963. FRANK, H.: Kybernetik — Wesen und Wertung. In: Alsleben, K. (ed.): Kybernetik und Organisation. Schnelle, Quickborn 1963. SCHOPENHAUER, A.: Über die vierfache Wurzel des Satzes vom zureichenden Grunde. 2nd edn. Hermann'sche Buchhandlung, Frankfurt 1847.

**Modulation**
Modulation
modulation
модуляция

*Control of a modulation-carrier according to the time variations of a modulator-signal.*
A modulation-carrier can be, for example, an *oscillation (carrier-oscillation) of the form

$$M(t) = A \cos \varphi(t) = A \cos (\Omega t + \varphi_o).$$

Let the time variation of the modulating sign be described by $s(t) = a \cos \omega t$. One modulates either the amplitude $A$ or the phase angle $\varphi(t)$ of the carrier-oscillation, and speaks of amplitude-modulation (AM) or phase-modulation (PM). The amplitude-modulated oscillation has the form

$$M(t) = A(1 + a/A \cos \omega t) \cos \varphi(t),$$

in which $a/A = m(m \leq 1)$ gives the degree of modulation. The modulation of the phase angle can result either by the modulation of the frequency $\omega/2\pi$ or by modulation of the zero phase angle $\varphi_0$ (frequency-modulation: FM; or zero phase modulation: zPM;). The frequency-modulated oscillation is described by

$$M(t) = A \cos (\Omega t + \Delta\Omega/\omega \sin \omega t)$$

in which $\Delta\Omega/2\pi$ is called frequency-deviation and $\Delta\Omega/\omega$ is called modulation index. zPM is closely related to FM. There are, however, other possible modulation-carriers, such as a beam of electrons of a cathode-ray tube (brightness modulation) or pulses.

**Moment**
Zeitquant, subjektives; SZQ; Moment
quantum subjectif de temps
время осознанного восприятия

*The greatest length of time between two successive events which can still be perceived as simultaneous.*
The hypothesis that our observation of time is not a continuous process, but is quantized into so-called 'moments' was first put forward by K. E. v. BAER; he estimated the number of moments experienced per second at 6 to 10. W. WUNDT, who also argued for 'the discrete nature of our observation of time', settled on an evaluation of moment at 1/16 sec. (0·0625 sec.); at this minimum spacing, periodic acoustic stimuli begin to fuse into one single sound (lowest audible approx. 16 c/s), periodic light stimuli fuse into one apparently moving flickering picture (lowest level of flicker, or 'fusion-frequency' in the sense of filming techniques below 18 c/s). BRECHER later proved that even periodic tactile stimuli fuse into one impression of vibration at this level (lowest level of perception of vibration: 18 c/s; in BRECHER's experiments this level was reduced by the use of both stimulants and tranquilizers to approx. 12 c/s). However, stimuli of constant intensity with regard to their duration can only be properly compared if the duration is shorter than 1 moment. BRECHER was able to show, however, that this ability ends as soon as the product of intensity and duration is kept constant, whilst the duration itself, and therefore also the intensity, is varied: two stimuli of different duration seem to have the same length if both have an effect of less than 1 moment; but a proper time comparison is possible as soon as one of them lasts longer than 1 moment. With an

average transmission speed of signals by *nerves of 60 m/sec., a distance of twice 2 metres (the greatest length of the centrifugal plus the greatest length of the centripetal nerve paths) is covered in 1/15 sec. (i.e. in 1 moment), so that one must assume that 'the consciousness releases further information only when signals on the direct consequences of the previous information have been fed back' (K. STEINBUCH, *Automat und Mensch*). In digital *computers the working speed is limited by the fact that despite a finite transmission speed of signals and finite switching time, certain events in various locations of the machine must be simultaneous (or of a defined chronological sequence), which is achieved by quantizing the time into elementary units (cf. *clock). Accordingly N. WIENER assumes the existence of a clock in the brain; he sees the effect of this clock in *alpha-waves (8–12 c/s). According to ROHRACHER's experiments (*Einführung in die Psychologie*), it would be better to regard *beta-waves (14–18 c/s) as 'the most recently formulated organic basis on conscious experience', which is, of course, a new argument for the value of moment. The explanation of moment by a central clock independent of stimuli is also given by the fact that the correct judgement or assessment of the sequence of two stimuli affecting two different organs does not end abruptly as soon as the objective time difference sinks below 1 moment, but becomes gradually less probable (because the probability decreases, the subjective limit between two moments falls exactly between the stimuli); from the relative frequencies of correct judgements in mass tests, this would lead to an acceptance of moment as between 1/17 sec. and 1/15 sec. *Information psychology has the hypothesis of a binary *coding of perception content when it enters the *short-term memory, whose *capacity for recording *information is approx. 16 bits/sec. (results of experiments produced a total range of 10–25 bits). According to a theorem of *information theory this can be achieved by binary sequences of a density of 16 bits/sec. (cf. *bit, *HUFFMANN tree). Beta-waves would then be understood as the effects of a binary coding of information and the ability of chronological separation would be directly associated with the capacity of information recording of the short term memory: $C_k = 1$ bit/moment.

The theory of moment as the rhythm of a central clock (beta-waves) is not undisputed, but can only claim to be a useful model idea. A model to oppose this idea has not so far been developed. The main objection lies in the difficulty in describing the development of the neuro-physiological structures (closed chains of *neurons, neuron circuits for binary encoding, etc.) which are required by the model.

BAER, K. E. von: Die Abhängigkeit unseres Weltbildes von der Länge unseres Moments. Auszug eines 1864 veröffentlichten Referats. Reprinted as Beihift 3 (1962) of Grundlagenstudien aus Kybernetik und Geisteswissenschaft Band 3, Verlag Schnelle, Quickborn 1962. BRECHER, G. A.: Die Entstehung und biologische Bedeutung der subjektiven Zeiteinheit,—des Moments. Zeitschrift für vergleichende Physiologie, Bd. 18, No. 1 (1932) pp. 204–43. FRANK, H.: Eine probabilistische Bedeutung des Zeitauflösungsvermögens. Grundlagenstudien aus Kybernetik und Geisteswissenschaft, Band 4, H. 2 (1963).

**Monitor (I)**

Monitor

monitor

монитор; контрольно—измерительный прибор; контрольный аппарат

*Control screen in a television studio.*

**Monitor** (II); **program supervisor**
Monitor; Überwachungsprogramm
monitor
монитор

*A program for the complete or partial control of the course of one or more calculation programs.*

A monitor lightens the tasks of the operator and programmer of a computer by taking over one or more of the following functions:

1 co-ordination during the simultaneous processing of several programs or sets of instructions by the automatic observation of the time rule for *communication between the units of a computer as well as the allocation of storage space for the individual programs;
2 co-ordination during the non-simultaneous processing of several programs by the general arrangement of input and output units (for example, the time consuming task of manually changing magnetic tape is greatly reduced).
3 *error-detection or other actions with erroneous data, certain faulty programs or machine-parts.

**Monostable multivibrator**
Kippschaltung, monostabile
monoflop; multivibrateur monostable
одноперекидная схема; одностабиль. ный вибратор

*See* *Multivibrator

**Monte-Carlo method**
Monte-Carlo Methode
méthode Monte-Carlo
метод Монте-Карло

*Method of simulating the behaviour of a system whose physical components and internal processes can in part be described only by laws of probability.*

By means of a *random number generator numbers are produced in order to determine the component movements by the use of *probability distribution. The behaviour of the whole system is then calculated by the use of these random movements. By frequent repetition of this process one can obtain data for statistics which will help to determine the probable behaviour of the whole system.

**Morphogram**
Morphogramm
morphogramme
морфограмма

*Concept in cybernetical logic which is obtained by the abstraction of the concept of pattern of reflection.*

The morphogram abstracts from the concept of the logical value, especially of the 'foreign' value. The 15 value sequences of the pattern of reflection thereby become 15 units of the morphogram; on the other hand, by inserting the values 1, 2, 3 and 4 of the pattern of reflection, the so-called standard form of morphogram is obtained. The structure-units of the morphogram represent the invariants for all logics which operate with values. If a logic is not treated from the point of view of values, but from the point of view of the occurring morphograms, then one speaks of a morphogrammatic system.

The purpose of the concept: the basis of a cybernetical logic which can be gained from the complete abstraction of contents or meanings. An abstraction which cannot be taken further is necessary, since cybernetics only deals with such structures and invariants.

**Morphogrammatic compound**
morphogrammatische Kette
chaîne morphogrammatique
морфограмматическая цепь

*A linking of individual *morphograms in such a way that the first and the last position of a morphogram is at the same time the first or last position of another morphogram.*

Such morphogrammatic compounds have shown themselves to be necessary as only bivalent logic can use a limited number of individual morphograms. If a morphogram contains a third value, then binary logical constants must supply nine positions for possible value-occupancy. This results in a morphogrammatic compound of three morphograms, in which the 1st, 2nd, 4th and 5th positions represent the first morphogram, the 5th, 6th, 8th and 9th form the second morphogram, which means that the third morphogram consists of the 1st, 3rd, 7th and 9th positions. Longer morphogrammatic compounds of more than three morphograms are produced if one uses numbers of any magnitude one chooses. A morphogrammatic compound produces a relatively simple structure for polyvalent logics, on the condition that the number of variables remains constant. If one increases the number of values as well as that of the variables, complicated structures result.

**Multiple-address machine**
Mehradressmaschine
machine à adresses multiples
многоадресная машина

*Electronic computer whose instructions contain more than one *address.*

There are two types of multiple-address machines. In the first type the giving of one address denotes the next address, i.e. the store-location in which will be found the next instruction which has to be carried out, whereas the others are operand addresses. The machines have no *sequence control register. They are mainly calculating machines which use a *magnetic drum store, as the working store. *Computing time depends on the optimal programming, i.e. the arrangement of the program in the store in such a way that the store location under the magnetic head is precisely the one whose content is needed at that particular moment for processing. Machines of this type are called $n + 1$ address-machines, especially $1 + 1$ address-machines and $2 + 1$ address-machine.

In the second type only operand addresses are given. The two addresses of a two-address machine designate especially the store locations in which are the two operands which are to be connected. Normally these machines have no *accumulator. In a three-address machine, the third address shows where the result is to be stored.

SPEISER, A. P.: Digitale Rechenanlagen. Springer-Verlag, Berlin, Göttingen, Heidelberg 1961.

**Multivibrator**
Multivibrator; Kippschaltung
multivibrateur
спусковая схема; триггерная схема; релаксационная схема; мультивибратор

*A circuit which can adopt two different circuit states one after the other. The switch from one state to the other is used for the production and shaping of *pulses.*

There are astable multivibrators, monostable multivibrators, bistable multivibrators and Schmitt triggers.

The astable multivibrator (relaxation generator) switches periodically between its two circuit states and thereby produces rectangular pulse trains. It is a pulse generator. Its range lies between

10 pulses/sec. and $10^7$ pulses/sec. With the monostable multivibrator (univibrator, or monoflop) a certain circuit state is the steady state. If a trigger pulse exceeds a threshold, the monostable multivibrator switches to the other state, remains there for a period of time $\tau$ and then switches back to the stable position; that means: a trigger pulse releases a rectangular pulse of duration $\tau$. $\tau$ is independent of the duration and shape of the trigger pulse. A monostable multivibrator can be regarded as a very simple *neuron-model. With a Schmitt trigger a certain circuit state is a steady state in a similar way. If a trigger pulse exceeds a threshold, then the Schmitt trigger switches to the other state. In contrast to the monostable multivibrator, it only remains there for the same length of time that the trigger pulse is above the threshold.

The bistable multivibrator (flip-flop) can stay in either of the circuit states any length of time. It is brought into one of the circuit states by a trigger pulse. It stays there until the next trigger pulse, which switches it back into the former circuit state. It acts like a switch which is switched on and off by trigger pulses following one upon the other. Multivibrators are mostly built with *transistors.

Meinke, H.; Gundlach, F. W. (eds.): Taschenbuch der Hochfrequenztechnik. 2nd edn. Springer-Verlag, Berlin, Göttingen, Heidelberg 1962. Neeteson, P. A.: Flächentransistoren in der Impulstechnik. Philips Techn. Bücherei, Eindhoven 1960.

# N

**Negation**
Negation
négation
отрицание

*Unary logical connective with the symbols* — *or* ~ *and the meaning* 'not'.

Truth-table:

| | | |
|---|---|---|
| $a$ | $T$ | $F$ |
| $\bar{a}$ | $F$ | $T$ |

**Negative entropy**
Negentropie
négentropie
негэнтропия

A term sometimes used in *information theory for average *information. The word calls attention to the difference from *entropy, but cannot be used as a better term for *average information*, with the result that it has recently been avoided.

**Nerve**
Nerv
nerf
нерв

*A cable-like structure consisting of a bundle of nerve-fibres surrounded by a sheath.*

The function of nerve-fibres (the *axons of *neurons) is the unattenuated conduction of pulse-sequences. Afferent fibres conduct information to the *central nervous system, efferent fibres conduct information away from it. Both types of fibre are contained in a nerve. The *membrane of the nerve fibre acts as a conductor. The fluid surrounded by the conductor has a different composition to the fluid outside it. The ion permeability of the membrane changes during a pulse. This causes an electrical disturbance which excites the neighbouring sections of the conductor. By this mechanism, the excitation is conducted along the nerve-fibre.

**Neuristor**
Neuristor
neuristor
—

*Any system which is capable of non-attenuated conduction of *pulses according to the *all-or-none law.*

Real nerve-fibres (cf. *nerve) are examples of neuristors, but this concept is reserved for artificial systems. A system which consists of various layers, one of which is made of a resistant material with a high temperature-coefficient (thermistor), was examined. However, no system working in this way was technically realized. But systems built up from neuristors, in which the adjacent pulse-conducting paths can share the same energy-source, permit the execution of logical operations of their signals. It is possible to construct a neuristor computer.

CRANE, H. D.: Neuristor Studies. Technical Report 1506-2, Stanford Research Institute, 1960. CRANE, H. D.: The Neuristor. In: Foerster, H. v.; Zopf, G.W. (eds.): Principles of Selforganization. Pergamon Press, London 1962.

**Neuron**
Neuron
neurone
нейрон

*A cell as a part of the nervous system with the special characteristics of excitability by which it can conduct information.*

A typical neuron consists of a cell-body with short branchlike extensions (cf. *dendrite) and one longer extension (cf. *axon). The dendrites effect the connection to further neurons and have a stimulating or an inhibiting effect on the cell. If a sufficiently large number of stimulating connections becomes active, the cell is excited and transmits a pulse along the axon. The length of an axon is between a few millimetres and approx. one metre.

McCULLOCH and PITTS developed a simplified mathematical model of a neuron, cf. *neuron model. See also under *excitation and *nerve.

MCCULLOCH, W. S. and PITTS, W.: A logical calculus of the ideas immanent in nervous activity—Bull. of Math. Biophysics 5, 115, 1943.

**Neuron model**
Neuronenmodell
modéle neuronique
модель нейрона

*Neuron models are systems with the help of which one tries to reproduce important functions of *neurons. They represent *analogue computers, which help in the treatment of neurophysiological problems.*

Neuron models can be subdivided according to the model-substance, the features reproduced, and their task. With regard to model-substance, one can differentiate between mathematical logic models, chemical-physical models and technical models.

Corresponding to the three parts of a neuron (*synapse, cell with *dendrites and *axon) there are models for the axon, the cell-membrane and for the whole neuron. More modern electronic axon-models have been developed in Japan, the U.S.A. and Germany. HODGKIN and HUXLEY (England) produced an excellent mathematical membrane-model. Many whole-neuron models have been developed in the U.S.A., in England, Holland, Italy and Germany ranging from greatly simplified logical systems to extremely complicated electronic apparatus. The time course of the membrane-potential can be reproduced by the course of the voltage $u_M$ (see diagram).

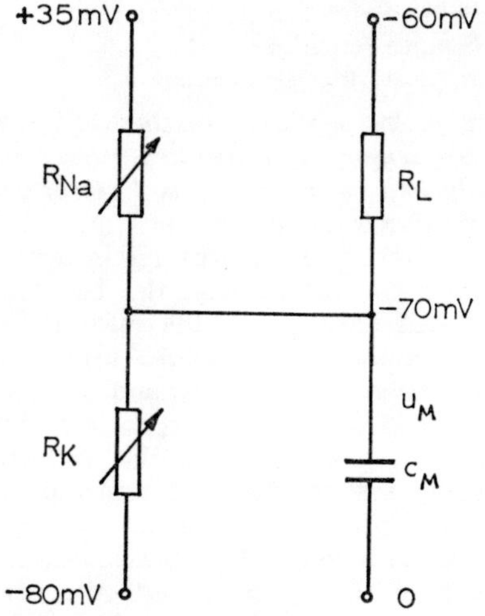


Neuron model

A depolarization is effected mainly by reducing $R_{Na}$, and a hyperpolarization by reducing $R_K$. $R_{Na}$ and $R_K$ can be influenced either by pre-synaptic pulses via the input channels, the synapses, (production of post-synaptic potentials), or by $u_M$ on two feedback paths (cf. *action potential). The functions of the feedback paths were obtained for a special membrane by HUXLEY and HODGKIN. KÜPFMÜLLER produced simple approximation equations for the description of the input channels. The neuron models which have been developed furthest show post-synaptic potentials, temporal and spatial summation, threshold value, action potential with post-hyperpolarization and *refractory period, as well as, in some cases, symptoms of fatigue and threshold variation. Neuron models should help in the clarification of information processing in the nervous system. Their advantage is that they can be properly observed, that disturbing influences can be avoided, and that extensive parameter variations can be undertaken.

HODGKIN, A. L.; HUXLEY, A. F.: A quantitative description of membrane current and its application to conduction and excitation in nerve. J. Physiol. 117 (1952), pp. 500–44. KÜPFMÜLLER, K.: Die nachrichtenverarbeitenden Funktionen der Nervenzellen In: Aufnahme und Verarbeitung von Nachrichten durch Organismen. Hirzel, Stuttgart 1961. ECCLES, J. C.: The physiology of nerve cells. Johns Hopkins Press, Baltimore 1957. JENIK, F.: Electronic neuron models as an aid to neurophysiological research. Erg. Biol. 25 (1962), pp. 206–45.

**Noise**
Rauschen
bruit
фон; шум; хаотический шум

*Noise or disturbance whose cause is determined by the quantized structure of the electrical charge-carrier.*
In conductors, *semi-conductors, gases, etc., electrical charge-carriers execute statistical movements due to temperature; this statistical movement produces unwelcome disturbances in the electrical circuit. One talks of white noise if the same intensity exists in all the frequency ranges in the amplitude-spectrum (cf. *spectrum) of the noise source. The probability of the occurrence of certain ordinate values of the true variable process then follows GAUSS's normal distribution. In contrast to white noise, band-limited noise is also called coloured noise.

KLEEN, W.: Schwankungserscheinungen. In: Meinke, H.; Gundlach, F. W. (eds): Taschenbuch der Hochfrequenztechnik. Springer-Verlag, Berlin, Göttingen, Heidelberg 1956.

**Non-conjunction**
*See* *SHEFFER'S stroke.

**Non-equivalence; exclusive disjunction**
Antivalenz
antivalence
отрицание однозначности; исключающее ,или»‘ неэквивалентность

*Binary *logical connective with symbol* $\not\equiv$ *or* $\sqcup$. *Two statements are non-equivalent if their entry in the truth table produces the value T.*
Truth table:

| | | | | |
|---|---|---|---|---|
| $a$ | $T$ | $T$ | $F$ | $F$ |
| $b$ | $T$ | $F$ | $T$ | $F$ |
| $a \not\equiv b$ | $F$ | $T$ | $T$ | $F$ |

The expression in terms of *negation, *disjunction and *conjunction (cf. *Boolean algebra) is as follows:

$$a \not\equiv b = (a \vee b) \wedge (\bar{a} \vee \bar{b})$$

**Nonlinear element**
nichtlineares Glied
élement non linéaire
нелинейный элемент

*A circuit element in which its characteristics depend on the magnitude of the applied signal.*
Whilst a nonlinear element can be understood on the one hand as a general term for all the disturbing nonlinear parameters of a circuit, special circuit characteristics can be achieved by introducing nonlinear elements. Nonlinear elements can be normal switching elements under special operational conditions (saturated *transistors, *diodes operated in the quadratic range of their characteristic curves, saturated magnetic elements, etc.) or especially elements designed with nonlinear features, as for example VDRs (voltage dependent resistors).

SCHÄFER, O.: Theorie elektrischer Schaltvorgänge. In: Steinbuch, K. (ed.): Taschenbuch der Nachrichtenverarbeitung. Springer-Verlag, Berlin, Göttingen, Heidelberg 1962, para. 1.5.

**Non-specific system; non-specific afferents**
Bahn, unspezifische
système d'afférents non spécifiques; substance réticulée
путь (связь) неспецифический

*The pathway which branches off from every sensory tract, crosses the main brain and re-enters at the level of the projection cortex areas.*
The information processing in a sensory-organ system (e.g. the acoustic) is based partially on the information conduction in two parallel arms, the *specific system (afferent) and the non-specific system. The non-specific system passes, for example in the acoustic sensory system, from the upper olive, via the Formatio reticularis, which is at the same time a link in the converging chain of the optical and tactile non-specific system, via the corpus geniculatum to the acoustic projection cortex. The excitation of the projection cortex fields through the excitation on the specific system is dependent on the influence of the non-specific system. Through the non-specific system there also result the influences of the autonomic system and of the sleep-wake-control.

MAGOUN, H. W.: Brain stem and higher centres. In: Nerve Impulse, Transact. of the fifth Conf. 11–93. J. Macy, New York 1954. MAGOUN, H. W.: The waking brain. Charles C. Thomas, Springfield Ill. 1958. KEIDEL, W. D.: Beispiele und Probleme einer kybernetischen Physiologie des ZNS und der Sinne. In: Berichte über den 23. Kongress der Deutsch. Ges. für Psych. Verlag für Psychologie (Hogrefe). Göttingen 1963.

**Nor-function**
PEIRCEscher Pfeil; Nor-Funktion
flèche de PEIRCE
стрелка Пирса

*A binary *logical connective with the symbol* $\downarrow$ or $\overline{\vee}$; *in this the nor-function* *corresponds to the propositional function, in which the propositions are connected by 'neither-nor'.*

| | | | | |
|---|---|---|---|---|
| $a$ | $T$ | $T$ | $F$ | $F$ |
| $b$ | $T$ | $F$ | $T$ | $F$ |
| $a \downarrow b$ | $F$ | $F$ | $F$ | $T$ |

The expression in terms of *negation, *disjunction and *conjunction (cf. *Boolean algebra) is as follows:

$$a \downarrow b = \bar{a} \wedge \bar{b} = \overline{a \vee b}.$$

Negation and disjunction and therefore all other binary logical connectives can be expressed solely in terms of nor-function alone:

$$\bar{a} = a \downarrow a, a \vee b = (a \downarrow b) \downarrow (a \downarrow b)$$

**Number**
Ziffer
chiffre
цифра

A *character from a *repertory of $B$ characters to which the whole numbers 0, 1, 2 . . . $B - 1$ are allotted in a $1 - 1$ correspondence. In this, $B$ is the basis of numerical representation.

**Number representation**
Zahlendarstellung
représentation des chiffres
представление чисел

*The form of expression of numerical values.*

A unified representation of all numerical values is of great importance in automatic computing. There are two distinct types of representation: (*a*) with a fixed point, and (*b*) with a floating point. In the former, a sequential place-value is allotted to each place in a sequence of numbers, e.g. sequential powers of 2 or 10. The radix point is treated by the *arithmetic unit as at a definite place during processing, mostly on the left- or right-hand end of a word. Calculation is then by fractions in the first case, and whole numbers in the second. The point itself does not appear explicitly. A programmer can, of course, imply a point after any position in the number-sequence. This imaginary point shifts in multiplication and division. The results of such calculations must therefore be brought back to the correct position once more by shift operations.

In calculations with fixed points, the range of numbers is limited to a certain power of the radix according to the length of the word.

This disadvantage does not arise when using a floating point. A floating point number $G$ is represented by the product of two factors, $G = M \times B^E$. The first part, the mantissa $M$, is a fixed point number, usually a fraction. The second part is a power of the radix $B$. This radix is mainly 2 (in binary machines) or 10 (in decimal machines). Of the second factor, only the logarithm, i.e. the exponent $E$, needs to appear. $E$ gives the actual location of the decimal point. For automatic processing of numbers, it is of advantage if no negative exponents occur. Hence a set amount, e.g. 50 or 128 is added.

Example: 12345 53 ≡ 123. 45.

The range of representable numbers is for example:

$$0{\cdot}1 \times 10^{-50} \leq z < 0{\cdot}1 \times 10^{50}$$

in the decimal system, and

$0{\cdot}5 \times 2^{-128} \leq z < 0{\cdot}5 \times 2^{128}$ in the binary system. Usually the results of operations with a floating point are automatically normalized, i.e. the mantissa is shifted to the left—with a simultaneous adjustment of the characteristic—until a number other than 0 appears in the first position. By this, all locations of the mantissa are used for the maximum attainable accuracy in computing.

**Nystagmus**
Nystagmus
nystagmus
нистагм

*Involuntary rhythmical movements of the eyeballs in a straight line. These consist of one slow and one faster movement, the latter bringing the eyeball back to its original position.*
A distinction is made between horizontal and vertical nystagmus, although circular movements have been observed.
In the pathological state, nystagmus is a sign of injury to the labyrinth or the cerebellum. In healthy people, nystagmus can be produced by stimulation of the labyrinth (injection of cold or warm water into the outer acoustic meatus, BARANY's caloric nystagmus) or by the rotation of the test-subject around the longitudinal axis of his body. If the test-subject is told to follow a strip on a rotating cylinder with his eyes, he may show nystagmus (opto-kinetic nystagmus).

# O

**Oarsman**
Ruderer
rameur
гребец

*Paradigm for the level or instance of physical work performed in a socio-technical system; one of the levels of cybernetics (See* *cybernetics, levels of). *The transfer of the function of the oarsman to machines forms the content of classical machine *techniques.*

**Object language**
Objektsprache
langage-object
язык предмета

*A language which is described in another language.*
If a language $S_1$ is discussed in a language $S_2$, then $S_1$ is called an object language, and $S_2$ the *meta language.

STEGMÜLLER, W.: Das Wahrheitsproblem und die Idee der Semantik. Springer, Wien 1957.

**Off-effect; off-response**
Off-Effekt
réponse de fin
off-ответ

*Excitation response to the end of a stimulus.*
Off-response is produced essentially by relay stations (cf. *neuron) which are sensitive to changes in stimulation, and whose excitation (action-potential sequence) rises sharply at the end of a stimulus and falls again after a short while. One speaks of on- and off-neurons in the cortical section of the sensory-organ system (the eye); this purely on-off behaviour forms the essential contrast to peripheral neurons, which in general show no switching-on of their excitation, but only an influence on the sequence frequency of their action potential, In a slow *evoked response, the variation in potential, which results from the integration of several off elements through the excitation states, is called off-response.

GRANIT, R.: The organization of the vertebrate retinal elements. Ergeb. der Physiol. 46 (1950), pp. 31–70. HARTLINE, H. K.; RATLIFF, F.: Inhibitory interaction of receptor units in the eye of limulus. J. Gen. Physiol. 40 (1957), pp. 357–76. KATSUKI, et al.: Activity of auditory neurons in upper levels of brain of cat. J. Neurophysiol. 22 (1959), pp. 343–59.

**On-effect; on-response**
On-Effekt
réponse de début
on-ответ

*Excitation response to the start of a (longer) stimulus.*

On-response is produced essentially by relays (cf. *neuron) which are sensitive to changes in stimulation, and whose excitation (action-potential sequence) rises sharply at the start of a stimulus and falls again after a short while. On-elements exist within both the sensory cell and areas of the central nervous system. One talks, for example, of so-called on- and off-neurons in the cortical area of the sensory-organ system (the ear); this purely on-off behaviour forms the essential difference to peripheral neurons, which as a rule show no switching-on of their excitation, but only a modulation of the sequence frequency of their action potential. In the eye, the retina (in actual fact, part of the brain) shows a differentiation of the sensory cells into on-off elements and continually conducting elements. In a slow *evoked response, all the long variations in potential which arise from the integration of several on-elements via the excitation states are called on-responses.

GRANIT, R.: The organization of the vertebrate retinal elements. Ergeb. der Physiol. 46 (1950), pp. 31–70. HARTLINE, H. K.; RATLIFF, F.: Inhibitory interaction of receptor units in the eye of limulus. J. Gen. Physiol. 40 (1957), pp. 357–76. KATSUKI, et al.: Activity of auditory neurons in upper levels of brain of cat. J. Neurophysiol. 22 (1959), pp. 343–59. JUNG, R.: Korrelationen von Neuronentätigkeit und Sehen. In: Jung, R.; Kornhuber, H. (eds.): Neurophysiologie und Psychophysik des visuellen Systems. Springer-Verlag, Berlin, Göttingen, Heidelberg 1961.

**On-off controller**
*See* *Bang-bang servo

**Open-loop amplification**
Kreisverstärkung
extension de domaine

The *transfer-function of a circuit with the *feedback loop cut open is occasionally called open-loop amplification, especially in respect of electronic amplifiers.

**Open-loop control**
Steuerung
commande
управление

*A mechanism or process for influencing certain output values of a system by one or more input values.*

Whereas a feedback control system always has a feedback of the *controlled condition and a comparison with the index value, the hall mark of open-loop control is the signal or energy flow which continually exerts an influence from the input towards the output. Its block diagram has therefore no closed circuits but is in the form of a series connection, perhaps with parallel paths, if several control influences work in combination. The advantage of open-loop control over closed loop control is that it is simpler and cheaper, and moreover there is no instability through oscillation. Its disadvantages are its sensitivity to disturbances and its greater dependence on variations of individual control elements of the whole system.

OPPELT, E.: Kleines Handbuch technischer Regelvorgänge. Verlag-Chemie, Weinheim. DIN 19226 Normblatt über Regelungstechnik und Steuerungstechnik.

**Operand**
Operand
opérande
исходное число; функтор

*Any content of a *register to which an operation is applied.*
In an extended sense an operand is not only a participant in an arithmetical operation, but any arithmetic, Boolean or other value which participates in an *operation.

**Operant conditioning**
*See* *Conditioning, instrumental

**Operation**
Operation
opération
операция

*Any actions in a *computer triggered off by an *instruction.*
Processes triggered off by an instruction can proceed completely or partially simultaneously, or one after the other. In any case they lead to permanent changes at one or more locations. Arithmetic or *logical connectives specify known operations. Further operations are: shifting, comparison, the setting of *registers, the reading of magnetic tape etc. Electronic computers can according to their size carry out from 10 to 20 or several hundred operations.

**Operationalism**
Operationalismus
operationalisme
операционализм

*An attitude of mind stressed by BRIDGMAN, which developed from empiric positivism.*
BRIDGMAN holds the view that it is not one of the functions of science to formulate more than so-called 'operational concepts', i.e. concepts, ideas or values which can give rise to practical operations by a direct deduction, in other terms actions which modify in some way or other the experimenter's perceptible field, or the observer's environment. Operationalism therefore imposes a strict limitation on the interpretations of the phenomena of the surroundings which can be made by reasoning, compared to the number of all operations which could be imagined. *Cybernetics, as well as *information theory, cannot introduce a concept which is not absolutely essential for the realization of operations. This axiom which comes from Ockham's principle (*Entia non sunt multiplicanda praeter necessitatem*) has its technological correspondence in the realizability principle. One should not imagine, for the building of a simulation model, any device or part which it is not possible to make actually available at the current level of technology.

MOLES, A. A. Sociodynamique de la culture. Mouton Ed., den Haag, 1967.

**Optimalizer**
Optimalwertkreis
circuit à valeur optimale
оптимизатор

*Feedback control system for the control of optimal value.*
If a *controlled condition $x$ is dependent on two or more *regulating variables ($y_1$ and $y_2$) there results in many machines or processes a process-function $\eta = f(y_1, y_2)$, which shows a maximum for a constant $x$. (Example for $\eta$: the degree of efficiency of a combustion-engine which can be regulated by fuel mixture and ignition-timing, or yield from a chemical process). In a case such as this, an optimalizer permits control at maximum degree of efficiency or maximum yield. In order to achieve

this, an optimalizer possesses (as well as feedback, comparison unit, and the regulator) an evaluation device for ascertaining the degree of control efficiency. This can consist of an analogue computer which calculates a correcting signal (to increase the degree of efficiency) by means of a test oscillation (cf. *test signal) of the regulating variable. Other optimalizers use special digital *computers, which produce test-steps for the regulating values and evaluate the associated alterations of the controlled condition and of the degree of efficiency, until a maximum is achieved in the latter.

STEINBUCH, K. (ed.): Taschenbuch der Nachrichtenverarbeitung. Springer-Verlag, Berlin, Göttingen, Heidelberg 1962.

**Optimize; optimalize**
Optimalisieren
optimaliser
оптимализировать

Alteration of its own index-value setting by a learning *regulator or controller until such time as an optimal-value is reached for the index-value.
In an extended sense the automatic setting of the parameters of a *feedback control system in such a way that the feedback control system adopts an optimal control-behaviour.

OPPELT, W.: Kleines Handbuch technischer Regelvorgänge. Verlag Chemie, Weinheim 1956. TRUXAL, J. G.: Entwurf automatischer Regelsysteme. R. Oldenbourg, München and Wien 1960.

**Order**
Ordnung
ordre
порядок

*Evenness in the sequence of terms (e.g. characters) or their connection; any connection of quantitative, qualitative, mechanical or teleological reference.*

The growth of *entropy destroys order. Entropy is a measure of disorder. A perfect order is complete equality and is equal to zero-entropy.
Let there be given any organized and mathematically represented system: then the BOLTZMANN-SHANNON equation can be applied to its individual parts.
A value is obtained which can be called entropy or difference-entropy; this has no connection with thermodynamic entropy; it is nevertheless a measure for the comprehensive unity of the system, in fact, a measure for its order state.

BRILLOUIN, L.: Science and Information Theory. Academic Press. Inc., New York. BONSACK, F.: Information, thermo-dynamique, vie et pensée. Gauthier-Villars, Paris 1962. MOLES, A. A.: Über konstruktionelle und instrumentelle Komplexität. Grundlagenstudien Band I, Heft 1 (1960).

**Organization**
Organisation
organisation
организация

*Just as in other branches of science, organization is used in cybernetics with its everyday meaning.*
More precisely, organization can be understood as a concept of general system theory. It then refers to both the structure and to the reciprocal action between parts of the system. In other words: one describes the position and the effect of each component of a system within the whole structure; this can only happen with reference to other parts of the same system (and often to its surroundings). In complicated systems or aggregates of living organisms, a knowledge of organization (in the above sense) is of the utmost importance. For example, this is the case in the theory of games, in eucology and in experimental psychology of small groups (cf. *mathematical group dynamics). There is an

extensive literature on the organization of business firms, which need not be gone into here. According to L. v. BERTALANFFY the problem of life is largely one of organization. By the expression 'biological organization' is meant not only the structure and internal relationships of an organism, but often also their dynamic consequences, such as the ability of a creature to construct complicated end-products from simple raw materials. In questions of organization, the theory of *graphs can often be used to advantage. In this way N. RASHEVSKY formulated the principle that the total of biological characteristics of an organism can be represented as the set of nodes of a directed graph, and that such graphs can be transformed into each other by a transformation dependent on parameters which must still be suitably chosen (principle of biological epimorphism). For a somewhat different interpretation of similar graphs or diagrams we refer the reader to R. ROSEN's theory of M-R systems (compare RASHEVSKY). Let us merely mention that KEMENY and SNELL have used the theory of graphs as an essential aid to the study of certain problems of social organization. *Blockdiagrams or structure diagrams are often used as the first step in the description of the organization within a system: structure formulae of chemical compounds and technical plans of electronic apparatus are examples of these. Just as in statistics the average value and the scattering give some information on distribution, one can try to characterize organization or its degree by numerical values. H. QUASTLER finds useful for this the difference between the total information and the sum of the information of the individual component parts. D. M. McKAY suggested defining the structural information content of a system in the same way.

Quastler, H. (ed.): Information Theory in Psychology. The Free Press, Glencoe, Illinois 1955. Rashevsky, N.: Mathematical Biophysics: Physico-mathematical foundations of Biology. Vol. II, 3rd edn. Dover Publications, New York 1960. Kemeny, J. G.; Snell, J. L.: Mathematical Models in the Social Sciences. Ginn & Co., Boston, New York, Chicago 1962. Krupp, S.: Pattern in Organization Analysis. Chilton Co., Philadelphia, New York 1961. Eulenberg, F.: Das Geheimnis der Organisation. Duncker & Humboldt, Berlin 1952.

## Originality

Originalität
originalité
оригинальность

*In a message, something which was not foreseeable or predeterminable.*

Every message contains a certain amount of originality which lies between the following two extremes:

1 the message corresponds to the limitation of the number of characters to the minimum necessary for its transmission;

2 the message is pure *redundancy. It can be shown that maximum originality corresponds to a patternless message which is completely incomprehensible.

Redundancy enables the receiver to perceive and to understand *patterns. In a given situation there is an optimal level of redundancy (i.e. of originality) which can be attained, thanks to the process of informational accommodation (cf. *probability learning).

Moles, A. A.: Théorie informationnelle et perception esthétique. Flammarion, Paris 1958. Bense, M.: Ästhetische Information. Agis, Baden-Baden. Frank, H.: Kybernetische Grundlagen der Pädagogik. Agis, Baden-Baden 1962.

## Oscillation

Schwingung
oscillation
колебание

*The temporal variation of a physical variable in which certain characteristics of the variation process are repeated.*
Let $x(t)$ denote the momentary value of a physical value. Periodic oscillations are a special class of oscillations; for these, $x(t + T) = x(t)$ is fulfilled; in this, $T$ stands for the duration of the cycles of the oscillation. The reciprocal value $1/T$ gives the number of cycles per unit time; $1/T$ is called the frequency $f$ of periodic oscillations. It is measured in cycles per second (or Herz units). Harmonic oscillations are an important type of cyclic oscillations, and are described by $x(t) = A \sin(\omega t + \varphi)$. In this, $A$ stands for the amplitude of the oscillation (sinusoidal oscillation); $\omega$ represents the circuit frequency and is given in $s^{-1}$; $\omega = 2\pi f$. The total angle $\omega t + \varphi$ is called the phase angle; $\varphi$ is the zero phase angle.

**Output** (I)
Ausgabe
sortie
выдача; вывод

*Concept from electronic data processing.*
The output of *information (calculation results, logical decisions, organization instructions, etc.) in automatic computers can be produced optically (control desk or electric typewriter) or with the help of an output medium, on which the information is stored long enough to be decoded into script. Output media of this type are: (*a*) punch cards (output speed approx. 250 cards per minute); (*b*) punched tape (150 characters per second); (*c*) magnetic tape (approx. 60,000 characters per second); (*d*) line-printers with approx. 800 characters per second; (*e*) typewriters (teleprinters) with approx. 10 characters per second; and (*f*) special apparatus such as cathode ray tubes, graph plotters, microfilm instruments, etc.
From the output media named under (*a*) to (*c*) the information can be transformed 'off line', i.e. independently of the operation of the rest of the computer, into script in the teleprinter, punch card reader or line printer or be processed further in sorting machines, etc. For the further processing of information with conservative data-processing systems (sorters, accounting machines) punched tape and punch card output is particularly suitable. The fastest *input and output possible is achieved with magnetic tape machines (cf. *magnetic tape store), the installation of which is, however, only worth while for large computers with a high calculation speed and which process a large amount of data.

KNÖDEL, W.: Programmieren von Ziffernrechenanlagen. Springer-Verlag, Wien 1961.

**Output** (II)
Ausgang
sortie
выход; выходное устройство

*Place in a machine at which it exerts direct influence on its surroundings; also this effect itself. This effect can be of an energetic or informational nature.*

**Output quantity, output value**
Ausgangsgrösse
grandeur de sortie; valeur de sortie
выходная велинина

*A value which quantitively distinguishes the output, i.e. the direct effect of the machine on its surroundings.*
Output quantities are dependent on the *input quantities of a machine in a way which is given by the physical laws that are the basis of the machine.
An output quantity forms the information carrier of an outgoing piece of

*information; this carrier has to record the semantics corresponding to the *input quantity in question. Here the problem of comprehension or of meaning arises, which however can be solved by a more exact and precise representation of the corresponding semantics. This problem represents a fringe area of information theory and psychology.

COUFFIGNAL, L.: Kybernetische Grundbegriffe. Agis, Baden-Baden 1962. OPPELT, W.: Kleines Handbuch technischer Regelvorgänge. Verlag Chemie, Weinheim 1956.

# P

**Pandemonium**
Pandemonium
pandemonium
пандемоний

*A class of *learning machines for *pattern recognition.*

The distinguishing mark of such a machine is the parallel operation of a series of calculating elements which were termed 'demons' by SELFRIDGE. In the simplest form of this system, there exists for each class formed from different patterns one demon which produces an output signal. The largest output signal determines the class of the pattern to be classified. As several classes can show a series of common features, a more effective automaton is necessary to ascertain the features of the patterns by computational demons. The computational demons feed the cognitive demons corresponding to the different classes. Algorithms are given for the selection and the modification of the computational demons.

SELFRIDGE, O. G.: Pandemonium, a paradigm for learning. In: The Mechanization of Thought Processes. H.M.S.O., London 1959.

**Parallel operation**
Parallelsystem
opération parallèle
параллельная система



*A digital *computer which permits the simultaneous processing of the individual digits of a word.*

*Arithmetic unit and *store must be organized in parallel for this, i.e. a row of information channels corresponding to the length of the word must be provided. The operation speed which, compared to a *serial* operation, is considerably higher is only obtained at a similarly much higher cost. The series-parallel-system offers a compromise between speed and cost.

SPEISER, A. P.: Digitale Rechenanlagen. Springer-Verlag, Berlin, Göttingen, Heidelberg 1961.

**Parametron**
Parametron
paramétron
параметрон

*Structure element in digital *computers.*

The parametron was discovered almost simultaneously in 1954 by E. GOTO (Japan) and J. v. NEUMANN (U.S.A.) as a structure element for computers. There are two kinds: *magnetic core parametrons and *diode parametrons. In principle the parametron is an oscillating circuit whose inductance or capacitance is periodically altered at the frequency of a pump-oscillation. The physical effect which is here used is called parametric excitation.

In a resonant circuit of this type, an *oscillation with the circuit frequency $\omega$ can be produced under certain conditions, if the circuit frequency of the pump-oscillation applied is $2\omega$.
Sub-harmonic $\omega$ can only be excited in two stable phase-positions which are different by 180°. The *binary digits 0 and 1 can be represented with the two possible phases of parametric oscillation 0 and $\pi$. Nonlinear switching-elements are used as variable reactances in the megnetic core parametron. In the diode parametron, coils with pre-magnetized cores are used as variable inductance. Semi-conductor diodes are used as variable capacitance.

GOTO, E.: The Parametron, a Digital Computing Element which utilizes Parametric Oscillation. Proc. IRE 47 (1959), p. 1304. BILLING, H.; RÜDIGER, A.: Das Parametron. In: Steinbuch, K. (ed.): Taschenbuch der Nachrichtenverarbeitung. Springer-Verlag, Berlin, Göttingen, Heidelberg 1962, pp. 510–21. SCHMITT, E.: Das Parametron. Theorie und Schaltkreisc. Moser-Verlag, Garmisch-Partenkirchen 1961.

**PARKINSON's Disease**
PARKINSONsche Krankheit
maladie de PARKINSON
болезнь Паркинсона

*A disease characterized by disturbances in the muscle-tone; hypertonia of the extrapyramidal type and involuntary movements (PARKINSON'S tremor); evident during the rest state (while the sufferer is at rest).*
PARKINSON's tremor is characterized by involuntary, rhythmical muscle-contraction, whose frequency is approx. 5–7 c/s; both agonistic and antagonistic groups are affected and exchange of contractions from one group to the other often occurs (alternative shaking). Parkinson's disease is caused by injury of the corpus striatum and especially of the nucleus niger (the groups which are decisive in movement control and posture). In senile PARKINSON's syndromes, these injuries are abiotrophic or vascular, whilst in post-encephalic PARKINSON's syndromes there is normally some inflammatory injury.

**Pattern**
Gestalt
forme
форма; вид; образ

*In the context of information theory a *message which does not appear accidental to an observer.*
In agreement with COURNOT and BOREL this assumes that the observer has *a priori* some idea of what a random message could be, that is, a message constructed from *equi*probable elements. The concept of *pattern* is therefore linked to the concept of predictability and the inner organization of a message. Every *super-character which appears in a message is a pattern, yet the concept of pattern is more comprehensive than that of the super-character or of the *sub-routine.
The existence of patterns is evidently connected with the existence of a receptive observer who will perceive and classify the pattern.

MOLES, A. A.: Information Theory and Aesthetical Perception, Univ. of Illinois Press 1966. MEYER-EPPLER, W.: Grundlagen und Anwendungen der Informationstheorie. Springer-Verlag, Berlin 1959.

**Pattern of reflection**
Reflexionsmuster
tableau de réflexion
——

A concept in cybernetical logic which is obtained by generalization and the formalizing of four digit value sequences in traditional propositional logic. The pattern of reflection also has four digits and is classically positive, although the second and third positions can be occupied by 'foreign' values, i.e. by logical

positions which do not belong to bivalent classical values. The value-sequences 1, 2, 2, 2, and 2, 1, 1, 1 which in classical logic represent independent values are identical as patterns of reflection. Patterns of reflection with foreign values are for example: 1, 2, 3, 2, and 1, 4, 3, 2; altogether there are 15 various patterns of reflection of which eight can be interpreted as classical values; the remaining seven patterns supplement the classical sector to a generalized positional-value logic.
The purpose of the concept is the logical representation of the characteristic feature of our consciousness to produce a synthetic unit from various reflection centres, and of the technical simulation of this process.

**Pattern recognition**

*See* *Character recognition

**Perception**
Wahrnehmung
perception
восприятие; перцепция

*The process by which an organism obtains knowledge of its environment, i.e. in which representations of data of its environment are formed in the organism.*
*Stimuli from outside an organism or within its own body lead via receptors to physiologically demonstrable *excitations which produce sensations. But perception contents go far beyond information on individual physical or chemical data of environment. There must therefore occur yet another integration of the individual sensation-data in the organism. This process can be thought of almost as a drawing of unconscious conclusions in the sense of HELMHOLTZ's theory, in which the sensation-data given at that moment are combined with the contents of stored experience. Research into the nature of this process of integration often makes use of the phenomena of three-dimensional space perception, of certain constancy phenomena, or of perceptual illusions. Gestalt psychology utterly denies the existence of individual classifiable sensation-data, and rejects the necessity of experience for perception. Some modern theories (e.g. BRUNSWICK, BRUNER, POSTMAN, McCULLOCH) accept that the perceiving organism forms, on the basis of experience, hypotheses about the data which are to be perceived; it examines these hypotheses by random samples from the total of possible sensations.

ALLPORT, F. H.: Theories of Perception and the Concept of Structure. New York, London 1961.

**Perceptron**
Perceptron
perceptron
перцептрон

*A class of *learning machines. A model of physically well-defined neuron networks.*
Perceptron is the name given (by F. ROSENBLATT) to networks which are constructed of simplified *neurons. They consist of sensory units, association units, and response units. Depending on the structure of the network, several types of perceptron can be distinguished. The sensory unit produces a pulse if it is excited by a stimulus. An association unit has inhibiting and stimulating inputs, and crosses from the binary state $e = -1$ into the state $e = +1$ if the sum of its inhibiting and stimulating values exceeds a given threshold $\Theta$. Its output value is $\alpha \times e$, in which $\alpha$ stands for the adjustable weight-factor. The response unit is active ($r = +1$) if the

sum of its input values is positive; otherwise it is not active ($r = -1$).
In the simplest perceptron (see diagram) the association units are connected *stochastically with the sensory units; the response element is connected to all the association units. For every pattern projected on all the sensory units the response unit produces an output value $r = +1$ or $r = -1$, and thereby subdivides each pattern into two classes. By a suitable influence of the weight-factors $\alpha$ (reinforcement strategy) during the learning phase, every pattern can be allocated to one of the two classes during the testing phase.
By extending the simple perceptron, perceptrons can be obtained which have several consecutive, feedback or interconnected association units with several response units.

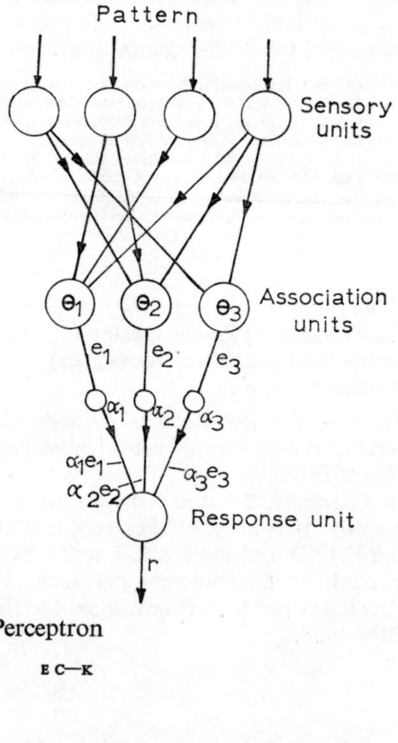

Perceptron

ROSENBLATT, F.: Principles of Neurodynamics. Spartan Books, Washington 1962. ROSENBLATT, F.: Perceptrons and Cognitive Systems. In: Billing, H. (ed.): Lernende Automaten. R. Oldenbourg, München 1961.

**Perturbance**
*See* *Disturbance

**Pilot**
Lotse
pilote
лоцман; проводник
*Paradigm for the level or instance of *information processing in a *feedback control system. From the Greek word for 'steersman' and 'pilot' WIENER formed the expression *'Cybernetics'* (1948).
DUCROCQ has shown that in Greek shipping the function of the pilot was distinguished from that of the steersman after the time of PLUTARCH at the very latest. Whilst the steersman, by operating the rudder, participates in the conversion of power which is essential for the movement of the ship, the function of the pilot is limited solely to *information processing. The products of this information processing (i.e. steering instructions) can only become effective by steering measures being coordinated with them by the steersman. The messages processed by the pilot are on the one hand *actual values, namely the results of his observation of the situation at the time, and on the other hand stored (i.e. retained in his memory) *index values, namely the features of the goal of which the *captain has informed him.
The pilot function can easily be extended from the nautical sphere (cf. *cybernetics, levels of), for example to a system for controlling the water level of a basin with inlet and outlet. In this example, the index value is the level of water desired (by the captain), and the actual

value the measured level. For the pilot, the positive or negative difference between *index value* and *actual value* is the *sign of too high or too low a water level, from which he deduces the steering instruction, *close* or *open tap* in accordance with, in this case, a predetermined strategy. Whilst this meaning of pilot function is directly relevant to cybernetical *social science, for engineering cybernetics and cybernetical biology it is only of heuristic importance, that is, it represents an *as if* approach. Information processing in automata and physiological systems operates on the basis of the level of the signals, not on the level of signs (i.e. *consciousness is an irrelevant concept) and is only projected on the informational level instead of the physical because of its convenience.

There are three distinct stages of the function of pilot:

1 a debased pilot function which renounces continuous measurements of the actual value, and deduces a steering program (a plan or strategy) from the index value together with the initial actual value which was measured only once; this program is altered neither in its content nor in the frequency between the captain-commands during the course of its execution (Pilot Type 1).

2 a simple pilot function which ascertains the next instructions after an algorithm used in conjunction with the measured values of the actual value which has changed as a result of the execution of the instructions already given (Pilot Type 2).

3 an extended pilot function which, without any such algorithm (i.e. without knowledge of the optimal strategy because it has no knowledge of conformity in the effects on the actual value of instructions already carried out) approaches only gradually an optimal strategy by experience of the effect of previous instructions (Pilot Type 3).

In systems with a pilot of the first type one talks of *open-loop control. In this the pilot function is debased to such an extent that the only differences between it and the co-ordinating function of the steersman are: (1) just as before the *output has no direct effect on the conversion of power; and (2) the output of the pilot does not result for the present as a function of the *input (initial actual value and index value) but is given in the form of single instructions in a temporal sequence (i.e. by using time channels).

In systems with a pilot of the second type one talks of a simple feedback control system.

Systems with a pilot of the third type are called self-organizing systems (or self-adapting, adaptive, self-optimalizing, etc.) (cf. *self-organization).

Wiener, N.: Kybernetik. Econ-Verlag, Düsseldorf 1963. Ducrocq, A.: Die Entdeckung der Kybernetik. Europ. Verlagsanstalt, Frankfurt 1959. Frank, H.: Kybernetik—Brücke zwischen den Wissenschaften. Part I. Umschau-Verlag, Frankfurt Bd. 61, H. 14 (1961, pp. 417–20). Frank, H.: Kybernetik—Wesen und Wertung. In: Alsleben, K. (ed.): Kybernetik und Organisation. Schnelle, Quickborn bei Hamburg 1963.

**Pitch**

Zeichenteilung; Zeichenabstand

espacement des caractères (signes)

расстояние образов

*Measure for the distance between the vertical centre lines of two neighbouring characters.*

In Germany, 2·3 and 2·4 mm are frequently used in typewriter script. Both the E 13 B and the CMC-7 script have a pitch of 8 characters per inch. 10 characters per inch is envisaged for the IBM 1428.

**Polyvalence**
Mehrwertigkeit
multivalence
многозначность; многовалентность

*A feature or characteristic which *mathematical logic sometimes ascribes to proposition variables.*

In contrast to the *principium exclusi tertii*, according to this concept propositions do not have to be either true or false, but can also have a third truth-value (tertium) or even more. The significance of these truth values (*uncertain*, etc.) is disputed.

G. GÜNTHER tries to justify a polyvalent logic by pointing out that in ARISTOTLE the logical bivalence *true/false* corresponded to the metaphysical bivalence *be/think*; as *cybernetics demands at least three metaphysical levels (subject-object-reflexion process, or even I-you-it) in order to be able to grasp philosophically the process of communication, then a logic that is at least trivalent is also essential.

GÜNTHER, G.: Das Bewusstsein der Maschinen Agis, Baden-Baden 1957. GÜNTHER, G.: Idee und Grundriss einer nicht-aristotelischen Logik. Meiner, Hamburg 1959. GÜNTHER, G.: Analog-Prinzip, Digital-Maschine und Mehrwertigkeit. Grundlagenstudien Band 1, No. 2 (1960). GÜNTHER, G.: Ein Vorbericht über die generalisierte Stellenwerttheorie der mehrwertigen Logik. Grundlagenstudien Band 1, No. 4 (1960).

**Predictor**
Optimalfilter
predicteur
оптимальный фильтр

A *filter which, from a noisy signal-spectrum presented at the input, delivers the signal-function extrapolated by the forecast-time $\tau$ at the output. A prestipulation of this is that the signal satisfies certain conditions.

SCHLITT, H.: Systemtheorie für regellose Vorgänge. Springer-Verlag, Berlin, Göttingen, Heidelberg 1960.

**Probabilistic approach**
Wahrscheinlichkeitsverfahren
approche probabiliste
вероятностный подход (способ)

*A principle of information processing in higher centres of the sensory-organ system.*

As in sensory-organ systems constructed according to the principle of a *focalized-diffused-excitation the divergence of conducted information is predominant in the higher centres, a probabilistic approach is necessary for the information processing which takes place there. The effect of divergence is that a peripheral *excitation of a closely defined receptor area always results in an excitation of a larger cell group in higher centres. The end-product of the information processing which has to be stored or made known to the consciousness then occurs by statistical mediation or by *autocorrelation via the excitation states of several *neurons.

ROSENBLITH, W. A.: Sensory performance of organisms. Rev. Mod. Physics 31, pp. 485–91 (1959).

**Probability**
Wahrscheinlichkeit
probabilité
вероятность

According to A. N. KOLMOGOROFF probability is nowadays introduced axiomatically as a measure. The connection with experience is obtained by the following principles: if one carries out the basic random experiment frequently ($N$ times), and if the event $A$ occurs $n$ times with the probability $P(A)$ then the relative frequency $n/N$ will lie very near to $P(A)$. R. v. MISES defines probability directly as the limit of relative frequency, but this definition leads to inconsistencies. The old definition of LAPLACE presupposes *a priori* equally probable results of the random experiment and defines the probability of an event as the number of experiment results favourable to this event divided by the number of all experiment results. The probability of an event $A \in \mathfrak{B}$ of a *field of events or probability field $(\Omega, \mathfrak{B}, P)$ is a non-negative number with the axiomatically required properties:

1 $P(A)$ exists for every $A \in \mathfrak{B}$.
2 $P(A) \geq 0$
3 $P(\Omega) = 1$
4 For any $A$, $B \in \mathfrak{B}$ and $AB = 0$ (empty sets, impossible event) the following is valid:

$$P(A + B) = P(A) + P(B)$$

5 Even for any calculable number of $A_i$, $i = 1, 2, 3, \ldots$, $A_i \in \mathfrak{B}$, $A_\mu A_\nu = 0$ for $\mu \neq \nu$ the following is valid:

$$P(\Sigma A_\nu) = \Sigma P(A_\nu),$$

($\sigma$-additive of the measure of probability).

Probability is therefore an $\sigma$-additive standardized measure. For calculable sets of events $\Omega$ is taken for the $\sigma$-algebra the set of all subsets $A < \Omega$, i.e. the potency set $\mathfrak{P}(\Omega)$.

KOLMOGOROV, A. N.: Grundbegriffe der Wahrscheinlichkeitsrechnung. Dtsch. Vlg. d. Wissenschaften, Berlin 1960. MISES, R. von: Wahrscheinlichkeitsrechnung und ihre Anwendung in der Statistik und der theoretischen Physik. Beuticke, Leipzig and Wien 1931. RICHTER, H.: Wahrscheinlichkeitstheorie. Springer-Verlag, Berlin, Göttingen, Heidelberg 1956. GNEDENKO, B. W.: Lehrbuch der Wahrscheinlichkeitsrechnung. Akademie-Verlag, Berlin 1957.

**Probability, subjective**
Wahrscheinlichkeit, subjektive
probabilité subjective
вероятность, субьективная

The *probability with which a receiver (characterized by a finite scheme) expects a character from a transmitter with the same repertory. Subjective probability (of the receiver) can agree with objective probability (of the transmitter) (as for example in the process of throwing dice) but they are generally different. (cf. *information, subjective). If the subjective probabilities of the receiver are not identical with those of the transmitter schemes, then the subjective information of a message sent by the transmitter is greater than the objective information.

**Probability density**
Wahrscheinlichkeitsdichte
densité de probabilité
плотность вероятности

If for a *random variable the *probability distribution function $F(x)$ can be differentiated for every $x$ and if $F^1(x) = p(x)$, then $p(x)$ is called the density of the probability distribution. The following relation is then valid:

$$F(x) = \int_{-\infty}^{x} p(x)\,\mathrm{d}x.$$

The function $p(x)$ has the following properties:

1 $p(x) \geq 0$
2 for any $x_1$ and $x_2$,

$$P\{x_1 \leq \xi \leq x_2\} = \int_{x_1}^{x_2} p(x)\,\mathrm{d}x$$

is valid
3 if $p(x)$ is constant in $x$, then
$P\{x \leq \xi \leq x + \mathrm{d}x\} = p(x)\,\mathrm{d}x$
4 $\int_{-\infty}^{+\infty} p(x)\,\mathrm{d}x = 1$

Example: the probability density function of normal distribution is

$$p(x) = c \times e - \frac{(x - a)^2}{2\sigma^2}$$

in which $c = \dfrac{1}{\sigma\sqrt{2\pi}}$.

$p(x)$ has a maximum in $x = a$ and turning points for $x = a + \sigma$. The abscissa axis is an asymptote for $x \to \pm\infty$. The form of the curve is the well-known normal distribution curve; it depends on the two parameters $a$ and $\sigma$.

**Probability distribution**
Wahrscheinlichkeitsverteilung
distribution de probabilité
распределение вероятности

The probabilities with which individual values of a discrete random variable $\xi$ occur is called the probability distribution of this value. The probability distribution function (distribution function in short) $F(x)$ appropriate to the value $\xi$ is defined as the *probability $P\{\xi < x\}$ if $\xi$ adopts a value which is smaller than $x$, therefore by $F(x) = P\{\xi < x\}$. For example, in dice-throwing with a true dice, the probability of $P$ of the dice result $\zeta$ being less than 2·8 is a value of $2/6 = 1/3$; accordingly, $F(2{\cdot}8) = 1/3$ is valid. Represented as a curve, a probability distribution in the shape of a 'staircase' curve results for throwing a true dice (see diagram).

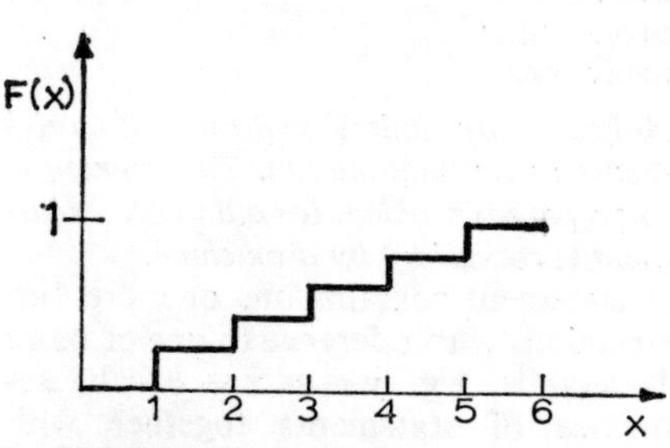


Probability distribution

Further examples of distribution functions are:
(*a*) the binomial distribution function

$$P_n(m) = \binom{n}{m} p^m q^{n-m}$$

(*b*) the POISSON distribution function

$$p_n = \frac{\lambda^n e^{-\lambda}}{n!} \quad (n = 0, 1, 2, \ldots)$$

(*c*) the normal distribution function

$$\Phi(x) = \frac{1}{\sigma\sqrt{2\pi}} \int_{-\infty}^{x} \exp\left(-\frac{(z-a)^2}{2\sigma^2}\right) dz$$

with $\sigma < 0$, $a =$ constant.

The probability distribution of any random variable is a continuously increasing function, whose values lie between 0 and 1 and satisfy the conditions $F(-\infty) = 0$ and $F(+\infty) = 1$. Every function which satisfies these conditions can be taken as a distribution function.

A distribution function can be defined in several dimensions. The definition of probability distribution is the basis of more advanced topics of probability theory and statistics.

GNEDENKO, B. W.: Lehrbuch der Wahrscheinlichkeitsrechnung. Akademie-Verlag, Berlin 1957.

**Probability field; field of events**
Feld
champ
поле

*A set of a finite number of events together with their probabilities. Should the number of events not be finite then the operation combining subsets of all possible events must also be defined.*

In the simplest, and in practice the most important, case a field $X$ is a set of a finite number (namely $u(X)$ of events $x_1, x_2, \ldots, x_u$, of which exactly one will certainly occur; in this, the probability $p(x_i)$, that $x_i$ will occur for $i = 1, 2, \ldots, u$, is given. The ordered set of the probabilities

$$\{p(x_i), \ldots, p(x_u)\}$$

is called the probability vector of $X$. The ordered sets of the pairs

$$\{x_1, p(x_1); \ldots; x_u, p(x_u)\}$$

is called the scheme of $X$. $u$ is the order of the field.

The limitation to a finite number of events can be avoided by the following definition:

A field or probability-field is a triple $(\Omega, \mathfrak{B}, P)$, consisting of any finite, enumerable or non-enumerable set of events $\Omega$ of element events $\omega \in \Omega$, a Boolean $\sigma$-algebra ($\sigma$ event-algebra, Boolean $\sigma$-ring) of subsets, the events of $\Omega$ and the probability measure, the probability of $P$ on $\mathfrak{B}$.

**Berger, E. R.; Piloty, H.: Erläuterungen zu den in der Informationstheorie verwendeten Begriffen der mathematischen Statistik. NTZ 1 (1963), pp. 49–52.**
**Rényi, A.: Wahrscheinlichkeitsrechnung. VEB Wissenschaft, Berlin 1962.**

## Probability learning

Wahrscheinlichkeitslernen; informationelle Akkomodation
accomodation informationnelle
вероятностный яподход

*The (approximate) recording or learning of the objective frequency distribution of objects of perception, especially of characters, without these relative frequencies necessarily becoming directly available to conscious processes (cf. *maximum effect).*

The most important empirical principle of *information psychology states that the time required for the apperception of *characters or other events (also for the reaction to these) are those which (at least on average) are proportional to the (average) information content of these characters or events. As *information* is calculated from probabilities, these must be stored in the brain (and internalized probabilities deviate from the values named in conscious evaluation of relative frequencies). These stored values can only come from experience. If now the objective frequency distribution alters, then the stored *subjective probabilities* (cf. *probability, subjective) deviate from the objective relative frequencies, as does the subjective from the objective information. But as, according to a principle of information theory, the average subjective information is larger than the average objective information, apperception and reaction times are lengthened on an average. The learning of the new probabilities therefore means a saving in time through a decrease in the average subjective information. The convergence of the subjective probabilities towards the objective relative frequencies is called probability learning, and the associated convergence of subjective information towards objective information is called informational accommodation. The two terms therefore mean practically the same thing.

**Frank, H.: Kybernetische Grundlagen der Pädagogik.—Eine Einführung in die Informationspsychologie. Agis, Baden-Baden 1962.**

## Program

Programm
programme
программа

*A (generally finite) sequence of statements to an *automaton. To program is to prepare a problem for automatic treatment (processing) by a machine.*

A statement contains one or more *instructions with reference to one or more *operands, e.g. $y \leftarrow a.x + b$. The sequence of statements together with particulars or conventions of the successor $B$ to every statement $A$, as well as a commencement-statement (start-instruction) $A_0$, forms a program. Data are defined by a program, i.e. the statements are sets of instructions for the processing of information. The results of a program form a subset of the data defined in the program. The information-content concerning the information recorded and the statements contained in a program cannot be enlarged by a program. A program can be physically connected to a machine, or it can be inserted in a certain *code into an erasable *store.

The statement sequence: 1. $x \leftarrow 0$; 2. $y \leftarrow 1 + x$; 3. $x \leftarrow y.y$; 4. 'go to statement 2' forms an infinite program; the statement sequence: 1. $x \leftarrow 0$; 2. $y \leftarrow 1 + x$; 3. $x \leftarrow y.y$; 4. 'if $x < 10$ go to statement 2, otherwise to statement 5; 5 stop' forms a finite program. The statements are written in a *programming language.

IVERSON, K. E.: A Programming Language. New York and London 1962.

**Programming language**
Programmierungsprache
langage de programmation

---

**Language in which a *program is written. All statements to an *automaton in a programming language must be unambiguous.*

If statements in a program, which are made accessible to an automaton according to a strict set of rules (cf. *code), are executed directly by this automaton, then one speaks of a *machine language. In this, a statement corresponds to a single *instruction. Machine languages clearly correspond to classes of automata. The description of a machine language is therefore also part of the description of this class.

If a program (i.e. source program) which has been set up for a certain automaton has been written not in the pertinent machine language but in a pseudo-language (cf. *pseudo-code), then a translation into an object program by means of a super-program on a *computer is necessary. If by this the pseudo-language becomes a machine language by a transformation of the automaton, then one talks of a simulation or an interpreting super-program. This super-program is fed into the *store, it interprets the source program instruction by instruction, and executes the resulting instructions of the object program. Two automata which are equivalent to the universal *TURING machine can simulate each other without limitation.

If there results a translation from the pseudo-language into the machine language (in which the results of each source program must be retained in the pertinent object program), then the super-program is called a generating program or a compiling program. If the translation consists of a re-coding or arrangement of symbols, then it is called an *assembler. In this, several instructions in the object program may correspond to one statement in the subject program (macro-instructions) which are realized by subroutines. If a transformation of the *syntax of a language is necessary, then the generating program is called a *compiler. (In general, the use of a generating super-program is more economical than the use of an interpreting one, as the translation time in a program which is run through several times only occurs once with the former.)

Programming languages which can be made accessible to an automaton by an assembler for direct processing are called machine-orientated. The complete translation of two program languages into each other by a compiler is not always possible; in certain circumstances some is left over for simulation (since, for example, instructions and data in machine languages are processed in the same way, when there is a different instruction-structure the meaning of an *operation can only be recognized when all information referring to it is available, and this may not be the case until the object program is run through). A program language for the description of tasks within a certain class of problems without taking into account any particular automaton or a real subset of all automata is called a problem-orientated language. Problem-orientated languages greatly facilitate the writing of a program. They are used predominantly for mathematical and technical problems (cf. *ALGOL, *FORTRAN), in business (cf. *COBOL) and logical problems (theorem-proving programs).

**Propagation time**
*See* *Transit time

**Propositional functions**
logische Funktionen
fonctions logiques
логические функции

*Functions which arise from the application of *logical connectives to logical variables.*
According to the classical conception, a proposition is either true or false (theorem of bivalence).
A propositional function is a function whose values and arguments are propositions. Propositional functions formed with logical connectives are extensional in the sense that the truth-value of the function-value results clearly from the truth-values of the arguments. A propositional function can therefore be represented by a truth-table.

HERMES, H.: Einführung in die mathematische Logik. Teubner Verlag, Stuttgart 1963. LORENZEN, P.: Formale Logik. Gruyter, Berlin 1958.

**Pseudo-code**
Pseudocode
pseudo-code
псевдокод

*An *instruction code used for the writing of a *program which is not identical to the *machine code allocated to the *automaton used (cf. *programming language).*
Pseudo-codes help to simplify the programming. There exist pseudo-codes which are intended for use with one given class of automata (machine-orientated languages) and pseudo-codes which facilitate the description of tasks of one given class of problems (problem-orientated languages).
The processing of a program written in a pseudo-code presupposes in a separate operation the translation into the machine language by means of a translator (cf. *assembler and *compiler) or the interpretation (cf. *simulator) of each pseudo-instruction which results at the same time as the processing.

**Psychology of groups**
*See* *Group dynamics

**Psychophysics**
Psychophysik
psychophysique
психофизика

*An area of psychology which is concerned with the relations between *stimuli and their relationship in the experience of an organism.*
If a physically or chemically describable stimulus reaches a *receptor tuned to it in a living organism, then under certain conditions a relationship in the experience of the organism concerned can be shown; this relationship is called *sensation*. All stimuli of a certain modulation (e.g. electro-magnetic *oscillations) vary in different dimensions (e.g.

frequency and intensity of the oscillations). In order to be able to produce a sensation, a stimulus must lie within these dimensions which are each limited by two **absolute thresholds*. Electromagnetic oscillations which alight on the eye only produce a sensation of light if both their frequency and their intensity lie between the corresponding thresholds. Stimuli beneath the pertinent *lower absolute threshold* do not produce sensation. In the same way, above the *upper absolute threshold* no sensation can be proved with different dimensions of individual stimulus modulation; however, in some cases it can be shown that there is simply a change of type of sensation. For example, there are upper thresholds for the intensity of sounds; these thresholds differ according to frequency and a sensation of sound changes to a sensation of pain when they are exceeded.

In psychophysics a special meaning is attached to the *difference threshold; a difference threshold is the amount by which the condition of a stimulus in one dimension must be altered so that the resultant new stimulus is distinguishable from the output stimulus. Most research in this field is concerned with the difference threshold for stimulus intensity. According to WEBER's law (E. H. WEBER 1843) the quotient of the amount of necessary alteration in intensity $\Delta S$ and the intensity of the output stimulus $S$ forms a constant $c = \Delta S/S$ for every type of stimulus. FECHNER (1860) assumed that any two stimuli, which are separated by an equal number of difference thresholds, have equal differences of a hypothetical *strength of sensation R*. From the statement $\Delta R = c \times \Delta S/S$ there results by a limiting process $dR = c \times dS/S$ and by subsequent integration FECHNER's law $R = K + c \log S$. More recent research has shown that WEBER's law represents only a very rough approximation of the real facts. So when a stimulus gets nearer and nearer to the absolute thresholds of its modulation substantially larger difference thresholds can be proven than result from WEBER's law. To register strength of sensation, processes are used to-day which are not deduced from the concepts of difference thresholds. For example, two stimuli of different intensity are given, and test-subjects are asked to distribute a specified number of points to these stimuli in such a way that the point-ratio corresponds to the ratio of the intensities felt. In other experiments test-subjects are asked to set a variable stimulus in such a way that it bisects a perceived intensity difference between two given specified stimuli. This and other methods have produced various theories and functions for the connection between stimulus intensities and strengths of sensation. The connections which have been discovered can be described very well by STEVEN's power law $R = k(S - S_0)^n$ in which $R$ represents the strength of sensation, $S$ the stimulus intensity, and $K$ and $n$ two parameters, whose values are specific for the various stimulus modulations.

GUILFORD, J. P.: Psychometric Methods. New York 1954. STEVENS, S. S.: The Psychophysics of Sensory Functions. American Scientist 1960. (Of historical importance: WEBER, E. H.: Annotationes Anatomicae et Physiologicae, de Tactu. Leipzig 1851.)

**Pulse; impulse**
Impuls
impulsion
импульс

*A brief deviation of a variable (e.g. current, voltage, charge) from its steady-state. In mechanics: time-integral of power:* $I = \int \mathfrak{K} dt = m.\mathfrak{v}$.

Pulses are described by their direction, their shape, their amplitude, their duration, their rise time and their fall time. The direction is positive and negative. Their shape is described as for geometrical patterns, e.g. rectangular, trapezium, saw-tooth or exponential pulses. The amplitude is the maximal deviation of the value from its steady state; where necessary, a differentiation between positive and negative amplitude. In physiology, impulses with 1, 2 or 3 deviations are called mono-, di- and tri-phase pulses. The pulse duration is defined as the length of time in which the pulse value deviates from the steady state by more than a certain amount (50 per cent or 10 per cent of the amplitude). Rise time or fall time is given by the length of time which the pulse value needs to rise from 10 per cent to 90 per cent or to fall from 90 per cent to 10 per cent of the amplitude value. The pulse variations during the rise time and fall time are called the leading and trailing edges. The pulse between the leading and trailing edges is called the amplitude. Several pulses following one upon another are called a pulse-train.

JUNG, R.: Die Tätigkeit des Nervensystems. Handbuch der Inneren Medizin, V/1, Springer-Verlag, Berlin, Göttingen, Heidelberg 1953. STEINBUCH, K. (ed.): Taschenbuch der Nachrichtenverarbeitung. Springer-Verlag, Berlin, Göttingen, Heidelberg 1962.

## Pulse function

DIRACstoss

fonction de DIRAC

импульс Дирака

*Idealized (rectangular) *impulse of duration* $\varepsilon$ *and height* $1/\varepsilon$ *for the boundary-case* $\varepsilon \to 0$.

The rectangle form is of no consequence and is only meant to help explain the facts. The only thing that is important is the surface area of the impulse of the value 'one' with an infinitely short duration. A pulse function has a constant amplitude spectrum independent of frequency of the value 'one', and a phase spectrum independent of frequency of the value $\frac{\pi}{2}$ (cf. *spectrum).

Because of the exceptional shape of the spectrum, a pulse function is frequently used as a test signal in *system theory. If the input signal of a system is a pulse function, then the output signal is called the impulse response. A system is completely described by the impulse response in a similar way as by the transfer function. Impulse response and transfer function are related to each other by the FOURIER transformation.

FETZER, V.: Einschwingvorgänge in der Nachrichtentechnik. Porta Verlag, München: Verlag Technik, Berlin 1958. WUNSCH, G.: Moderne Systemtheorie. Geest & Portig, Leipzig 1962.

## Punch card

Lochkarte

carte perforée

перфорированная карточка; перфокарта

*Information carrier in modern data-processing.*

A punch card is a piece of card approximately 19 × 8 cm in size on which the *information of a character (i.e. a number, a letter or technical sign) is punched in approx. 80 colums (IBM, REMINGTON) or 90 columns (REMINGTON, etc.). Each piece of information is then in the shape of a small (rectangular) perforation, or a combination of such perforations. In each column 12 different perforations are possible. The coding of the information in such perforation combinations is performed automatically by the punch.

A punch of this kind can be either manually operated or take its information from other information carriers (magnetic tapes, the store of a com-

puter, etc.). Punch cards can be scanned, sorted or duplicated mechanically or photo-electrically. Their use is to store data and instructions (cf. *program) of electronic computers or other data-processing apparatus for technical, scientific or business purposes.
Punch cards are processed with the help of tabulators (from the punched data sums, differences or balances, tables and lists can be written depending on the card-groups). Invented in 1890 by Dr. H. HOLLERITH.

**Punch card reader**
Lochkartenabtaster
lecteur de cartes perforées
устройство для чтения перфокарт

*Apparatus for the reading of *punch cards.*

A punch card reader is a device in modern data processing which can scan punch cards mechanically (by contact-brushes) or photo-electrically (by photo-cells), in other words, 'read' the information. The information of a card is passed by a punch card reader to, for example, a computer or directly to sorting or duplicating apparatus.
Nowadays, punch card readers can read some 500 punch cards per minute (e.g. IBM 7070). This speed is too low for modern computers. So the information contained on the punch cards is re-stored (with the help of punch card readers) on the other information carriers (*magnetic tape stores, *magnetic core stores), which serve as the input medium of the computer.

**Punched tape**
Lochstreifen
bande perforée
перфорированная или перфораторная лента; перфолента

*Information carrier in data-processing apparatus.*

Tape of parchment paper or similar material, approx. 17 mm wide—although other widths are used—on which the *information of a character sequence (numbers, letters, technical signs, etc.) can be recorded. The information here is in the shape of a single (round) hole or a combination of up to eight such perforations, which are arranged next to each other as the 'column' of the tape. A further hole in each column serves to carry the tape into the punch and reading apparatus.
The coding of single characters is done (for example in teleprinter code) by a puncher, perhaps a teleprinter with an attached punched tape transmitter. If on teleprinter the key G is pressed, then a hole-combination corresponding to this G is punched on the tape, and the tape is carried forward the width of one column.
Punched tapes are used in postal teleprinters and in input and output with computers. In *input the information is obtained from the punched tape by mechanical scanning (up to 150 characters per sec.) or photo-electric scanning (up to 1000 characters per sec.). The *output of punched tape is achieved by mechanical punching.

KNÖDEL, W.: Programmieren von Ziffernrechenanlagen. Springer-Verlag, Wien 1961.

**Pushdown store**
Speicher nach dem Stapelprinzip
LIFO store
——

*A *store in which a chain of information of any length can be stored, whereby the sequence of access to the elements of the information chain is the reverse of the sequence of storing; the information* *stored last is the first to be called* (*LIFO: last in, first out*).

Stores according to this principle play an essential part in programs for the translation of natural and formal languages with a bracketed structure. In respect of the capacity of representation, these automata stand between finite automata and *TURING machines (cf. *grammar).

BAUER, F. L.; SAMELSON, K.: Maschinelle Verarbeitung von Programmsprachen. In: Hoffmann, W. (ed.): Digitale Informationswandler, pp. 227–68. Vieweg, Braunschweig 1962. MEYER-EPPLER, W.: Informationstheorie. Springer Verlag, 1959. MOLES, A. A.: Information theory and aesthetical perception. Univ. of Illinois Press 1967: OETTINGER, A. G.: Automatic Syntactic Analysis and the Pushdown Store. In: Jacobsen, R. (ed.): Structure of Language and its Mathematical Aspects, pp. 104–229. Proc. Symp. Appl. Math. XII, Amer. Math. Soc. Providence, Rhode Island 1961.

# Q

## Quant

Quant
quantum
квант

In principle, science can incorporate all physical phenomena of our environment into a system of measurement which can belong to one of two categories—continuous and discontinuous measurement. The world of the individual can be understood as a system of discontinuous and digital variables. On the other hand, the length of a table or the strength of an electrical current is characterized by a continuous variable. The majority of those values which an observer may measure as being continuous by a standard individual to man show themselves to be discontinuous as soon as they are measured by a smaller standard. In fact, such values consist of simple elements, quants. Hence the conception of *quantification is connected to the concept of a system of measurement. The concept of quantification helps in the atomistic theory of the divisibility of matter. However, it also appears in connection with the input value in an observer and in connection with measurement if and when the observation is continued far enough into detail, into the microscopic. Although the concept of quant originated from M. PLANCK's examination of light beams, it is a question of a general concept independent of any particular method of observation. In *psychophysics, for example, one has come to interpret perceptive values as consisting of a given number of quants, such as the pitch of a note or the strength of light. In this the quants are perception-quants or perception-elements. In *cybernetics this type of perception-quant or perception-element is sometimes regarded as corresponding to the elementary pulses of the nervous system.

WIESER, W.: Organismen, Strukturen, Maschinen. S. Fischer, Frankfurt/M. 1962. MOLES, A. A.: Théorie de l'Information et Perception Esthétique. Flammarion, Paris 1958.

## Quantification

Quantisierung
quantification
квантование

*A mental process by which the observer*

*divides a stochastically fluctuating continuous value into a given number of *quants selected at will.*
For ideal quantification the value of the elemental quantum should, in theory, be chosen in such a way that it is larger than the fluctuation (oscillations, random impulses) to which the phenomena can be subjected. MILLER showed that in those fields in which the attribution of a measurement depends on the judgement of the observer, such as in the social sciences, it is sufficient to establish 7 quants for each dimension, e.g. 7 social classes, 7 colours in the spectrum, 7 stages within each opposition of qualifiers that appears in the *semantic differentials.

MILLER: The magical number 7 (plus or minus one). American psychological Journal 1957. OSGOOD, SUCI, TANNENBAUM: The Measurement of Meaning, University of Illinois Press 1956.

# R

**Random**
*see* *Stochastic

**Random number**
Zufallszahl
nombre aléatoire
случайное число

*A random number is a *random variable which adopts numerical values, in particular integral values.*

**Random number generator**
Zufallszahlengenerator
générateur de nombres aléatoires
датчик случайных чисел

*A machine or *program for the production of *random numbers.*
With the help of program-controlled *computers *pseudo-random numbers* can be produced by a determined process; these pseudo-numbers show the same statistical distribution as real random numbers, e.g. equal distribution, normal distribution, POISSON distribution.
A program which produces random numbers of this type is called a random number generator. There are various methods of doing this, e.g. from a specified number, half of the digits are masked, the rest squared and again masked. After sufficient iteration of the process, the numerical sequences produced can be regarded as (uniformly distributed) random numbers.

**Random variable**
Zufallsvariable; stochastische Variable; Zufallsgrösse
variable aléatoire; nombre aléatoire
случайная переменная

In probability theory, random variable is the term applied to a value which is capable of various numerical values under the influence of random circumstances. The value which is adopted by such values can only be stated with probability, not with certainty. This adopted value changes at random from test to test.
A random variable is given by: (*a*) giving its value-repertory, i.e. those values which it can adopt (*b*) giving the probabilities with which it adopts these

values (e.g. its probability distribution function).
Example: the results of dice throwing are taken from the value repertory (1, 2, 3, 4, 5, 6). With a genuine dice these are accepted or adopted with the equal probability $p = \frac{1}{6}$.
The number of phone calls made by subscribers within a certain period of time also adopts an integral value which depends on random circumstances. There is a certain probability distribution for this, according to which the capacity of the telephone exchange, for example, can be calculated. The speed of gas molecules is introduced as a random variable in the theory of gasses. It changes depending on collisions with other molecules. These collisions occur stochastically and can be described statistically.
Exact definition: every random variable $\xi$ is a function $f(e)$ in the set of events $E$ (or $\Omega$) of the elementary events $e \varepsilon E$. $\xi$ is called a random variable if this function $f(e)$ with regard to the probability field ($E$, $\mathfrak{B}_u$, $P$) defined by the set of events $E$, is measurable, i.e. that for every BOREL measurable set $A\xi$ of $\xi$, the set $A_e$ of $e$ with $f(e) \leqslant A\xi$ belongs to the set $\mathfrak{B}_E$ of random events so that for them a probability $P\{\xi \subset A\xi\} = P\{A_e\}$ is defined.
If the set $A\xi$ satisfies the inequality $\xi < x$ then $P\{A_e\} = P\{\xi < x\} = F(x)$ is the distribution function of the random variable $\xi$.

GNEDENKO, B. W.: Lehrbuch der Wahrscheinlichkeitsrechnung. Akademie-Verlag, Berlin 1957.

**R. C. circuit (differentiating or integrating)**
RC Glied
relais RC
RC-звено; резистивно-емкостное звено

*A passive *four-terminal network easy to realize.*
In a more precise sense, consisting of one resistance and one capacitor. According to the circuit the R.C. circuit possesses differentiating or integrating characteristics; as a filter it is like a high-pass or a low-pass filter so that an input time-function is either accentuated or smoothed. With a set frequency, use is made of its ability of phase-rotation (phase shifter).

SCHÄFER, O.: Theorie elektrischer Schaltvorgänge. In: Steinbuch, K. (ed.): Taschenbuch der Nachrichtenverarbeitung. Springer-Verlag, Berlin, Göttingen, Heidelberg 1962, para. 1.5.

**Reaction**
Reaktion
réaction
реакция; противодействие

*Largely voluntary unit of behaviour of an organism which can be interpreted as the response to a *stimulus.*
In psychology the concept of reaction is often clearly separated from the concept of action. In this case, one can only consider as reaction that behaviour which is triggered off by a stimulus from outside the organism. Any other behaviour is action. Some authors, however, regard all behaviour as reactive and introduce a theoretical stimulus as part of a model-idea (cf. *behaviourism) in the absence of any external stimuli. In experimental psychology it is useful to define classes of reaction whose elements, according to the formulation of the questions, fulfil certain conditions of *invariance (e.g. the class of all right-hand turns carried out by an organism in a labyrinth). Several classes which are possible in a certain stimulus situation, which cancel each other out and which contain all possible reactions, have certain probabilities which depend on

different controllable variables. Between the occurrence of an external stimulus and the quickest reaction there always elapses a short time-span called reaction time. The length of this time in man varies according to type of connection of the stimulus reaction and other influences, but is within the range of 30 msecs (reflex of patellar tendons) to 20 secs (blushing and turning pale).

HOFSTÄTTER, P. R.: Psychologie. Fischer Lexikon 6, Frankfurt 1957.

**Reading machine**
*See* *Character reader

**Reafferent principle**
Reafferenzprinzip
réafférence
обратная афферентация

*A general circuit system in the body which at every level of synaptic information processing compares the issue and the execution of instructions, and which, in case of failure, sends back to higher centres a report demanding correction.*
If instructions issued from a controlling centre run via a relay station to an effector, then a delayed excitation (efferent-copy) is branched off at the relay station of the efferent signal-sequence and compared to the report on the execution of the instruction by the effector. If the efferent copy and reafferent do not agree, then a message (exafferent) will return to the controlling centres, and exert some effect on the original efferent in the sense of a *feedback control system, although the reafferent principle cannot be regarded as a simple feedback control system (see diagram). The reports which are fed back can sometimes penetrate as far as the *consciousness and give rise to recognition. A visual example of the reafferent principle is eye-movement and the co-ordination of the eye-hand system.

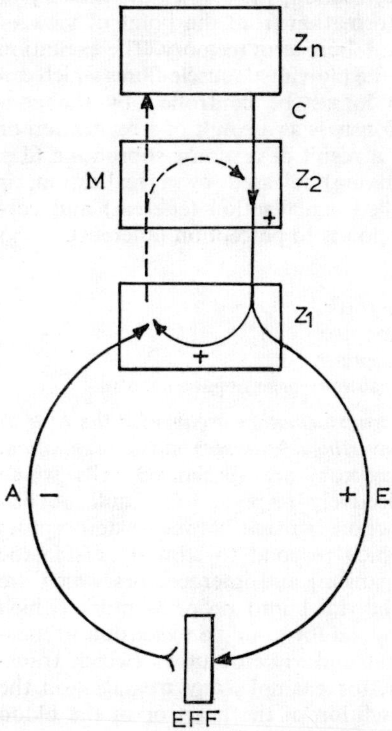


Reafferent principle: A—afferent; C—control; E—efferent; EFF—effector; M—message (exafferent); $Z_n$ $Z_1$ $Z_2$—centres

HOLST, E. v.; MITTELSTAEDT, H.: Das Reafferenzprinzip. Naturwiss. 37 (1950), pp. 256–72. HOLST, E. v.: Zentralnervensystem und Peripherie in ihrem gegenseitigen Verhältnis. Klin. Wschr. 29 (1951), pp. 97–105.

**Realization**
Realisation; Verwirklichung
réalisation
реализация; осуществление

*A conscious movement of the muscles for reaction to external events.*

Realization corresponds to *apperception. The latter is the recording of information, the former the delivery of information from the point of view of the *short-term memory. The excitation of the individual muscle-fibres which can no longer be controlled by the consciousness as a result of a realization or as a result of a motor subroutine (e.g. walking) released by a realization, is called signalization (efferent) and corresponds to perception (afferent).

**Receptor**
Rezeptor
récepteur
рецепторы; рецепторные нейроны

*A transformation organ with the task of converting a *stimulus into an *excitation.* Receptors are specialized cells which selectively respond to stimuli. A distinction is made between exteroceptors (which respond to stimuli outside the organism) and interoceptors which are subdivided into proprioceptors (which respond for example to tension in muscles) and visceroceptors (which transfer, for example, any messages on the condition of the heart or of the blood vessels, etc.).

As the most important part of the sensory organs receptors are capable of responding to stimuli with a series of successive excitations, i.e. the strength of the stimulus is encoded into a pulse-frequency modulated series of action potentials of the same amplitude (cf. *all-or-none law), as the membrane of the receptor cell can repeatedly run through depolarization and repolarization phases (cf. *encoding). Before encoding there takes place a transformation of the stimulus in the receptor; it is a measurable alteration in potential dependent on the stimulus parameters which guide the encoding process. The *thresholds of a receptor group are different, so that with a rise in strength of stimulus the number of excited receptors also rises.

A distinction is made between receptors with proportional and differential behaviour; sensory-organ systems have both types of receptor (cf. *on-effect and *off-effect). The *adaptation based on receptor metabolism is also essential for the range adjustment of the sensory organs.

Field, J.; Magoun, H. W.; Hall, V. E. (eds.). Handbook of Physiology. Vol. 1 Neurophysiology: Am. Physiol. Soc. Williams and Wilkins Co, Baltimore 1959. Ranke, O. F.: Allgemeine Physiologie der Sinnesorgane. In: Lehmann, G. (ed.): Handbuch der gesamten Arbeitsmedizin. Urban and Schwarzenberg, München, Berlin, Wien 1962.

**Reciprocal action; interaction**
Wechselwirkung
action réciproque
взаимодействие

*Relationship and influence of the parts of a system (objects, people, etc.) to and on each other.*

Reciprocal action is the basis and starting-point of all systems with which *cybernetics is concerned. (*Feedback is a special case of reciprocal action.) Reciprocal action assumes that the system contains some contradiction or inconsistency (not in the sense of logic, but in the sense of two or more unstable states which exclude each other); this can consist of simply a constant swing between the two states of a system (e.g. temperature continuously stays between a certain constant minimum and maximum value when a thermostat is used).

On the other hand, reciprocal action can lead to an adjustment of a system to its environment (e.g. in living creatures). In this case, reciprocal action adopts HEGEL's meaning and functions as progress (spiral development); hence it is often given as an example of dialectic processes.

SPEISER, A.: Elemente der Philosophie und der Mathematik. Birkhäuser, Basel 1957. CVEKL, J.: Über materialistische Dialektik. Dietz, Berlin 1959. APOSTEL, L.: Matérialisme dialectique et méthode scientifique. Revue 'Socialisme' July (1960).

**Recognition**
Erkennung
reconnaissance
распознавание; опознавание

The unambiguous (usually not perceivably unambiguous) translation of any (digital or non-digital) *signal into a *character from a finite *repertory. So in automatic recognition (oral or visual character), output is always given in a *1-from-n-code*, if *n* is the range of the repertory. An example of automatic recognition processes is given by the learning matrix in the EB testing phase (cf. diagram in *learning matrix).

STEINBUCH, K.: Automatische Zeichenerkennung. MEYER-EPPLER, W.: Automatische Spracherkennung. In: Steinbuch, K. (ed.): Taschenbuch der Nachrichtenverarbeitung. Springer-Verlag, Berlin, Göttingen, Heidelberg 1962.

**Redundancy**
Redundanz; Weitschweifigkeit
redondance
избыточность; излишняя часть сообщения

*Concept in *information theory which is used mostly for a quantitative measure of the possible abbreviation of a character sequence (or a multi-dimensional arrangement of * characters) by use of better *encoding but using the same repertory of characters.*

Let $X$ be a finite *field of events of the order $u(X)$, let $H(X)$ be the average *information (or *entropy) defined by this field, and let $I_0(X) = \log_2 u(X)$ be the *information content of the field $X$. Then $R = I_0(X) - H(X)$ is the absolute redundancy of the field, and $r = R/I_0(X)$ its relative redundancy. The relative redundancy then reaches its maximum 1 if the *uncertainty $H(X)$ disappears, that is, if one of the events with the probability 1 can be expected. Conversely, the probability is zero if the uncertainty assumes its maximum $I_0(X)$. By the addition of redundancies a *message can be transmitted with a suitable *encoding to any degree of accuracy even through a disturbed *channel with a *channel capacity of any size down to and including zero (cf. *error-correction).

BERGER, E. R.; PILOTY, H.: Erläuterungen zu den in der Informationstheorie verwendeten Begriffen der mathematischen Statistik. NTZ Heft 1 (1963).

**Redundancy at the super-character level**
Superzeichenredundanz
redondance des supersignes
——

*If a receiver forms through super-characters a new repertory from the *repertory of its *characters, then in certain circumstances in a reverse process it can reduce the information of the original repertory by this manipulation.*

So, for example, a word in German (in the finite scheme of words used) has an average information of some 12 bits. As a word consists, on average, of 5·6 letters, the average information of one letter is 2·1 bit. As in the repertory of the alphabet one letter has the average information of 4·1 bit, there occurs in this way a redundancy at the super-character level of:

$$R_s = \frac{4{\cdot}1 - 2{\cdot}1}{4{\cdot}1} = 0{\cdot}49$$

(cf. H. ZEMANEK: Elementary Information Theory, 1959, for the numerical values). Redundancy at the super-character level is normally defined by the expression:

$$R_s = \frac{I^{(1)} - I^{(2)}}{I^{(1)}}$$

in which $I^{(1)}$ is the average information of a text $Z_i$ in the original scheme and $I^{(2)}$ is produced by all combinations of $n$ characters $z_i$ up to $m$ elements being formed as words, by the definition in this repertory of the average information, and by the latter being divided by the average number of letters. If in this process the relation $I^{(1)} > I^{(2)}$ is valid, then redundancy at super-character level occurs.

**Redundancy by steps**
Stufenredundanz
redondance de niveaux
ступенчатая избыточность

If a receiver forms by *super-characters a new repertory from the repertory of its characters then this transfer normally means a redundancy process which is called redundancy by steps. (In this way, for example, the information of a text $z_1\ z_2 \ldots z_8$, which in the repertory of characters $z_i$ is $I_1 = 8 \log_2 = 24$ bits, is summarily reduced in two characters to the information $I_2 = 2 \log_2 = 2$ bits. Redundancy by steps is iterative and can be defined in relation to the observed steps $\nu(\nu = 1, 2, \ldots)$ by the following expression:

$$R_{st} = \frac{I_\nu - I_{\nu+1}}{I_\nu},$$

if $I_\nu$ is the information at the $\nu$-th step and $I_\nu > I_{\nu+1}$. In the above example, the redundancy by steps $R_{st} = 0{\cdot}91$. Redundancy by steps plays an important part in processes of figure-perception, learning and thinking and also in aesthetics.

**Referent**
Referent
objet d'un signe
референт

*That which is referred to in a *character, i.e. what it indicates (source) or describes (meaning).*

The referent as an indicator is the source; for example, thunder points to lightning as its source, a fugue to its composer and his distinctive style.

The referent as a representation sign is its *meaning, given to it by convention (e.g. *circle* means ○), or by being conditioned by the same cause (crackling in a wireless during a storm means imminent thunder).

MALDONADO, T.: Beitrag zur Terminologie der Semiotik. Hochschule f. Gestaltung, Ulm 1961.

**Refractory period**
Refraktärzeit
période réfractaire; temps de latence
———

*Duration of the inexcitability or decrease in excitability of excitable biological function-units.*

Due to dependence of excitability on metabolism, excitable function-units in the body such as *nerves or muscle-fibres always have a refractory period, shortly after the start of and during an *excitation. This phase of inexcitability can be divided into an absolute refractory period, in which no further excitation can occur, and a relative refractory period, during which the excitability is once more present, although at first only to a small extent.

REIN, H.; SCHNEIDER, M.: Einführung in die Physiologie des Menschen. 11th edn. Springer-Verlag, Berlin, Göttingen, Heidelberg 1960, p. 550.

**Regeneration**
Regeneration, biologische
régénération
регенерация

*The replacement or renewal of a destroyed or lost organ or *structure.*

Plants and animals are capable of repairing small injuries to their structure. This ability presupposes the existence of *communication between the cells which regenerate, although very little is known about this. The ability of regeneration is limited in higher animals by the high degree of specialization of the individual cells which can only reproduce themselves to make new specialized cells. In lower animals, the ability of regeneration is much higher: for example, crustaceans can grow new limbs in place of those which have been lost. Planaria cut in two regenerate complete new individuals from the two halves. Precisely this characteristic was used in research into the mechanism of learning. The new planaria which developed from the tail-sections showed a much higher retention of the *conditioning of the original planarium than those regenerated from the head-sections. Higher animals are not capable of regenerating their *central nervous system after injury; this is, however, possible in amphibians. SPERRY and others have shown in experiments that severed bundles of nerve-fibres show connecting structures after being severed similar to those present beforehand. It is clear that the fibre-ends at the point of bisection have the ability—probably chemical—to identify the corresponding fibre-ends in the severed bundle.

SPERRY, R. W.: Mechanisms of Neural Maturation. In: Stevens, S. S. (ed.): Handbook of Experimental Psychology. Wiley, London 1951.

**Register**
Register
registre
регистр

*A *store in information processing systems which is distinguished by special characteristics.*

Most data-processing machines have only at central points (e.g. in the *arithmetic unit) individual registers (e.g. *accumulator) into which all numbers from the store must be transported, if they are to be connected with each other. Registers are often used as *shift registers whose contents can be shifted by means of clock pulses to the left or right or cyclicly. A special group of registers in electronic *computers is formed by *index registers, which are used for *address-modification.

SPEISER, A. P.: Digitale Rechenanlagen. Springer-Verlag, Berlin, Göttingen, Heidelberg 1961.

**Regulating variable**
Stellgrösse
grandeur réglante
регулирующая величина; регулирующее воздействие

*See under* *Feedback control system, especially sections 1 and 2

**Regulator; controller**
Regler
régulateur
регулятор

*See under* *Feedback control system, especially sections 3 and 4

**Rejection value**
Rejektionswert
valeur de rejection

---

A term used in cybernetical logic for a logical value which lies outside a given alternative. Rejection value therefore transcends the system of classical bivalent logic, in which one value is always chosen from the offered alternatives. The classical system thereby becomes a subsystem, in which the rejection value represents a 'foreign' value. From the morphogrammatic point of view (see *morphogram), the purpose of rejection value is to construct a cybernetical logic which is capable of logically representing, by the introduction of various degrees of reflection, the analogous structure of the neural system and the synthetic unity of the various grades of reflection of human consciousness.

**Relay**
Relais
relais
реле

*An electro-magnetically operated switch.*
A relay consists of a soft iron core with one or more windings, one movable armature and several contact springs. If a current flows through a winding the relay attracts its armature magnetically. This operates the contacts which close the circuit (normally open contacts), open it (normally closed contacts), or divert it (diverting contacts). As it is at the moment the most frequently used type of switch (e.g. in telephone transmission) there are countless types of relays.
A rather different form, which is nowadays frequently used because of its short switching time, is the reed relay (also herkon). In this two metal elements are fused in a small glass bulb filled with protective gas (to prevent oxydation).

HEBEL, M.: Das Fernmelderelais. R. Oldenbourg, München 1956. RENSCH, H.: Der hermetisch abgeschlossene Kontakt Herkon. Elektrotechnische Zeitschrift 12, H. 12, (1960) p. 295.

**Repertory**
Repertoire; Zeichenvorrat
répertoire
репертуар

*A set of the *characters of a *code (cf. *alphabet, *probability field.)*

**Repertory, subjective**
Repertoire, subjektives
répertoire subjectif
субъективный репертуар

If one measures the *information of a *message on the finite scheme of a transmitter (e.g. the sequence of letters on the scheme of the alphabet) then this information does not need to agree with the subjective information actually recorded by a receiver—not even if the subjective and objective schemes are identical. For if the receiver is capable of forming *super-characters then it can alter the information transmitted by the transmitter by changing the repertory, which in general leads to a decrease of the information.
By the subjective repertory of a receiver one understands that repertory in which the in-going messages are actually recorded by the receiver (e.g. the transfer of a letter-repertory to a word-repertory and the sentence-repertory in reading).

**Reproductive storing**
Zeichenreproduktion
reproduction des caractères (signes)
воспроизведение или репродукция образов

*The representation or storage of a character within the character reader in a form appropriate to the recognition process.*
The signals which arise during character scanning must be processed in such a way that the features describing the character can be obtained from them. As logical decisions are most easily carried out with electrical trip circuits, the characters must generally be produced electrically.
The reproduction consists, in digital processes in the most complicated case, of the digital representation of the scanned black-white distribution of the

pattern inserted; this representation is quantized according to surface and optical density. In simpler cases, the reproduction consists of the storage of available features (criteria of shape, line elements, points of intersection, etc.) or, for example, with special scripts in the counting of the black or white code-elements along certain tracks.
In analogous character processing, no information is lost in scanning and here the reproductive storing can consist of a precise analogous electrical reproduction of the scanned character (e.g. for electrical correlation processes).

STEINBUCH, K.; KAZMIERCZAK, H.: Grundlagen und Anwendungen der automatischen Zeichenerkennung. In: Jahrbuch des elektrischen Fernmeldewesens. 1960/61.

**Requisite variety**
Requisite variety
requisite variety

The principle of requisite variety states that the abundance of alternative control actions which a control mechanism is capable of executing must be at least equal to the abundance of the spontaneous fluctuations which have to be corrected by the control mechanism if the control mechanism is to function effectively.
This principle originates from ASHBY and is roughly equal to SHANNON's tenth theorem, which refers to a noisy communication channel with a correcting channel. The spontaneous fluctuations of a *feedback control system correspond to the noise of the communication channel, and the control actions to the signals in the correcting channel.

ASHBY, W. R.: Requisite variety and its implications for the control of complex systems. Cybernetica 1 (1958), Heft 83. SHANNON, C. E.; WEAVER, W.: The Mathematical Theory of Communication. University of Illinois Press, Urbana 1949.

**'Residue' phenomenon**
'Residue' Phänomen
phénomène de résidu

*Division of the function of the acoustic sensory-organ system into the analysis of frequency and periodicity.*
Not all sound frequences are projected approximately tonotop only at the end of the *specific system (specific afferent) in the acoustic projection-cortex area, but rather, there are periodic complex sound-sequences of low frequency (important up to approx. 300 c/s) which produce no excitation of certain cell-groups which can be locally described, although they do produce subjective sensations of comparable pitch. It can be assumed that the perception of periodicities of this type is connected with excitations in the range of non-specific afferents, and that both the location and the type of processing of the frequency analysis are different (cf. *autocorrelation function).

SCHOUTEN, J. F.: Philips Techn. Rev. 5 (1940), pp. 286–94. LICKLIDER, J. C. R.: A duplex theory of pitch perception. Experention, Basel, 7 (1951), pp. 128–34. BOER, E. de: On the 'residue' in hearing. Ph.D. Thesis, Amsterdam 1956. KEIDEL, W. D.: Physiologie des Hörens. Klin. Wschr. 37 (1959), pp. 1205–17.

# S

## Sampled data control

Abtastregelung
régulation par impulsions
система дискретных данных с сбратной связью

*Control whereby the controller measures the control-value $X(t)$ only at certain intervals.*

The control loop is periodically interrupted. If the sample frequency is at least twice as high as the highest frequency contained in $X(t)$, then $X(t)$ can be re-assembled from the individual sampled values. The whole of the information contained in $X(t)$ is recorded by the controller (cf. *sampling theorem).

OLDENBOURG, R. C.; SARTORIUS, H.: Dynamik selbsttätiger Regelungen. Band 1. R. Oldenbourg, München 1951. OPPELT, W.: Kleines Handbuch technischer Regelvorgänge. Verlag Chemie, Weinheim 1960. SOLODOWNIKOW, W. W.: Grundlagen der selbsttätigen Regelung. Oldenbourg, München and Berlin 1959.

## Sampling theorem

Abtasttheorem
théorème d'échantillonage
теорема Котельникова

*States that a time function $f(t)$ whose frequency spectrum lies in the *frequency range* (0 *to* $B$ c/s) *is clearly defined by its ordinates at equidistant points which are* $1/2\ B$ *seconds apart.*

The sampling theorem is fundamental for the use of the information theory on continuous signals, because it allows the representation of a continuous signal of finite duration by means of a finite number of parameters. The same result could be obtained by the representation of the signal by the coefficients of its *FOURIER series, but this cannot be easily extended to the case of signals of infinite duration.

SHANNON, C. E.; WEAVER, W.: The Mathematical Theory of Communication. University of Illinois Press, Urbana 1949. SHANNON, C. E.: Communication in the presence of noise. Proc. I.R.E. Vol. 37 pt. 10 (1949).

## Self-organization

Selbstorganisation
autoorganisation
самоорганизация

*A comprehensive, general concept for the properties of self-reproduction, production of structural order or growth in connection with inorganic mechanisms.*

By self-organization one understands primarily thinking models whose aim is an exchange of information between a system and its environment, an exchange which permits adaption to the situation at hand. Self-organizing systems are based on the ability to recognize and to learn, and can be regarded as the preliminary steps towards achieving artificial *intelligence. In so far as the construction of an inner organization corresponding to the conditions of environment is concerned, there are some *programs for *computers by which the possibilities of self-organizing models are examined.

HAWKINS, J. K.: Self-organizing system, a review and commentary. Proc. IRE 49 (1961), pp. 31–48. YOVITTS, M. C. et al.: Self-organizing systems 1962. Spartan Books, Washington 1962.

## Semantic differential

Polaritätsprofil; semantisches Differential
différential semantique

———

*A method of comprehension of the connotations of concepts or any other perceivable data.*

Semantic differential was developed

almost simultaneously by HOFSTÄTTER and OSGOOD working independently of each other. A concept, or any other perceivable data (pictures, colours, sounds of instruments, etc.), is comprehended, in so far as the connotative meaning is concerned, by being arranged by different test-subjects on several scales which are spread between two adjectives of opposite meaning. The pairs of adjectives (e.g. hard-soft, happy-sad, etc.) are called polarities. For a concept which has been assessed, the arithmetical average of the arrangements can be formed for each polarity-scale. The vector of the average values forms the semantic differential of the assessed concept. OSGOOD takes this analysis further by calculating correlations (cf. *correlation coefficient) between the scales. A *factor analysis of the resultant intercorrelation matrix leads to a number of factors which are understood as orthogonal co-ordinates of a multi-dimensional *semantic space* in which the assessed concepts can be located. HOFSTÄTTER obtains a semantic space by factor analysis of the correlations between the profiles of different assessed concepts, which can be interpreted as the measured values of the similarities. This space has at least three statistically assured dimensions which can be described by an orthogonal co-ordinate system, whose axes can be placed by the positions of the concepts *male*, *female*, and *loneliness*.

HOFSTÄTTER, P. R.; LÜBBERT, H.: Die Untersuchung von Stereotypen mit Hilfe des Polaritätsprofiles. Zeitschrift für Markt- und Meinungsforschung 1 (1958). HOFSTÄTTER, P. R.: Über Ähnlichkeit. Psyche 9 (1959). OSGOOD, C. E.; SUCI, G. J.; TANNENBAUM, P. H.: The Measurement of Meaning. Illinois Univ. Press, Urbana 1957.

**Semantics**
Semantik
sémantique
семантика

*Representation of the meaning of a formalized *language in a *meta language.*
A calculus defined by syntax (formal system) becomes a formalized language (see *languages, formalized) by interpretation. By interpretation is understood a projection of the expressions of a calculus to items and relations which are not normally of a linguistic nature, and which are already known independently of the calculus.
In classical propositional logic (cf. *Boolean algebra) this interpretation occurs by allotting the expressions truth values. If in an interpretation an expression has the value *true*, then this interpretation satisfies the expression. If the expression is satisfied by any interpretation, then it is called generally valid. Generally valid expressions of propositional logic can be obtained as sentences of a propositional calculus.

CHURCH, A.: Introduction to Mathematical Logic. Princeton University Press 1956. HERMES, H.: Einführung in die mathematische Logik. Teubner Verlag, Stuttgart 1963.

**Semi-conductor**
Halbleiter
semi-conducteur
полупроводник

*Material whose electrical conduction lies somewhere between the conduction of metals and that of insulators.*
In a more precise sense one understands by *semi-conductor* structure elements built up on the basis of semi-conductive materials (cf. *diodes, *transistors). Diodes are used in rectification, transistors are used in amplifiers and as control switches.

SPENKE, E.: Elekronische Halbleiter. Springer-Verlag, Berlin, Göttingen, Heidelberg 1956. DOSSE, J.: Der Transistor, ein neues Verstärkerelement. R. Oldenbourg, München 1960.

**Semiotic aspects of characters**
Zeichenfunktion
fonction de signes
функция образа

*The various functions of a sign or *character (a) in an examination solely of the character itself, (b) in an examination of what it denotes, and (c) the statement of what it aims at.*

The syntactical semiotic aspect abstracts from the *referent and from the receiver and examines only the probability of the occurrence of the characters (statistical aspect), the laws according to which characters are combined to form *supercharacters (constructive aspect), and finally the ability of the characters to encode diverse meanings (semantic aspect).

The semantic semiotic aspect abstracts only from the receiver (and the source) and consists of the function of encoding of the meaning with its various probabilities (statistical aspect), its coherence (constructive aspect) and its ability to be a description of the goal (pragmatic aspect).

The pragmatic semiotic aspect consists of the statement triggered off by the character with the *imperative which it expresses. This statement is triggered off by the imperative meeting the normative-ideological prior decision of the receiver or its actual goal. The imperatives can again become of interest with regard to their various probabilities (statistical aspect) or with regard to their location of a strategy or of a normative-ideological system.

FRANK, H.: Kybernetische Grundlagen der Pädagogik. Ch. III, Agis, Baden-Baden 1962.

**Semiotics**
Semiotik
semiotique
семиотика

*General theory of language characters.*

The object of semiotics is *language. A language in the most general sense is characterized as follows: it consists of an *alphabet with a supply of *characters and rules, according to which words can be formed from the characters.

A language which is used in communication is called a communicative language. To this type belong the formalized languages of science as well as natural languages in the sense of linguistics. Scientific semiotics, according to MORRIS and CARNAP, can be divided into three areas: *syntax, *semantics and pragmatics.

Syntax is limited to propositions regarding the formal structure of the character sequence; the meaning of the latter is considered in semantics, whilst in pragmatics the users of the language are included.

CARNAP, R.: Einführung in die symbolische Logik. Springer, Wien 1954.

**Sequence control register**
Befehlsfolgezähler
compteur ordinal
счетчик команд

*Part of the *control unit of a *computer.*

In the sequence control register the *address of an *instruction which is being carried out is stored and increased by 1. This gives the address of the following instruction, provided that the instruction which has just been carried out is not a jump instruction.

**Sequential coding**
Reihenverfahren
procédé des séries; méthode des séries
однокоординатная адресация

A process to represent *characters $A_i$ of an *alphabet $i$ by characters $A_j$ of an alphabet $j$, in which a character $A_j$ is allocated to every character $A_i$. For the representation of $n$ characters according to sequential coding, up to $n$ different symbols are necessary.
Example: Roman numerals.
Alphabet $i$:
1st no.; 2nd no.; 3rd no.; etc.
Alphabet $j$:
I II III

ZEMANEK, H.: Elementare Informationstheorie. R. Oldenbourg, Wien and München 1959.

**Serial operation**
Seriensystem
opération série
последовательная система

*A system in which the *characters of a word are transmitted in a channel in sequence and processed sequentially.*
One must distinguish between series-series-operation and series-parallel-operation. In series-series-operation the characters of a word (and within these also the code elements from which the characters are formed) are transmitted and processed in sequence, whilst in series-parallel-operation the characters of a word are transmitted and processed in sequence, but the code elements of the characters are transmitted and processed in their own channels simultaneously and independently of each other.

**Series-parallel-system**
Serien-Parallelsystem
système série-parallèle
последовательно—параллельная система

*Concept in the construction of programmed computers.*
A distinction is made between parallel-operating machines and series machines. The difference can be demonstrated by a simple calculation operation: numerical computers encode the numbers of the decimal system into a system of *binary characters, in which the individual decimal numbers are normally represented by 4 to 7 binary numbers. In parallel machines all digits of this system are processed simultaneously in a calculation operation; any carries which may be necessary are executed in a further beat. In series machines each figure is treated individually from right to left one after the other; carries are taken into account immediately. Series machines need only one channel for the transmission of information in the *arithmetic unit. The *computing time depends on the length of the word. Parallel machines are technically not so economical (several channels) but work much more quickly. To take advantage of both types, many machines are constructed as series-parallel-machines. The treatment of the binary characters which correspond to a decimal number is parallel. The processing of the individual decimal numbers is carried out in series.

KNÖDEL, W.: Programmieren von Ziffernrechenanlagen. Springer-Verlag, Wien 1961.

**Servomechanism**
*See under* *Feedback control system

**Set point**
*See* *Index value

**SHEFFER's stroke; non-conjunction**
SHEFFERscher Strich
opération de SHEFFER
штрих Шеффера

## She

*A binary logical connective with the symbol | or $\overline{\wedge}$ and meaning 'not both'.*
Truth table:

| | | | | |
|---|---|---|---|---|
| $a$ | $T$ | $T$ | $F$ | $F$ |
| $b$ | $T$ | $F$ | $T$ | $F$ |
| $a \mid b$ | $F$ | $T$ | $T$ | $T$ |

The expression in terms of *negation, *disjunction and *conjunction (cf. *Boolean algebra) is as follows:

$$a \mid b = \overline{a \wedge b} = \bar{a} \vee \bar{b}$$

Negation and disjunction and therefore all other binary logical connectives can be expressed by SHEFFER's stroke:

$$\bar{a} = a \mid a$$
$$a \vee' b = (a \mid a) \mid (b \mid b)$$

## Shift register
Schieberegister
registre coulissant; registre de décalage
регистр сдвига

*A *register used in information processing systems which permits the shifting of stored information by one position in response to a shift pulse.*

Between the individual elements for the storage of individual *bits there are auxiliary stores which during transfer take over for a short time the information of the preceding location. Flip-flops are frequently used for bit-stores and capacitors for the auxiliary stores. Simple linear shift registers can be used as series-parallel-*transducers, since a code-word being inserted location by location can be read simultaneously from all the register locations and vice versa.

Feedback shift registers permit additional shifting in a ring, whereas normally digits leaving the register are lost. A shift register can serve as the *arithmetic unit or the *accumulator of a *computer. According to the use made of them, there are parallel linear shift registers (e.g. in *series-parallel-systems), or two or more dimensional shift registers which can be used in *registration centring.

SPEISER, A. P.: Digitale Rechenanlagen. Springer-Verlag, Berlin, Göttingen, Heidelberg 1961.

## Short-term memory
Kurzspeicher
mémoire phosphorescente
оперативная память; временная память; оперативное запоминающее устройтво

*A model conception in the *theory of information which is considered as realized by those central-nervous instances or levels whose function is connected with *consciousness.*

The recording of only one consciousness-content can take place in every *moment (narrowness of the consciousness). This recording (cf. *apperception) can extend over several moments if the *information of what is being recorded is great enough. HOFSTÄTTER says that the *super-characters (e.g. figures), which become conscious in this way, go through a development ('actual genesis') which, under suitable conditions, leads from diffuse, strongly dynamic initial states (i.e. 'prefigures' or 'figure seeds') to pregnant and clearly articulated 'final figures'. The recording speed of the short-term memory is $C_k = 16$ bit/sec. of subjective information. Whatever is recorded in the short-term memory remains present in the consciousness for the *duration $T$ by retaining the sequence, unless it is prolonged in the consciousness by the application of attentiveness. The storage capacity of the short term memory is at the most $K_k = C_k T$, i.e. lies between 100 and 160 bits. (For information-theory reasons a maximum of 32 signs can be present in the consciousness at one time:

'narrowness of the consciousness' in the second meaning of this expression.) A linear *shift register with 160 binary locations and a constant shift pulse of 1 moment has been suggested as the crudest information-theory model of a short-term memory.

HOFSTÄTTER, P. R.: Psychologie. S. Fischer Verlag, Frankfurt/M. 1957. FRANK, H.: Kybernetische Grundlagen der Pädagogik—eine Einführung in die Informationspsychologie, Agis, Baden-Baden 1962.

**Sign**

*See* *Character

**Signal**

Signal; Zeichenträger
signal
сигнал

*A physical state (beam of a signalling lamp, distribution of printer's ink on paper) or a process (flow of speech-modulated current through a telephone cable, spread of a sound wave) which serves to transmit *messages.*

If a physical system at a point in time $t_i$ can accept a condition $S$ or can transmit the process of development $S$ during the period of time from $t_i$ to $t_i + \Delta t_i$, and if $S$ is perceived by a receiver, then $S$ is called a signal. The physical system whose condition or development is $S_x$ normally represents a *channel.

STEINBUCH, K.: Automat und Mensch. 2nd edn. Springer-Verlag, Berlin, Göttingen, Heidelberg 1963.

**Similarity**

Ähnlichkeit
similitude; resemblance
сходство; подобие

*Connection between similar objects. Transformation which does not alter the form of the objects but their dimensions in a given relationship. In this, characteristic dimensionless terms for the structure or for the function of a class of objects remain unaltered.*

In geometry, similarity is the product of homothety rotation and translation. In physics, especially applied physics, rules have been developed by which measurements of one machine may be obtained from another or from a *model where certain dimensionless terms remain constant. This permits the transfer of rules of construction (e.g. in tests on scale models). In cybernetics, experience has shown that functional models are more advantageous in use than structural models; so *analogy is preferred to similarity. In psychology, similarity possesses a meaning very close to 'parity, equality'.

BRUN, E.; MARTINOT-LARGARDE, A.: Mécanique des fluides. Vol. I, pt. I, Dunod, Paris 1959. FELIX, L.: Exposé moderne des mathématiques élémentaires. pp. 367–70. Dunod, Paris 1962. HOFSTÄTTER, P. R.: Über die Ähnlichkeit. Psyche 9 (1955).

**Simulation of strategic games**

Simulation strategischer Spiele
simulation de jeux stratégiques

———

*Imitation of a mathematical *model for the execution of a game by means of a *program in an *automaton.*

In the theory of games, *algorithms are developed which permit the treatment of certain games by means of *computers. If the game is dependent on random events or if random decisions are necessary, then these can be defined by a *random number generator. Incomplete *information on situations in the game can be completed by experience of the program. If this information influences the decisions, then the program can improve its playing ability by analogy to learning processes (cf. *learning).

**Simulator**
Simulator
simulateur
моделирующее счетно- решающее устройство; симулятор; имитирующее устройство

*Imitation of a *model for certain actions. This simulation can be achieved analogously (cf. *analogous) or by a program in a *computer.*

An analogue device simulates processes of a similar behaviour, such as multiplication by OHM's law. In general, simulation facilitates the execution of experiments if the model is already available or can be produced economically. Simulation of a process may take place with either a different time-scale or the same 'real time' scale.

In computers, a program which alters the behaviour of the automaton and thereby permits the processing of another program written in a *pseudocode, is called a simulator or an interpreting system. This simulator must be available throughout the processing time of the pseudo-program; it interprets the program written in the pseudo-language instruction by instruction and carries them out. A simulator therefore results in a transformation of the computer used into another with another *machine code. Occasionally, even a program used to imitate certain processes is called a simulator, e.g. in the *simulation of strategic games.

**Source; transmitter**
Quelle
source
источник

The part of the information system in which the *message originates is called the source. Mathematically, a source $[A, q]$ is a *stochastic process with the *alphabet $A$ and the probability-measure $q$. For a definition of the source the probabilities $q(A)$ of all finite sequences of letters from $A$ must be given.

GRELL, H. (ed.): Arbeiten zur Informationstheorie, I, II. Dtsch. Vlg. d. Wissenschaften, Berlin 1957. HENZE, E.: Einführung in die Informationstheorie. Beiheft 3, Elektronische Datenverarbeitung, 2nd edition 1965.

**Source; ergodic**
Quelle, ergodische
source ergodique
эргодический источник

A *source is called ergodic if a chronological shift with probability 'one' mixes not only parts of the *message space, but the whole message space.

A set of messages $S$ is called invariant (cf. *invariance) if the shift-operator
$T: Tx = x'$,

$$x = \{\ldots, x_{-1}, x_0, x_1, x_2, \ldots\};$$
$$x' = \{\ldots, x_0, x_1, x_2, x_3, \ldots\}$$

does not alter the probability of $S$:

$$q(TS) = q(S).$$

A source is called ergodic if from

$$q(TS) = q(S)$$

there results either

$$q(S) = 0 \text{ or } q(S) = 1,$$

hence this subset of messages has the probability 0, or is the whole message space.

GRELL, H. (ed.): Arbeiten zur Informationstheorie, I. Dtsch. Vlg. d. Wissenschaften, Berlin 1959. HENZE, E.: Einführung in die Informationstheorie. Beiheft 3, Elektronische Datenverarbeitung, 2nd edition 1965.

**Source, stationary**
Quelle, stationäre
source stationnaire
стационарный источник

A *source $[A, q]$ is called stationary if its probability-theoretic structure is invariant (cf. *invariant). If $S$ is any $q$-measurable set of messages, a $q$-measurable subset of the *message-space of the source, i.e. of the infinite series $\{x_i\}$ $x_i \in A$, in which $A$ is the alphabet of the source, then

$$q(TS) = q(S)$$

must always be valid with the shift-operator $T$ which shifts the message

$$x = \{\ldots, x_{-1}, x_0, x_1, x_2, \ldots\}$$

by one time unit, in other words where

$$Tx = x'$$

with

$$x' = \{\ldots, x_0, x_1, x_2, x_3, \ldots\}.$$

GRELL, H. (ed.): Arbeiten zur Informationstheorie I. Dtsch. Vlg. d. Wissenschaften, Berlin 1957. HENZE, E.: Einführung in die Informationstheorie. Beiheft 3, Elektronische Datenverarbeitung, 2nd edition 1965.

**Specific system; specific afferent**
Bahn, spezifische
voie spécifique; afférent spécifique
путь (связь)специфический

*Direct connection including several central-nervous relay-stations between the peripheral transformation organ (cf. *receptor, *sensory cell) and the primary cortical projection area specific to the pertinent sensory-organ system.*

In the acoustic sensory-organ system the specific system, built up for example in the sense of a convergence-divergence-switch, passes from the hair cells of the basilar membrane through several relay nuclei of the central *nervous system (cochlear nuclei, trapezoid bodies, upper olive, lemniscus lateralis, colliculus superior and inferior, corpus geniculatum mediale) to the primary acoustic projection cortex. Specific systems have self re-exciting chains radiating from the individual relay stations, bilateral intermeshing and the branching-off of the *non-specific system across the main brain.

KEIDEL, W. D.: Grundprinzipien der akustischen und taktilen Informationsverarbeitung. Ergebnisse der Biologie, 26 (1961), pp. 213–46.

**Spectrum**
Spektrum
spectre
спектр

*The frequency or spectral representation of a time-function.*

In information theory, the spectrum of an absolutely integrable time-function $F(t)$ is understood to be the FOURIER transform

$$f(\omega) = \frac{1}{\sqrt{2\pi}} \int_{-\infty}^{\infty} e^{-i\omega t} F(t)\, \mathrm{d}t.$$

The time-function then has the spectral-representation

$$F(t) = \frac{1}{\sqrt{2\pi}} \int_{-\infty}^{\infty} e^{i\omega t} f(\omega)\, \mathrm{d}\omega.$$

In the case of a periodic function $F(t)$ with the period $T$, the spectrum has discrete lines at the frequencies

$$\nu/T,\ \nu = 0, \pm 1, \pm 2, \ldots$$

with the amplitudes $a_\nu$. The time-function then has the FOURIER series

$$F(t) = \sum_{\nu=-\infty}^{\infty} a_\nu\, e^{i\nu \frac{2\pi t}{T}}.$$

The power spectrum is the integral $H(f) = \int_{-\infty}^{f} h(\nu)\, \mathrm{d}\nu$ of the power spectral density $h(f)$—if it exists—which is the FOURIER transform of the *autocorrelation function $\varphi(\tau)$ of $F(t)$:

$$h(\nu) = \frac{1}{\sqrt{2\pi}} \int_{-\infty}^{\infty} e^{-2\pi i \nu \tau} \varphi(\tau)\, \mathrm{d}\,\tau.$$

In this, $F(t) = X_t(\omega)$, $\omega \in \Omega$ fixed can also be a realization of a *stochastic process.

FETZER, V.: Einschwingvorgänge in der Nachrichtentechnik. Porta-Verlag, München and Verlag Technik, Berlin 1958.

**Speech recognition**
Spracherkennung, automatische
reconnaissance automatique du langage
автоматическое опознавание (узнавание) речи; машинное распознавание устной речи

*A clear automatic identification of character units (spoken words, syllables, phonemes) of a language on the basis of the acoustic signal. The reproduction of the corresponding ability in man.*

Digital signals are deduced from the spoken sound signal by linear and non-linear signal processing or by complex analysis in *computers; the pattern of these signals clearly represents the linguistic units independent of the situation and the speaker.

A complete and faultless automatic recognition of speech would only be possible if practically all intelligent skills were capable of automization: at the present moment, however, this is a utopian dream. An automatic recognition of articulated sounds does seem possible, however, if certain conditions regarding the articulation are observed, namely that it be especially clear, slow and split up into words or even syllables. Even the recognition of speech such as this is extremely complicated. It is impossible to estimate the cost, both financial and in effort, of a satisfactory solution to this problem.

All that is possible to-day is the recognition of limited vocabularies (or, more generally, of sequences of acoustic complexes, i.e. of codes constructed specially for automatic recognition).

MEYER-EPPLER, W.: Automatische Spracherkennung. In: Steinbuch, K. (ed.): Taschenbuch der Nachrichtenverarbeitung. Pp. 831–43. Springer-Verlag, Berlin, Göttingen, Heidelberg 1962. SCHNELLE, J.: Automatische Spracherkennung. In: Frank, H. (ed.): Kybernetische Maschinen. S. Fischer, Frankfurt/M., Reihe Welt im Werden 1964.

**Spike**
Spike
spike
спайк

*See* *Action potential

**Stability**
Stabilität
stabilité
стабильность; устойчивость

*The property of a system which enables it to return to its original state after a disturbance.*

If a variable *a* remains constant after a transformation *T*, then *a* is stable with respect to *T*. If a class of variable is unaltered after applying *T*, in which each individual variable does not have to remain constant, then this class is also stable with respect to *T*. With continual transformation the variables form a state of stability which is not altered by *T*. One also says that the transformation for the variable *a* or for the class of variables is closed.

Stability is predominantly a concept of the mechanics of mass systems and more generally of the theory of any oscillation systems, especially in feedback circuits. Stability is defined differently by different writers, e.g. a process of oscillation or the solution of the differential equation system is said to be stable if the solution is limited, e.g. the values of the variables which adjust themselves as a result of finite input values or initial values cannot become infinitely large. According to LIAPUNOV a process determined by certain initial values is stable if processes which are determined by slightly different initial values are themselves only slightly different. A process is asymptotically stable if other initial values determine processes which approach the first with increasing time ($t \to \infty$). Of especial interest is the asymptotic stability to the static state (fading of all oscillations towards zero). It can often be established whether a process is stable without completely defining it, e.g. without calculating the solution of the differential equation. There are several algebraic and graphic criteria, especially for linear systems, which enable a decision on the question of stability to be made from the coefficients of the differential equation or of the *transfer function, or from the measured *frequency response.

Control circuits with *feedback are good examples of stable systems. The tendency of a system such as this to approach a certain state was often understood as a finality. In systems built by man, this finality was determined by the construction. Phylogeny shows that the finality of living organisms is only fictitious. It can be established that man selects from all possible machines those whose stability enables a continuous functioning. In this sense DARWIN's theory can be extended in such a way that only stable biological or mechanical systems survive.

The stability of a system is based on its *structure. With an increased development of its *organization, a system is not influenced by external disturbances or incidents. A stable system has its own standard of quantity and quality (in HEGEL's sense).

A system is ultra-stable if it remains unaltered by the most extreme disturbances or changes of its surroundings. If a disturbance goes beyond a certain level, then the ultra-stable system adopts another pattern of behaviour. These can be regarded as stages of a multi-stage function.

A system is multi-stable if it consists of several ultra-stable systems which are functionally connected at discrete moments.

KLAUS, G.: Kybernetik in philosophischer Sicht. Pt. 1, Ch. 5. Dietz, Berlin 1961. ASHBY, W. R.: An Introduction to Cybernetics. Chapman and Hall, London. MALKIN, J. G.: Theorie der Stabilität einer Bewegung. Oldenbourg, Berlin and München 1959. PETERS, J.: Einschwingvorgänge, Gegenkopplung, Stabilität. Springer-Verlag, Berlin, Göttingen, Heidelberg 1954.

**Steersman**
Steuermann
timonier
штурман; рулевой

*Paradigm for the level at which instructions are translated into intervention in the conversion of energy in a controlled system. In* 1948 *WIENER formed the expression* *cybernetics *from the Greek word for steersman (which later referred to the *pilot).*

The steersman reacts to the steering instructions of the pilot and by activating the helm intervenes in the conversion of energy which is necessary for the progress of the ship without, however (in contrast to the oarsman), making a physical contribution to the propulsion of the ship.

The function of the steersman can easily be generalized outside the nautical sphere (cf. *cybernetics, levels of). In transferring it to the spheres of technical systems or biological processes of control, it must be noted that one does not presuppose any conscious allocation of physical measures to *understood* characters or signs (in respect of their semantic and pragmatic semiotic aspect), but rather an alteration in the condition of a *correcting element causally induced by a *signal. Only for heuristic purposes is there here (more especially at the pilot level) a projection of the problem from the physical level to the intuitively more easily accessible informational level.

WIENER, N.: Kybernetik. Econ, Düsseldorf 1963. DUCROCQ, A.: Die Entdeckung der Kybernetik. Europäische Verlagsanstalt, Frankfurt 1959. FRANK, H.: Kybernetik—Brücke zwischen den Wissenschaften. Pt. I. Umschau, Frankfurt (1961).

**Step function**
Sprungfunktion
fonction de choc
скачкообразная функция; функция включения

*A time function which is zero for times $t < t_0$, and has the constant value 'One' for time $t > t_0$. The value for $t = t_0$ is not defined.*

A step function is distinguished by the simple form both of its variation with time and its *spectrum and is therefore often used, as is the *pulse function, as a test signal in *system theory and in control systems. If a step function is given as an input signal to a system, then the output signal obtained is called *step response. A linear system can be fully characterized by it.

FETZER, V.: Einschwingvorgänge in der Nachrichtentechnik. Porta-Verlag, München and Verlag-Technik, Berlin 1958. OPPELT, W.: Kleines Handbuch technischer Regelvorgänge. 2nd edn. Verlag Chemie, Weinheim 1956.

**Step response**
Übergangsfunktion; Sprungantwort
fonction de passage; choc de réponse
передаточная функция; переходная функция

*Time function of the output value of a *linear system which results from a step-like alteration of the input value of the value 'one'.*

The input function which causes step response at the output is therefore exactly expressed: $x(t) = \begin{cases} 0 \text{ for } t < 0 \\ 1 \text{ for } t > 0. \end{cases}$

Step response has the advantages in practice of simple measurability and of the clear representation of the transfer properties of a system. The relations of the step response $\varphi(t)$ to the other types of marking of a linear system can be represented mathematically quite simply. If, for example, $H(s)$ is the *transfer function then the LAPLACE transform of the step response is: $L\{\varphi(t)\} = \frac{H(s)}{s}$.

OLDENBOURG, R. C.; SARTORIUS, H.: Dynamik selbsttätiger Regelungen. Bd. 1. Oldenbourg, München 1951. OPPELT, W.: Kleines Handbuch technischer Regelvorgänge. Verlag Chemie, Weinheim 1960. SOLODOWNIKOW, W. W.: Grundlagen der selbsttätigen Regelung. Oldenbourg, München and Berlin 1959.

**Stimulus, physiological**
Reiz, physiologischer
stimulus
раздражитель

*All states, within or outside an organism, which can be physically or chemically defined and which stimulate excitable function units (especially *receptors).*

In sensory physiology one describes as adequate stimuli for a sense organ those stimulus modalities (such as deviations in pressure, electro-magnetic waves) which firstly are appropriate to the anatomic function of the sense organ and secondly can release an *excitation with a minimum of energy. The range of intensity within which the stimulus can cause excitation in its wake is limited amongst other things by upper and lower *thresholds (*absolute threshold and intensity threshold). Strengths of stimuli can also be divided into temporal, local or absolute differences of two amounts of energy, which at that moment are capable of producing different excitations. (*See* *Difference threshold, local-, time- and space thresholds). Before *encoding into a conducted nervous excitation a stimulus-transformation takes place in the *receptor.

However, any incident excitation (action potential sequence) in a combined action of excitable function-units which takes place purely within an organ can be called the stimulus of the excitable function unit at which it is directed.

REIN, H.; SCHNEIDER, W.: Einführung in die Physiologie des Menschen. 11th edn. Springer-Verlag, Berlin, Göttingen, Heidelberg 1960, p. 550. RANKE, O. F.: Allgemeine Physiologie der Sinnesorgane. In: Lehmann. G. (ed.): Handbuch der gesamten Arbeitsmedizin. Urban and Schwarzenberg, München, Berlin, Wien 1962.

**Stimulus, psychological**
Reiz, psychologischer
stimulus
раздражитель

*Any factor which can affect an organism in such a way that the latter shows patterns of behaviour which are influenced by this factor.*

This concept is not used as uniformly in psychology as might be desired in the interests of clarity. Sometimes stimuli are understood as all given facts or states outside an organism, or physiologically within the body belonging to the organism, which can be defined physically or chemically and which can excite a *receptor. (Apart from this, an intervening variable in some theories (cf. HULL) is called a drive stimulus, in so far as its function in the theory is to trigger off patterns of behaviour.) Every stimulus has a sensory modality and an intensity. For every stimulus modality (e.g. pressure variations, electro-magnetic oscillations of certain frequencies) the range of the intensities (which are a condition for the effectiveness of the factor as a stimulus) is limited by an upper and a lower threshold (cf. *psychophysics). The total of all stimuli which affect an organism at one time is the stimulus field. Facts or states whose existence outside the organism can be chemically or physically proved are often called stimuli and in some theories are often taken as infinite sets of stimulus elements from which an organism takes a random sample in perception.

HOFSTÄTTER, P. R.: Psychologie. Fischer Lexikon 6, Frankfurt 1957.

**Stochastic; random**
stochastisch; zufällig
stochastique; aléatoire
стохастический; случайный

*Stochastic is simply a synonym for random (in older literature also 'statistical').*

**Stochastic process, stationary**
stochastischer Prozess, stationärer
processus stochastique stationnaire
стохастический процесс

A stochastic process $\{X_t, t \in T\}$ is called strictly stationary if its distribution functions of the *random variables

$$X_{t_1}, X_{t_2}, \ldots, X_{t_n}$$

and

$$X_{t_1+\tau}, X_{t_2+\tau}, \ldots X_{t_n+\tau}$$

are identical, i.e. if its probability theoretical structure is invariant (cf. *invariance) to a time shift. The multidimensional distribution functions

$$F t_1 t_2 \ldots t_n (x_1, x_2, \ldots, x_n)$$

then depend only on the differences

$$t_2 - t_1, t_3 - t_1, \ldots, t_n - t_1.$$

The process is called weakly stationary

if the second moments exist, i.e.

$$E\{|X_t|^2\} < \infty$$

and the *autocorrelation-function

$$E\{X_t X_\tau\}$$

depends only on the difference $t - \tau$.

DOOB, J. L.: Stochastic Processes. Wiley, New York 1953. ROSENBLATT, M.: Random Processes. Oxford Univ. Press, New York 1962.

**Store; storage; memory**
Speicher
mémoire
аккумулятор; запоминающее устройство; накопитель

*A device for the storage of program, data and results in information processing systems.*

Information is mostly stored magnetically. The carriers used are of various types, e.g. magnetic tape, magnetic drums, magnetic discs or magnetic cores. With the exception of magnetic tape, an address is allocated to each store location in the store which is specified during reading and writing. A location can always accept a machine word. The most important measures of a store are *capacity and *access time.

SPEISER, A. P.: Digitale Rechenanlagen. Springer-Verlag, Berlin, Göttingen, Heidelberg 1961.

**Structure**
Struktur; inneres Gefüge
structure
структура; строение

*The interrelationship of elements of a system.*

In an extended sense structure is an abstract form which is transposed from the imaginary to reality.

The structural classification of a system results from the structure of its elements (anatomy) and not from their function or hierarchical position (physiology). The structural complexity $C_s$ is given by

$$C_s = -\sum_{i=1}^{n} p_i \log_2 p_i$$

with $p_i$ as the frequency of the element $i$.

Structural analogy, which leads to structural models, is in general heuristically less productive than functional analogy.

WIESER, W.: Organismen, Maschinen, Strukturen. S. Fischer, Frankfurt 1959. MOLES, A. A.: Über konstruktionelle und instrumentelle Komplexität. Grundlagenstudien, Band 1, No. 2 (1960).

**Subcortical nuclei**
subkortikale Kerne
noyaux sous-corticaux
субкортекс

*Parts of the grey matter inside the great brain and the peduncle.*

These nuclei surround the thalamus or the optic region formed from several nuclei whose main function is the relay of sensory pathways. Subcortical nuclei are also part of the relays for the control of movement (connection to the corpus striatum), as well as participating in cortical activating mechanisms (reticular thalamic system).

Moreover, subcortical nuclei include the corpus striatum (putamen, pallidum and nucleus caudatus, which belong to the systems of movement control), the red nucleus, the nucleus niger, and the subthalamic basal ganglion as relays in the extrapyramidal paths.

**Sub-routine**
Unterprogramm; Prozedur
sous-programme; sous-routine
подпрограмма

*A *program for the execution of a well-defined *algorithm, which in a program of a hierarchically higher stage can take over the solution of a subproblem.*

A distinction is made between a closed

and an open sub-routine, depending on whether the sub-routine can be used and stored independently of the main program. A sub-routine demands the observance of certain conventions regarding the preparation of the parameters used in the sub-routine, and a closed sub-routine demands also the saving of the address for its return to the main program.
Sub-programs for algorithms which are frequently used are kept in program libraries.

**Summation**
Summation
sommation
суммация

*Nonlinear integration of excitations in *synapses.*
Local summation is the name normally given to the integration of converging information in higher processing centres of the body. Local summation can be subdivided into temporal summation of individual excitations which occur at the synapses as a result of the large *time constants for the information and destruction of the excitatory substance. The excitatory state of the synapse can be increased stepwise with the number of pre-synaptic signals and with their sequence frequency. (cf. *decoding.)

ECCLES, J. C.: The psychology of nerve cells. John Hopkins Press, Baltimore 1957.

**Super-character; super-sign**
Superzeichen
super-signe

---

*A *character which itself consists of characters (e.g. a word consisting of sounds) or the sum total of equivalent characters (e.g. the perfect fifth represented by various chords, e.g. C—G, D—A, E—B, etc.).*
A super-character is produced from the *hierarchization of its sub-characters. Hierarchization can be based on class-formation or complex-formation. In this case, the super-character always contains less *information than each of its sub-characters; at least, in the first case the expectancy value of the information of the super-character never exceeds the sum of the expectancy values of the information content of the sub-characters. Hierarchization enables one to have an overall view of a complex message despite the limited recording ability and capacity of the *short-term memory.

**Surprise value**
Überraschungswert
degré de surprise

---

*Relationship of the *information of a *character or of an event to the *uncertainty which is removed by this information.*
Information is not a suitable measure for the value of surprise effected by a character or an event. If one is interested in what the next result of a roulette game will be, then one is faced with a *field of events $X$ of 37 equally probable possibilities: the uncertainty is therefore $H(X) = \log_2 37 \approx 5{\cdot}209$ bit. If the result is 11, then one is not unduly surprised by this information ($I \approx 5{\cdot}209$ bit). If however one is only interested whether in a roulette game zero turns up or not, then one is faced with a field $Y$ with two possibilities of different probability, and the uncertainty is only $H(Y) \approx 0{\cdot}147$ bit. If zero does turn up, then this result in the field $Y$ has the same information (approx. 5·209 bit) as 11 had in the field $X$; yet the surprise is

unmistakably much greater. A measure of the surprise $S(z_i)$ could be the quotient:

$$s(z_i) = \frac{I(z_i)}{H(Z)}$$

In our example one obtains from this:

$s$ (zero) $\approx$ 5·209 : 0·147 $\approx$ 35·556.

The other possible result in the field $Y$, i.e. zero does not turn up, has only the information $\log_2 37/36$ bit $\approx$ 0·040 bit, from which results the much smaller surprise value:

$s$ (not zero) $\approx$ 0·040 : 0·147 $\approx$ 0·270.

If the information (as in the example of field $X$) is equal to its expectancy value, then the surprise value is exactly equal to 1. If the constant repetition of a situation $Z$ results in *probability learning on the part of the observer, then the probability distribution in the field $Z$ depends on the point of time $t$. It then corresponds to the above relation:

$$s(z_i; t) = \frac{I(z_i; t)}{H(Z(t))}$$

The chronological density of the surprise resulting from the character or event $z_i$, namely

$$a(z_i) = \frac{1}{N} \sum_{t=1}^{N} \frac{I(z_i;t) \times T(i;t)}{H(Z(t))}$$

with $T(i; t) = 1$ if the event (character) observed at the point of time $t$ was $z_i$, otherwise $T(i; t) = 0$, is called the notability of $z_i$. If no probability learning occurs, this equation is simplified to $a(z_i) = h(z_i) \times s(z_i)$, in which $h(z_i)$ is the relative frequency of $z_i$. The measure of notability has been confirmed in many various ways in informational psychology (cf. *maximum effect).

FRANK, H.: Informationspsychologie und Nachrichtentechnik. In: Wiener, N.; Schadé, J. P. (eds.): Nerve, Brain and Memory Models. Elsevier Publishing Company, Amsterdam 1963. FRANK, H.: Information et Pédagogie. Cybernética, Namur, Band 1 VI, No. 1 (1963). FRANK, H.: Kybernetische Analysen. Schnelle, Quickborn 1964.

**Switching algebra**
Schaltalgebra
algébre des circuits
алгебра релейных схем; алгебра логики

*Mathematical formulation to describe switching processes.*

Switching algebra serves as a special application of *Boolean algebra in the analysis and synthesis of switching networks in information processing. The two values of the variables (polyvalent switching algebra is nowadays of little importance in switching circuits) correspond to switching states of the network, whose connection between input and output is represented by a switching function. A simple interpretation for a switching variable is a relay contact which is open unless closed by an excitation. Let the transfer function of an *adder be given as an example:

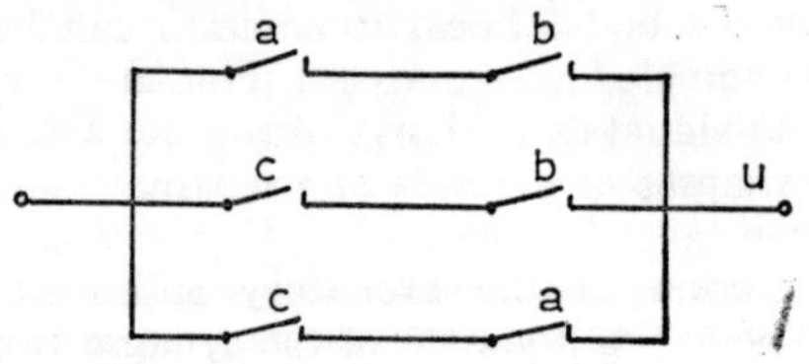


Switching algebra:

$$u = (a \mathbin{\&} b) \vee (b \mathbin{\&} c) \vee (a \mathbin{\&} c).$$

Contact $a$ is open if $a = 0$; contact $a$ is shut if $a = 1$.

It will be seen that this circuit is not optimal, but can be simplified by the use of the methods of switching algebra (minimization of switching networks). Technical realizations of such functions occur with the help of *logical circuits. In accordance with its connections with set theory and propositional logic, switching algebra is not dependent on time. By the introduction of delay elements and discrete cycles, however, even circuits with storage ability (sequential circuits) can be defined and treated by switching algebra.

ZEMANEK, H.: Logische Algebra und Theorie der Schaltnetzwerke. In: Steinbuch, K. (ed.): Taschender Nachrichtenverarbeitung. Springer-Verlag Berlin, Göttingen, Heidelberg 1962.

**Symbol**
Symbol
symbole
символ

Symbol has many meanings; in some formally or logistically orientated representations it stands for a *character independent of its meaning function; in non-formal contexts it may stand for a character together with a meaning, which, however, cannot be expressed explicitly and scientifically.

**Synapse**
Synapse
synapse
синапс

*The element which transmits information between excitable function-units in the body (cf. *neuron).*

The nerve-fibres (cf. *axon) transmit the excitation in them to other nerve-cell bodies and *dendrites at which they terminate, via synapses; in the same way, the connection between nerve and muscle occurs through a synapse (motor end-plate).

In principle, a neuron can be approached through synapses numbering from merely a few to a few hundred.

Structurally a distinction is made at this transmission point between a pre-synaptic fibre ending in a widening (or end-knob) at the neuron, a sub-synaptic membrane (membrane section of the cell) and the narrow space between the two (200–300 Å wide).

1 Excitatory synapses with a chemical transmitter.

Despite the narrow gap, pre- and post-synaptic positions are electrically completely disconnected. Only the chemical transmitter (e.g. acetylcholine) stored in the pre-synaptic position (end-knob) and released by the arriving electrical excitation, exerts an effect in that when it intervenes, part of the sub-synaptic membrane near the synapse is depolarized and 'excitatory post-synaptic potential' (EPSP) occurs intra-cellularly with a delay of some 0·3–0·6 msec. (within the range 1–2 msec., the resistance of the membrane is reduced from 1000 to 1 ohm by the effect of the transmitter in an area of approx. 10–20$\mu^2$). EPSP is not identical with *action potential (spike) which transmits the information leaving the cell-body, but represents a purely local alteration of potential (about 10 mV).

EPSP has a characteristic chronological development: a fast rise (1–20 msec.) and an approximately exponential return (1–120 msec.). In this, amplitude, not the development, is influenced by the sequence-frequency of the arriving pulses: *summation (cf. *decoding), which can be explained by repeated release of the mission transmitter. If the amplitude of EPSP or the sum of the amplitudes of all EPSPs at the neuron reaches a critical threshold, the result is an excitation of the whole neuron (amplifier effect) and an action potential (80–140 mV) as an output signal to the axon which continues the conduction. The excitation of the whole neuron is therefore dependent on the number of afferent excited fibres and their discharge frequency.

2 Excitatory synapses of the electrical transfer type.
Synapses of this type have a narrower gap, almost no latent period between EPSP and pre-synaptic spike ($< 0{\cdot}1$ msec.). It must be assumed that there is a direct transmission of the depolarizing current from the pre-synaptic to the sub-synaptic membrane; although only in one direction (rectifier effect).

3 Inhibitory synapses with chemical transmitter.
The excitation which arrives via an *interneuron with a short axon induces by a chemical transmitter (e.g. $\gamma$-amino butyric acid in invertebrates) a hyper-polarization of the sub-synaptic membrane, and 'inhibitory post-synaptic potential' (IPSP). The latter is practically the exact reverse of EPSP, and reduces the excitability of the nerve-cells.

4 Inhibitory synapses of the electrical transfer type.
In a few nerve cells (MAUTHEN cells), the axon is surrounded by a fine nerve-tissue which electronically affects the excitation conducted in the axon and inhibits it.

ECCLES, J. C.: The mechanism of synaptic transmission. Ergebnisse der Psysiologie 51 (1961), pp. 300–429.

**Syntax**
Syntax
syntaxe
синтаксис

*Description of the formal part of a formalized language (cf. *languages, formalized) in a *meta language.*

The elementary syntax of a formalized language contains the instructions for forming the calculus formalized in the meta language. A calculus is set up in this way:
The *alphabet is established by giving the basic characters (symbols, letters). By concatenation, finite character sequences are formed. From the set of all character sequences a subset is singled out according to certain rules. These special character sequences are called expressions or formulae. Some expressions serve as starting formulae (axioms) for deductions which are made by means of rules of inference. A rule of inference is a transformation rule for expressions, i.e. a relation which assigns certain expressions to certain $n$-tuples of expressions.
A finite sequence of expressions which contains only axioms or deduced formulae, is called proof (of the last expression of the sequence). The set of all expressions which can be deduced from the axioms is called a set of sentences.
The meta language used in the representation of syntax is called syntax language. Its rules must be effective, which means: (*a*) the sets of basic characters, expressions or axioms are decidable (*b*) the transformation relations on which syllogistic rules are based are decidable (cf. *decidability).
Under these conditions, the set of sentences of a calculus is capable of being enumerated, i.e. it can be represented as the value range of a calculable function upon the natural numbers.

CHURCH, A.: Introduction to Mathematical Logic. Princeton University Press 1956. LORENZEN, P.: Metamathematik. Bibl. Inst., Mannheim 1962.

**System theory**
Systemtheorie
théorie des systèmes
теория связи

*Theory of the influenceability of the output value of a system with given input*

*values by altering the characteristics of the system.*
In the frequency domain, the *spectrum of the output value can be calculated from the product of the spectrum of the input value and the *transfer function. In the time domain, the output time-function can be calculated by convolution of the input time-function with the pulse response. System theory discusses the special connections between the output functions and the various attenuation- and phase-functions by the use of special test-signals of the input.

KÜPFMÜLLER, K.: Systemtheorie der elektrischen Nachrichtentechnik. Hirzel, Stuttgart 1949. WUNSCH, G.: Moderne Systemtheorie. Geest & Portig, Leipzig 1962. SCHLITT, H.: Systemtheorie für regellose Vorgänge. Springer-Verlag, Berlin, Göttingen, Heidelberg 1960.

# T

## Tape store

*See* *Magnetic tape store

## Teaching machines

Lehrmaschinen
machines à enseigner
обучающие машины

**Automata which partially take over the functions of a teacher.*
Programs for teaching machines provide:

1 *Information from the *store given to the pupil in sections
2 Examination of the pupil by means of tests dependent on information previously imparted to him.

In general, a section with new information is only released if a certain test has been passed satisfactorily. Difficulties arise (as is generally the case with a mechanical test-evaluation) in that only one precise answer, or only a small quantity of precise answers, can be allowed for test questions. The technically simplest solution allows a choice only from the small quantity of answers to a question offered by the machine. *Communication between machine and pupil follows the pattern normal for *computers: *input and *output.

FRANK, H. (ed.): Lehrmaschinen in kybernetischer und pädagogischer Sicht. Klett, Stuttgart and Oldenbourg, München 1963.

## Techniques

Technik
technique
техника

*The method of applying available means in order to reach a pregiven goal.*
Depending on whether the means used are (*a*) of a purely physical or chemical nature, or (*b*) also include animals (apart from humans), or finally (*c*) include even humans, one talks of (*a*) machine-techniques, (*b*) bio-techniques (e.g. the use of beasts of burden or of trained animals in transport, agriculture, and even the control of rockets or (*c*) social techniques (work organization).
Depending on whether the goal to be reached is the mastering (1) of a function of the *oarsman, or (2) of a function of the *steersman or of the *pilot, one talks of (1) classical techniques or (2) cybernetical (non-classical) tech-

niques. (Engineering cybernetics is cybernetical machine techniques).
A distinction must be made between (1) the technical sciences, which develop theoretically the possible methods, and whose products are true or false propositions, and (2) actual techniques, which apply these processes and only by this produce ethically assessible results.

**Test signal generator**
Testwertgeber
évaluateur de tests
датчик нробной величины

*An active element in *learning machines which produces stochastic or systematic activity and thereby induces the machine to exert some influence on its surroundings.*

Adaption or learning occurs by evaluation of the activity produced by a test signal generator and the reaction of environment connected with it. Test oscillations can be produced in *feedback control systems by a test signal generator; these oscillations do not impair the control process (i.e. do not affect the value to be controlled), but provide a criterion of whether the system is working optimally (cf. *optimalize).

KAUFMANN, H.: Digitale Systeme in Regelkreisen. ZEMANEK, H.: Lernende Automaten. Both in: Taschenbuch der Nachrichtenverarbeitung (ed. Steinbuch, K.). Springer, Berlin, Göttingen, Heidelberg 1962.

**Theorem proving program**
Beweisprogramme
programme de démonstration
программа для построения доказательств

**Program to find proofs* (*formalized *languages*, **syntax*).

Presupposition for the possibility of a theorem proving program is the enumerability of the sentences of a formalized *language. It is decided by heuristic and non-heuristic (cf. *heuristics) theorem proving programs as to whether hypothetical processes should be used or not. Heuristic programs use statistical ratings (cf. *decision theory) for secondary aims (perhaps material gain through a move in chess, or disparity in a logical theorem, i.e. the number of terms in a subsidiary theorem which do not agree with a theorem which has to be proven). An abbreviation of the proving process can be made (*minimax strategy), without the guarantee, of course, that this chosen method will bring success.

Non-heuristic theorem proving programs exist for e.g. propositional calculus, (i.e. for treating the theory of truth-values and truth-functions). There are problems which cannot be solved mechanically (by means of a program)—cf. *decidability.

For setting up theorem proving programs there are problem-orientated *programming languages which permit, together with the use of symbols for logical combinations, the simple processing of lists of non-numerical information.

HERMES, H.: Aufzählbarkeit, Entscheidbarkeit, Berechenbarkeit. Springer-Verlag, Berlin, Göttingen, Heidelberg 1961. LORENZEN, P.: Metamathematik. Mannheim 1962.

**Theta waves**
Theta-Wellen
ondes thêta
тета-лучи

*Sinusoidal waves of the human *electroencephalogram.*

In normal test-subjects theta waves are recorded in the temporal-parietal area and occur singly or in the form of short bursts, mainly bilaterally and simultaneously. Their frequency lies between

4–7 c/s, their amplitude in the region of 50 $\mu$V. Theta waves are generally concealed by the surrounding electrical activity. The increase of theta waves can be attributed to psycho-effective disturbances (emotional conditions, frustration). The excitation centre of theta waves is at the thalamic level. In a pathological condition theta waves occur more frequently and more strongly. Between the ages of 2–15 years theta waves form the main part of the electrical activity of the brain, thereafter to be replaced by *alpha waves.

**Threshold** (I)
Reizschwelle; Wahrnehmbarkeitsgrenze
seuil d'excitation
порог возбуждения; порог раздражения

*The minimal amount of energy or time, to exceed which produces a specific *excitation, and whose variations produces an alteration of this specific excitation.*

In a *receptor or in a sensory-organ system, the absolute threshold is reached when the energy of the adequate *stimulus in certain stimulus-parameters exceeds the level given by intrinsic noise and intrinsic interference and a discernible excitation is observed, or a conscious sensation is perceived. This level is
(*a*) in the ear: $5{\cdot}0 \cdot 10^{-11}$ erg (continuous tone of sine waves between 1000 and 2000 c/s)
(*b*) in the eye: $1{\cdot}3$–$2{\cdot}6 \cdot 10^{-10}$ erg. (electro-magnetic wave of length 507 m$\mu$)
(*c*) in the skin: $0{\cdot}2$–$0{\cdot}4 \cdot 10^{-1}$ erg.
Its dependence on the stimulus parameters is established by the intensity threshold.
The successive threshold, which shows how large the difference between two successive stimuli must be in order for them to be recognized as separate, is about 10 per cent in the range of average intensities in all sensory organs. The difference in strength of stimulus which is necessary for distinguishing two stimuli offered simultaneously, is given by the simultaneous threshold (approx. 0·6 per cent in the eye). (Optimalizing of these difference-thresholds by *adaptation).
The local threshold, the ability to separate two stimuli at the location of the sensory cell, is dependent on the distance between the receptors and the *facilitation and *inhibition processes in the succeeding networks.
The time threshold gives the temporal resolution (fusion-frequency) of a sense organ; the space threshold marks the spatial resolution in the perception of distant objects.
In principle a (metabolically-dependent) threshold can be given for every excitable function-unit within an organism; this naturally varies according to the excitation triggered off (*all-or-nothing law).

RANKE, O. F.: Allgemeine Physiologie der Sinnesorgane. In: Lehmann, G. (ed.): Handbuch der gesamten Arbeitsmedizin. Urban & Schwarzenberg, München, Berlin, Wien 1962.

**Threshold** (II); **limen**
Schwelle; Limen
seuil
порог

*Used originally as a specialist expression in psychophysics to denote the limits of stimulation of *perception; more generally it is used for characteristic magnitudes or differences in these magnitudes which produce a specified reaction of a reagent with a certain probability.*

If facts are represented as points or vectors in a co-ordinate system formed from the relevant physical or psychological characteristics

$$m_i, (i = 1, \ldots, k;),$$

then the threshold of a certain reaction or response of a reagent (a receiver, a percipient or an information-evaluating system) is that set of points or vectors in which the reaction $A$ occurs under defined experimental conditions with the specified probability $0 > p(A) < 1$. As in many cases there is a difference between the parameters of the probability function of data which was collected by various experimental processes (e.g. by successive increment or by random variation of the characteristics), it is therefore essential for application to take into account the strategy of data collection. In most empirical definitions of threshold value only those values of one or two relevant characteristics are altered, whilst those of the others are kept constant. Thresholds obtained statistically from the reactions to single facts are called *absolute thresholds. *Difference thresholds are gained from reactions which refer simultaneously to two or more facts.

TORGERSON, W. S.: Theory and methods of scaling. Wiley, New York and London 1960.

**Time constant**
Zeitkonstante
constante de temps
постоянная времени

*The time interval which defines the value of growth- or fading-processes.*

Many growth- or fading-processes in physical systems can be described mathematically by a mathematical differential equation of the first order, which is the same as saying that the speed of change of a time-dependent value is proportional to the value itself. In this, the time constant is the reciprocal proportionality factor or the length of time the time-dependent value takes to rise or to sink to 1/e or the e-fold of the original value. A simple example of an electrical process of fading or decay is the discharge of a capacitor $C$ via a resistance $R$, in which the time constant of the reduction in voltage is given by the product $R.C.$ In radioactive fission, one talks of half-life.

**Time discriminability**
Gegenwartsdichte
épaisseur du présent
плотность существования

Reciprocal value of *moment. The given numerical values vary between 10 and 20 per sec.

MOLES, A. A.: Théorie de l'information et perception esthétique. Flammarion, Paris 1959.

**Toposcope**
Toposkop
toposcope
——

*A machine used in amplifying and representing bio-electrical potentials. The representation is two dimensional.*

Usually potentials are represented by intensity modulation. In some toposcopes the picture is produced on a cathode ray tube. LILLY used a neon lamp field. Usually the potentials of the scalp (EEG) or of the cerebral cortex are examined, but sometimes also those of the upper body as an electro-cardiogram (GOLDMAN). In the toposcope developed by WALTER and SHIPTON a field of small oscilloscopes is used, whose intensity-modulated beams are deflected in a circle by the amplified potentials simultaneously with the strongest components of the waves. This type of representation is useful in examinations of the phase relation between the electrical activity of various parts of the *brain.

WALTER, G.: Toposcopy. E.E.G. Clin. Neurophysiol. Suppl. 4 (1953).

**Transducer**
Wandler
transducteur
преобразователь; трансформатор; конвертер

*Transducers are devices for the analogous transformation of one form of energy into another. This transformation occurs directly or indirectly by controlling a generator of the second form of energy by means of the form of energy to be transformed.*

Only a few typical examples of the multitude of possible transducers are given here: microphones and loudspeakers are (direct) electrical-mechanical transducers, as are generators, electric-motors and electrical measuring instruments. An accumulator represents a chemical-electrical transducer. Thermo-elements are direct thermo-electrical transducers, resistance thermometers are indirect thermo-electric transducers, and photo-elements are indirect electromagnetic-electrical transducers.

KAZMIERCAK, H.: Wandler. In: Steinbuch, K. (ed.): Taschenbuch der Nachrichtenverarbeitung. Springer-Verlag, Berlin, Göttingen, Heidelberg 1962.

**Transfer function**
Übertragungsfunktion
transmittance isochrone
передаточная функция; функция иередачи

*Similar to *frequency response it is characteristic of the transfer properties of a *linear system.*

The dependence of the output $y(t)$ on the input $x(t)$ of a linear system can be described by the differential equation:

$$a_0\frac{d^n y}{dt^n}+a_1\frac{d^{n-1}y}{dt^{n-1}}+\ldots+a_{n-1}\frac{dy}{dt}+a_n y=$$
$$=b_0\frac{d^m x}{dt^m}+b_1\frac{d^{m-1}x}{dt^{m-1}}+\ldots+h_{m-1}\frac{dx}{dt}+b_m x$$

The transfer function of the system is then defined as the rational function

$$H(s)=\frac{b_0 s^m+b_1 s^{m-1}+\ldots+b_{m-1}s+b_m}{a_0 s^n+a_1 s^{n-1}+\ldots+a_{n-1}s+a_n}$$

of the complex variable $s=\delta+j\omega$. The imaginary part $\omega$ of $s$ has the meaning of angular frequency (cf. *oscillation); if $s$ is made equal to $j\omega$, then $H(s)$ is equal to the frequency response: $H(j\omega)=F(\omega)$. The real part $\delta$ has the meaning of the decay-constant ($\delta<0$) or the build-up constant ($\delta>0$) of an oscillation. The physical meaning of $H(s)$ can be characterized in the following way: if one chooses as the input function of the system the exponentially decreasing or increasing oscillation $x=x_0e^{(\delta+j\omega)t}$, then one obtains in the steady state the oscillation $y=y_0e^{(\delta+j\omega)t}$ with the same values $\delta$ and $\omega$; the complex number $y_0$ is defined as a function of $s$ by the following:

$$\frac{y_0}{x_0}=H(\delta+j\omega)=H(s).$$

Transfer function is also used by some authors with the same meaning as *frequency response.

GILLE, J. C.; PELEGRIN, M.; DECAULNE, P.: Lehrgang der Regelungstechnik. Band 1, R. Oldenbourg. München and Berlin 1960. SOLODOWNIKOW, W. W.: Grundlagen der selbsttätigen Regelung. R. Oldenbourg, München and Berlin 1959.

**Transfluxor**
Transfluxor
transfluxor
трансфлюксор

*A magnetic element with various flux paths.*

A transfluxor is a ferrite disc with several bored holes and with a rectangular hysteresis loop. Magnetic tubes of flux arise from the geometrical arrangement of the bored holes; the orientation of these tubes can be altered by electrical currents in the windings around the crossmembers between the holes. By single pulses in the master circuit of the transfluxor, the coupling between input and output circuits and hence the signal transmission between input and output can be established within a certain value. Transfluxors are used as storage elements for non-destructive read-out and as logical elements.

RAJCHMAN, J. A.; LO, A. W.: The Transfluxor. Proc. I.R.E. 44 (1956), pp. 312–32. DARRÉE, A.: Abfragen magnetischer Speicher ohne Informationsverlust. Frequenz 11 (1957), pp. 19–27 and pp. 38–42.

**Transinformation; transmitted information; mutual information**
Transinformation
information transmise; transinformation
трансинформация

*A measure of the alteration of the uncertainty regarding a situation B (e.g. nationality of a person) by the information on a situation A which is connected to it (e.g. the mother tongue of the person).*
If the random event $A_i$ in the *field of events $X$ of possible events has the information $I(A_i)$, and correspondingly if event $B_j$ in the field $Y$ has the information $I(B_j)$, and finally the double event $A_i \times B_j$ in the product field $X \times Y$ has the information $I(A_i \times B_j)$, then the transformation is:

$$T(A_i, B_j) = I(B_j) - (I(A_i \times B_j) - I(A_i)).$$

As the contents of the bracket signifies the conditioned information $(IA_iB_j)$ of $B_j$ when $A_i$ is known, then

$$T(A_i, B_j) = I(B_j) - IA_i(B_j)$$

is the decrease of the information contained in $B_j$ by the message $A_i$. $T(A_i, B_j)$ is also called the 'information' inherent in $A_i$ via $B_j$ in a general sense (as $T(A_i, B_j)$ can be negative). Often the transinformation

$$T(A_i, X) = H(Y) - HA_i(Y)$$

obtained via $Y$, or the transinformation

$$T(X, Y) = H(Y) - H_X(Y)$$

which is obtained via $X$ and $Y$ and hence never negative, are called transinformation. As $T(X, Y) = 0$ if $X$ and $Y$ are independent, $T(X, Y)$ is also used instead of the measure of correlation (cf. *correlation function) especially if $X$ and $Y$ are not *random variables.

JAGLOM, A. M. and I. M.: Wahrscheinlichkeit und Information. VEB Wissenschaft, Berlin 1960. ZEMANEK, H.: Elementare Informationstheorie. R. Oldenbourg, Wien and München 1959.

**Transistor**
Transistor
transistor
транзистор; полупроводниковый триод

*An active (amplifying) semi-conducting element.*
*Transistor* is a term formed from a combination of *transfer* and *resistor*. The transistor was developed in 1948 by BARDEEN and BRATTAIN. It consists of a semi-conducting material (today mainly of germanium or sicilium) which shows by the addition of certain chemical elements several zones which electrically behave quite differently (cf. *semi-conductor). Normally there are three zones, of which the two outer zones have principally the same characteristics which deviate from those of the middle zone (base). This leads to a distinction between pnp and npn transistors. In the npn type the charge carriers are electrons; in the pnp type they are holes (electron holes). The three zones

which have external connections are called emitter, base and collector. As well as the transistor, four zone devices also exist; the external connections are to auxiliary circuits (transistor tetrodes, etc.). Compared to a *vacuum tube, the base corresponds to the control grid, the emitter to the cathode, and the collector to the anode.
The transistor represents a four terminal network, and can be operated similarly to the vacuum tube in three types of circuit (common base, common emitter and common collector circuits). The characteristics of a transistor (e.g. input and output resistance, current amplification, frequency band width) depend greatly on the type of circuit.

**Transit time; propagation time; delay time**
Laufzeit
temps de propagation
задержка; время п(р)олета; продолжительность хода; время пробега; время запаздывания

*The length of time which physical parameters in the form of waves, pulses, etc. need as a result of their finite speed to cover a certain distance.*
Let $b$ stand for the transfer-angle of a system and $\omega$ the angular-frequency of waves. Then $b/\omega$ is the phase transit time, $\mathrm{d}b/\mathrm{d}\omega$ the group transit time; this is standard for the spread of signals. A transit time independent of frequency is ideal for signal transmission, as in this case no distortion of the signals occurs. In transit times dependent on frequency, signals are distorted.
Transit time can have a disturbing effect in feedback control systems, in information transmission and information processing. With transit time no synchronous operation is possible. Transit time is used technically for distance measuring (radar, sonar), for storage (cf. *delay line store), for producing oscillations, and for the selection of frequency. In the nervous system considerable transit times are found (up to 200 ms) caused by the low propagation speed in the nerve fibres (cf. *nerve). Transit time apparently has a great influence on information processing in the nervous system.

KÜPFMÜLLER, K.: Systemtheorie der elektrischen Nachrichtenübertragung. Hirzel, Stuttgart 1952. REIN, H.; SCHNEIDER, M.: Einführung in die Physiologie des Menschen. Springer-Verlag, Berlin, Göttingen, Heidelberg 1960. SCHIEF, R.: Koinzidenz-Siebschaltungen. Dissertation. Techn. Hochschule Hannover 1962. STEINBUCH, K. (ed.): Taschenbuch der Nachrichtenverarbeitung. Springer-Verlag, Berlin, Göttingen, Heidelberg 1962.

**Transjunction**
Transjunktion
transjonction
трансъюнкция

*An operation in cybernetical logic carried out with the help of a *morphogram and which demands more than two values for its occupancy of places.*
The expression ‘transjunction’ is a generalization of the classical terms *conjunction and *disjunction and means that the choice offered between two logical values or general logical places in favour of a ‘foreign’ value can be rejected. In this way, for example, the classical logical value of disjunction 1, 1, 1, 2 can adopt the form 1, 3, 3, 2 as a transjunction. The purpose of the concept is to transcend the bivalent classical system in the sense that logical intermediate values are included which describe an analogous structure.

**Translator** (I)
Übersetzer; Übersetzungsprogramm
traducteur
дешифратор; транслятор

*A distinction is made between *assembler and *compiler.*

**Translator** (II)
Zuordner
traducteur; coordinateur
декодирующее устройство; дешифратор

*A technical device for realizing a definite connection or co-ordination between two sets of signals.*

A translator produces from a set of binary signals $(x_1, x_1 \ldots x_m)$ a set of binary signals $(y_1, y_1, \ldots y_j \ldots y_n)$ according to a pregiven co-ordination instruction. This instruction is formulated according to the rules of *Boolean algebra, and realized in the translator by *logical circuits. As a rule, the technical execution of the translator does not permit a reversal of the co-ordination. Translators are used as code converters and as units for addition and multiplication in computers.

STEINBUCH, K. (ed.): Taschenbuch der Nachrichtenverarbeitung. Springer-Verlag, Berlin, Göttingen, Heidelberg 1962.

**Transmitted information**
*See* *Transinformation

**Transmitter**
*See* *Source

**Tremor**
Zittern
tremblement
дрожание

An involuntary rhythmical movement which occurs most frequently in the extremities, particularly the arms. It occurs in immobility (or more precisely in the persistence of a certain posture), for example in PARKINSON's disease, or in the execution of voluntary movements (intention tremor of the syndrome of the cerebellum).

Tremor is connected with injuries to the mechanisms of movement regulation (corpus striatum, cerebellum, extrapyramidal system).

The electromyographic analysis of tremor permits the examination of its frequency and its distribution over the various muscular groups.

**Trial and error**
Versuch und Irrtum; Lernen durch Erfolg
essai et erreur
проба и ошибка

*Process of reaching a goal, if there exists a priori only insufficient knowledge of the best method of solution.*

An automaton or an animal attempting to reach a goal has at any time several lines of action open to it, each of which excludes the others. The process of trial and error consists of trying the various alternatives one after the other and of evaluating their advantages until one is found which satisfies a criterion of success. In some circumstances it becomes necessary to reverse the effects of each alternative before the next alternative is tried. In most graduated optimalizing processes (cf. *optimalize) it is necessary in a continuous environment to retrace false steps. In some circumstances there exists a succession of known subgoals; here the success of a step can be measured by whether one of these subgoals has been reached or not. In yet other circumstances, the success of a step is given by a continuous measure of goal achievement. Trial and error implies a series of discrete, individually assessed steps, but also optimalization by continuous parameter variation.

ROSENBROCK, H. H.: An Automatic Method for Finding the Greatest or Least Value of a Function. The Computer Journal 3 (1960).

**Trigger**
Trigger
trigger; déclancheur
триггер; пусковое устройство

*A releasing circuit element, also the release pulse itself, or a storage circuit which remains marked from release until erasure.*
In oscillographs, a trigger serves to control the time base in order to obtain a picture of short processes on the screen. In this, the trigger circuit deduces the pulse from a certain criterion (e.g. a current exceeding a threshold value). The concept has also been transferred to the circuits in information techniques for a release pulse which results in a condition being altered in a defined way. Also used in neuro-physiology for exciting stimuli.

**TURING machines**
TURINGmaschinen
machine TURING
машина Тьюринга

*A mathematical model of an automatic computer. It serves to define precisely the concepts of *algorithm, *computability and *decidability.*
A mathematical model of an automatic computer must on the one hand reproduce all the characteristic features, yet on the other hand be simple and precise in its logical structure, in order to be of any use as a starting point for mathematical research. A model of this type was given by TURING in 1936.
A TURING machine has a finite *alphabet: $A = \{a_1, \ldots, a_m\}$, in which the data are represented. As a store it has a tape infinite in each direction, which is divided into single cells. Each cell can accept exactly one character of the alphabet. For the sake of completeness, the empty cells are allotted the character for empty (perhaps □). The information on the tape is processed in a so-called logical block. This has a finite set of states $Q = \{q_1, \ldots, q_n\}$. At every cycle of the machine, one cell is summoned, the character contained in it is read and, dependent on this and the present state of the logical block, a new character (which replaces the old one), a new state and the *address of the new working cell are ascertained. Only the addresses $A = \{R, L, M\}$, are permitted, which at the next cycle select the cell situated immediately to the right or left, or even the same cell location. The states attained by the logical block can be represented in a transition table or TURING table:

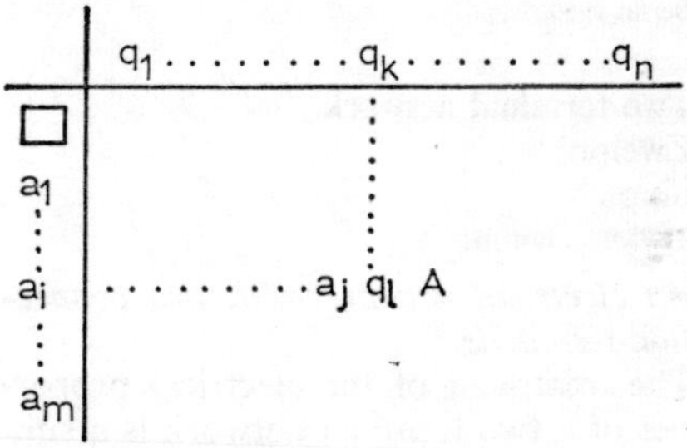


Transition table

The output triad $(a_j, q_l, A)$ belonging to the input pair $(a_i, q_k)$ stands at the intersection of the line and column marked $a_i$ and $q_k$.
A TURING machine works in the following way: the initial information is recorded on the tape, the machine is set at the first location and the logical block brought to the initial state. The calculation process is then executed automatically and is clearly defined by the transition table. The machine stops when tape inscription, working cell and state no longer change. A TURING

machine can only carry out one algorithm. However, universal TURING machines can be constructed which can realize any algorithm, or can simulate any TURING machine, and which themselves belong to the class of TURING machines. For this, the initial information and the TURING table of the machine to be simulated must be encoded in the alphabet of universal TURING machines and be recorded on the tape.
Universal TURING machines are models of stored-program computers.

HERMES, H.: Aufzählbarkeit, Entscheidbarkeit, Berechenbarkeit. Springer, Berlin-Göttingen-Heidelberg 1961. SHANNON, C. E.; MCCARTHY, J.: Automata Studies. Princeton Univ. Press, Princeton, N.Y. 1956. TRACHTENBROT, B. A.: Wieso können Automaten rechnen? VEB Verlag der Wissenschaften, Berlin 1959.

**Two terminal network**
Zweipol
dipole
двухполюсник

*An electrical network with two connection terminals.*
The treatment of the electrical properties of a two terminal network is a subject of network theory. The distinctive value is the generally frequency-dependent impedance $\mathfrak{Z}(\omega)$.
The elemental components of electrical engineering (resistors, capacitors, inductors) are two terminal networks.

ARTUS, W.: Einführung in die elektrische Nachrichtentechnik. R. Oldenbourg, München 1957.

**Type font**
Zeichensatz
signe-type
комплект (набор) знаков

*A set of characters, numbers and letters which is to be recognized by a character reader.*
In order to keep the technical expense of character readers within reasonable limits, often only certain sets of characters are permitted for recognition.
A type font of this kind consists of specially formed characters in order to make recognition as simple and accurate as possible for the machine. (CMC–7 and E 13 B for magnetic ink font, or the ASA–X.3.1. script for optical character readers). (*See also* *font standardization).

STEINBUCH, K.; KAZMIERCZAK, H.; Grundlagen und Anwendungen der automatischen Zeichenerkennung. In: Jahrbuch des elektrischen Fernmeldewesens. 1960/61.

**Type font, mutilated; noisy pattern; character deviation**
Zeichenveränderung; nichtideales Zeichen; reales Zeichen
altération des caractères (signes)
искажение образа

*Deviation of a character from the prototype agreed on.*
In the practical production of print or script some deviations from the prototype must occur. Some of the most frequent variations from the norm are misplaced letters, tilt, variations in gradation, interrupted flow of a line, or smudging. Characters in handwriting are most prone to mutilation or deviation. In the manufacture of *character readers a compromise must be made between expense and the range of variation which may be permitted (i.e. those characters which are still permitted for recognition with a pregiven error rate).

STEINBUCH, K.; KAZMIERCZAK, H.: Grundlagen und Anwendungen der automatischen Zeichenerkennung. In: Jahrbuch des elektrischen Fernmeldewesens. 1960/61.

# U

**Ultrastability**
Ultrastabilität
ultrastabilité
ультраустойчивость

*Extension of the principle of *homeostasis according to which a system of feedback paths is changed until the desired regulation is achieved.*

Every living organism keeps the values of certain internal variables within physiological limits. Artefacts often show similar functions of regulation. ASHBY applied the concept of ultrastability to systems in which the feedback paths are altered until they can achieve stable *closed loop control. ASHBY's definition of ultrastability includes only those cases in which the variations occur in finite steps every time the variables exceed given limits; however, continuous variations of the feedback paths are possible.

ASHBY, W. R.: Design for a Brain. 2nd edn. Chapman and Hall, London 1960. ASHBY, W. R.: An Introduction to Cybernetics. 3rd edn. Chapman and Hall, London 1958.

**Uncertainty**
Unsicherheit
incertitude
ненадёжность

Expectancy value for the *information of an imminent event or *character from a given *field of events (probability field). As uncertainty is equal to average information, it is defined by the same $H(X)$.

**Unit pulse**
Delta-Funktion
fonction delta
дельта—функция

Unit pulse is defined as follows: its value is zero for every value $x \neq x_0$, and infinite for $x = x_0$. The integral over $x$ is equal to 1.

$$\delta(x - x_0) = \begin{cases} \infty \text{ for } x = x_0 \\ 0 \text{ for } x \neq x_0 \end{cases}$$

$$\int_{\infty}^{-\infty} \delta(x - x_0)dx = 1$$

Unit pulses or series of unit pulses are used for describing shocks which disturb control systems or for describing random *noise.

# V

**Vacuum tube; valve**
Elektronenröhre
tube électronique
электронная лампа

*High-vacuum glass or steel container fitted with electrodes. Its use enables the control of the electric current produced in it.*

Vacuum tubes are used mainly as amplifying tubes. The simplest amplifier tube

has three electrodes (cathode, control grid and anode). In a vacuum tube an electric current is produced by a voltage between the anode and cathode and by heating of the cathode; this current can be controlled without energy by influencing the control grid potential. The amplifier effect stems from the large variation in the anode current caused by small variations in the voltage potential of the control grid. The electrical properties of the vacuum tube can be radically influenced by further electrodes such as screen grids and suppressor grids (pentodes), and also by an additional grid (hexode).
Apart from being used as low voltage amplifiers, vacuum tubes are also used as oscillators, high power transmitter valves and as rectifiers (cf. *diode).

Barkhausen, H.: Elektronenröhren. Hirzel, Leipzig 1951.

**Valence**
Valenz
valence
валентность; атомность

*A discrete numerical value which denotes the attraction which an object or a physical being has on another.*
Especially in chemistry, valence denotes a quantitative measure of the attraction of an element *A* with reference to an element *B*.
Valence is a specific property of the element *A* if it remains constant whatever the nature of the element *B*.
Valence is used in sociology and sociometry with the same meaning.

**Visible speech**
Visible Speech
visualisation du discours
видимая речь

*Any system which permits a clearly perceivable arrangement of acoustic phenomena and visual representation in one, two or three dimensions.*
Visible speech is the term applied especially to the system developed by Bell laboratories for making articulated speech visible on a two-dimensional diagram (speech frequency as a function of time). Each sub-frequency is represented at every moment by a dot, the opacity or optical density of which is proportional to its intensity at this moment. The diagram obtained in this way appears as a distribution of lines and dots which denote the time variation of the component of the sound; white areas correspond to missing components.
This diagram, called a sonagram, can be considered as a two-dimensional projection of the three-dimensional representation of a sound in intensity, frequency and time, on to the frequency-time plane, perhaps comparable to a geographical map. With the help of special equipment it is in principle possible to reproduce from the sonagram the original sound, at least within the limitations of accuracy of the original sonagram. Visible speech has become a concept which is applied generally to any objective correspondence between sound and picture. The same techniques applied especially to the representation of music or other acoustic phenomena.

Potter, R. K.; Kopp, G. A.; Green, H. C.: Visible Speech. Nostrand, New York 1947.

**Vocoder**
Vocoder
vocoder
вокодер

*A device for the reduction of frequency range in the transmission of speech.*
A vocoder (= voice coder) conducts

from the speech signal on the transmitter side characteristic parameters whose transmission requires a smaller band width than the original speech signal. On the receiver side, speech is reproduced synthetically from them. Parameters used in a channel vocoder are the basic frequency of the voice tone and the envelope of the *spectrum. The latter is also obtained from a number of band pass filters with attached rectifiers and stabilizing elements. The following are all well-known types of vocoder: channel vocoders; scan vocoders; pulse vocoders; response vocoders; resonance or formant vocoders; formant-moment vocoders (formoders); time-domain vocoders; recognition vocoders.

STEINBUCH, K. (ed.): Taschenbuch der Nachrichtenverarbeitung. Springer-Verlag, Berlin, Göttingen, Heidelberg 1962.

# W

**WEBER's law**
WEBERsches Gesetz; WEBER-FECHNERsches Gesetz
loi de WEBER
закон Вебера-Фехнера

*A law established by WEBER for extremely small stimuli, later extended by* FECHNER *to stronger stimuli.*

This law states that the strength of the sensation $R$ is proportional to the logarithm of the trigger-stimulus $S$, i.e. $R = \text{const.} \log S$. One result is that in an alteration of $\Delta S$ of the stimulus, the following alteration in sensation also occurs: $\Delta R = \text{const.} \Delta S/S$. The stimulus-alteration $\Delta S$ therefore leads to an alteration of sensation, which is diminished as the original stimulus is increased. The law is approximately fulfilled in light-and-sound-stimuli, and suggests the use of logarithmic scales.

**Word-time**
Wortzeit
temps d'un mot
длительность слова

*The time required to read a word from a drum.*

In drum computers (with a *magnetic drum store as the working store) the computing time needed is given in word-times; it is always a whole number of word-times.

GÜNTSCH, F. R.: Einführung in die Programmierung digitaler Rechenautomaten. De Gruyter, Berlin 1960.

# Z

**Zero-sum-game**
Nullsummenspiel
jeu à somme nulle
игра с нулевой суммой

*A game in which the sum of the gains of all players taking part is zero. Therefore payments for gains or losses are neither added nor deducted.*

Party games are usually classed as zero-sum-games, but not normally events in economics. By the addition of an imaginary player, every game can be changed into a zero-sum-game. There exist special tests for strategy in zero-sum-games (cf. *minimax strategy). Theoretical understanding permits *simulation (of strategic games).

NEUMANN, J. v.; MORGENSTERN, O.: Spieltheorie und wirtschaftliches Verhalten. Physica, Würzburg 1961.

**German-English word list**

absolute Beurteilung *f* — absolute judgement
Absolutschwelle *f* — absolute threshold
Abtastregelung *f* — sampled data control
Abtasttheorem *n* — sampling theorem
Adaptation *f* — adaptation
Addierwerk *n* — adder
Adresse *f* — address
Adressenmodifikation *f* — address modification
Adressensubstitution *f* — indirect addressing
Agnosie *f* — Agnosia
Ähnlichkeit *f* — similarity
Akkumulator *m* — accumulator
Aktionspotential *n* — action potential
Aktionspotential, monodales — action potential at a node of RANVIER
Akzeptionswert *n* — acceptance value
ALGOL — ALGOL; algorithmic language
Algorithmus *m* — algorithm
Alles-oder-Nichts-Gesetz *n* — all-or-none law
Alphabet *n* — alphabet
alphanumerisch — alphanumerical
Alpha-Wellen *pl. f* — alpha waves
Amplitudenfilter *m* — amplitude filter
analog — analogous
Analogie *f* — analogy
Analogrechner *m* — analogue computer
Anpassung *f* — matching
Antivalenz *f* — non-equivalence; exclusive disjunction
Aphasie *f* — aphasia
Apperzeption *f* — apperception
Apraxie *f* — apraxia
Äquivalenz *f* — equivalence, material
Äquivokation *f* — equivocation
Assembler *m* — assembler
Assoziation *f* — association
ästhetisches Mass *n* — measure of aesthetics
Ataxie *f* — ataxia
Auf-Zu-Regler *m* — bang-bang servo
Ausgabe *f* — output (I)
Ausgang *m* — output (II)
Ausgangsgrösse *f* — output quantity
Autokorrelationsfunktion *f* — autocorrelation function
Automat *m* — automaton
Automat, endlicher — automaton, finite
Automation *f* — automation
Axon *n* — axon

Bahn *f*, spezifische — specific system; specific afferent
Bahn *f*, unspezifische — non-specific system
Bahnung *f* — facilitation
Bandbreite *f* — band width
Bedeutung *f* — meaning
Befehl *m* — instruction
Befehl, bedingter — instruction, conditional
Befehlscode *f* — instruction code
Befehlsfolgezähler *m* — sequence control register
Begriffsbildung *f* — concept formation
Behaviorismus *m* — behaviourism
Berechenbarkeit *f* — computability
Beschreibungsfunktion *f* — describing function
Beta-Wellen *pl.f* — beta waves
Beurteilung *f*, absolute — absolute judgement
Beweisprogramm *n* — theorem proving program
Bewusstsein *n* — consciousness
binär — binary
Binärzeichen *m* — binary digit
biologische Regelung *f* — biological control
BIRKHOFFsche Übergang *m* — hierarchization

Bit *n* — bit
Blockschaltbild *n* — blockdiagram
BOOLEsche Algebra *f* — Boolean algebra
BUNSEN-ROSCOE-Gesetz *n* — BUNSEN-ROSCOE law

Chorea *f* — chorea
Codierung *f*, nachrichtentechnische — encoding
Codierung, sinnesphysiologische — coding (in nervous system)
Compiler *m* — compiler
Computer *m* — computer (digital)
Creativität *f* — creativity
Cryotron *n* — cryotron

Datenverarbeitung *f* — data processing
Decodierung *f*, nachrichtentechnische — decoding
Decodierung, sinnesphysiologische — decoding (of sensory information)
Delta-Funktion *f* — unit pulse
Delta-Wellen *pl.f* — delta waves
Dendrit *m* — dendrite
Deskriptor *m* — descriptor
Didaktik *f*, mechanische — didactics, mechanical
digital — digital
Digitalrechner *m* — computer, digital
Diode *f* — diode
DIRACstoss *m* — pulse function
Disjunktion *f* — disjunction, inclusive
Diskriminierung *f* — discrimination
Dissipation *f* — ambiguity
Dualzahl *f* — binary number

Ein-Aus-Regler *m* — bang-bang servo
Eingabe *f* — input (I)
Eingang *m* — input (II)
Eingangsgrösse *f* — input signal; input value
Elektrocorticogramm *n* — electrocorticogram
Electroencephalogramm (EEG) *n* — electroencephalogram
Electronengehirn *n* — electronic brain
Elektronenröhre *f* — vacuum tube; valve
elektronisch — electronic
endlicher Automat *m* — automaton, finite
endokrines System *n* — endocrine system
Engramm *n* — engram
Entropie *f* — entropy
Entropie, elektive — elective entropy
Entropie der Wahlklassen, elektive — elective entropy of choice classes
Entscheidbarkeit *f* — decidability
Entscheidungsgehalt *m* — information content
Entscheidungstheorie *f*, statistische — decision theory
Erkennung, *f* — recognition
Erregung *f*, physiologische — excitation

Faktorenanalyse *f* — factor analysis
FECHNERsches Gesetz *n* — FECHNER's law
Fehlererkennung *f* — error detection
Fehlerkorrektur *f* — error correction
FEINSTEINscher Satz *m* — FEINSTEIN's theorem
Feld *n* — probability field
Ferritkern *m* — magnetic core
Ferritkernspeicher *m* — core memory; core store
Filter *m* — filter
Flussdiagram *n* — flow diagram; flow chart
Formant *m* — formants
FORTRAN — FORTRAN language
FOURIERanalyse *f* — harmonic analysis
FOURIER-Integral *n* — FOURIER integral
FOURIER-Reihe *f* — FOURIER series
Freiheit *f* — freedom
Frequenzband *n* — frequency range

Frequenzfilter *m* — frequency filter
Frequenzgang *m* — frequency response; harmonic response
Funktionen *pl.f*, logische — propositional functions

GABORsche Informationszellen *pl.f* — GABOR information-cell
Gedächtnis *n* — memory
Gedächtnis eines Kanals — memory of a channel
Gegenwartsdauer *f* — duration
Gegenwartsdichte *f* — time discriminability
Gehirn *n* — brain
Generalisierung *f* — generalization
geregeltes System *n* — feedback control system
Gestalt *f* — pattern
Gestaltpsychologie *f* — Gestalt psychology
Grammatik *f* — grammar
Graph *m* — graph
Gruppendynamik *f* — group dynamics; psychology of groups
Gruppendynamik, mathematische — mathematical group dynamics
Gruppenentropie *f* — entropy of groups
Gruppenverfahren *n* — group coding

Halbleiter *m* — semi-conductor
HAMMING-Distanz *f* — HAMMING distance
harmonische Analyse *f* — harmonic analysis
Häufigkeit *f* — frequency
Hedonie *f* — hedony
Hemmung *f*, laterale — inhibition, lateral
Hemmung, zeitliche — inhibition, temporal
Heuristik *f* — heuristics
Hierarchieprinzip *n* — hierarchical principle
Hirnrinde *f* — cortex (of brain); cerebral cortex
Homeostase *f* — homeostasis
Homeostat *m* — homeostat
HUFFMANbaum *m* — HUFFMAN's tree

Ideogramm *n* — ideogram
Ikon *n* — icon
Imperativ *m* — imperative
Implikation *f* — implication
Impuls *m* — pulse; impulse
Indexregister *m* — index register
Information *f* — information
Information, ästhetische — information, aesthetical
Information, semantische — information, semantical
Information, subjektive — information, subjective
informationelle Akkomodation *f* — probability learning
informationelle Approximation *f* — informational approximation
Informationsästhetik *f* — informational aesthetics
Informationsdidaktik *f* — informational didactics
Informationserschliessung *f* — information retrieval
Informationspsychologie *f* — information psychology
Informationstheorie *f* — information theory
Informationstypographie *f* — informational typography
Informationswissenschaft *f* — informational sciences
Inhibition *f* — inhibition
Instanzen *pl.f*, kybernetische — cybernetics, levels of
Intelligenz *f* — intelligence
Intelligenz, künstliche — intelligence, artificial
Intelligenzquotient *m* — intelligence quotient
Introspektion *f* — introspection
Invarianz *f* — invariancy

Irrelevanz *f* — ambiguity
Istwert *m* — actual value

Kanal *m* — channel
Kanal, stationärer — channel, stationary
Kanalkapazität — channel capacity
Kapazität *f* — capacity (I: capacitance) and (II: storage capacity)
Kapitän *m* — captain
Kennlinie *f* — characteristic curve
Kerne *pl.m*, subkortikale — subcortical nuclei
Kippschaltung *f* — multivibrator
Kippschaltung, monostabile — monostable multivibrator
Kleinhirn *n* — cerebellum
kohärent — coherent
Kommandowerk *n* — control unit
Kommunikation *f* — communication
Komplexität *f* — complexity
Konditionierung *f*, instrumentale — conditioning, instrumental
Konditionierung, klassische — conditioning, classical or Pavlovian
Konjunktion *f* — conjunction
Konvergenz-Divergenz-Schaltung *f* — focalized-diffused-excitation
Korrelationsfunktion *f* — correlation function
Korrelationskoeffizient *m* — correlation coefficient
Kreisverstärkung *f* — open-loop amplification
Kreuzkorrelationsfunktion *f* — cross correlation function
Kurzspeicher *m* — short-term memory
Kybernetik *f* — cybernetics
Kybernetik, geisteswissenschaftliche — informational sciences
kybernetische Psychologie *f* — information psychology

Laufzeit *f* — transit time; propagation time, delay time
Laufzeitspeicher *m* — delay line store
Lehrmaschinen *pl.f* — teaching machines
Lernen *n* — learning
Lernen durch Erfolg — trial and error
Lernende Automaten *pl.m* — learning machines
Lernmatrix *f* — learning matrix
Lernmodelle *pl.n* — learning models
Lerntheorien *pl. f* — learning theories
Lesemaschine *f* — character reader; reading machine
Limen *m* — threshold (II)
Lochkarte *f* — punch card
Lochkartenabtaster *m* — punch card reader
Lochstreifen *m* — punched tape
Logik *f* — logic
logische Funktionen *pl.f* — propositional functions
logische Schaltungen *pl.f* — logical circuits
logische Verknüpfung *f* — logical connective
logischer Stellenwert *m* — logical value of occupancy
Logistik *f* — logic, mathematical
Logon *n* — logon
Lotse *m* — pilot

Magnetbandspeicher *m* — magnetic tape store
Magnetkopf *m* — magnetic head
Magnetplattenspeicher *m* — magnetic disc store
Magnetschrift *f* — magnetic ink font
Magnettrommelspeicher *m* — magnetic drum store
MARKOFFsche Kette *f* — MARKOV chain
MARKOFFsche Quelle *f* — MARKOV source
Maschinensprache *f* — machine code
Maximumeffekt *m* — maximum effect
MAXWELLscher Dämon *m* — MAXWELL's demon

McMILLANscher Satz *m* — McMILLAN's theorem
Mehradressenmaschine *f* — multiple-address machine
Mehrwertigkeit *f* — polyvalence
Membran *f* — membrane
Metasprache *f* — meta language
Minimaxverfahren *n* — minimax process
Modell *n* — model
Modulation *f* — modulation
Moment *n* — moment
Monitor *m* — monitor (I) and (II)
monostabile Kippschaltung *f* — monostable multivibrator
Monte-Carlo Methode *f* — Monte-Carlo method
Morphogramm *n* — morphogram
morphogrammatische Kette *f* — morphogrammatic compound
Multivibrator *m* — multivibrator
Musikanalyse *f*, mathematische — mathematical analysis of music

Nachricht *f* — message
Nachrichtenraum *m*; Nachrichtenmenge *f* — message space
Nachrichtenverarbeitung *f* — information processing
Negation *f* — negation
Negentropie *f* — negative entropy
Nerv *m* — nerve
Nervensystem *n*, autonomes — autonomic nervous system
Neuristor *m* — neuristor
Neuron *n* — neuron
Neuronenmodell *n* — neuron model
nichtlineares Glied *n* — nonlinear element
Nor-Funktion *f* — nor-function
Nullsummenspiel *n* — zero-sum-game
Nystagmus *m* — nystagmus

Objektsprache *f* — object language
Off-Effekt *m* — off-effect
On-Effekt *m* — on-effect
Operand *m* — operand
Operation *f* — operation
Operationalismus *m* — operationalism
Optimalfilter *m* — predictor
optimalisieren — optimize
Optimalwertkreis *m* — optimalizer
Ordnung *f* — order
Organisation *f* — organization
Organisationsmethodik *f* — social science
Originalität *f* — originality
Ortskurve *f* — locus

Pädagogik *f*, kybernetische — cybernetical pedagogics
Pandemonium *n* — pandemonium
Parallelsystem *n* — parallel operation
Parametron *n* — parametron
PARKINSONsche Krankheit *f* — PARKINSON's disease
PEIRCEscher Pfeil *m* — nor-function
Perceptron *n* — perceptron
Polaritätsprofil *n* — semantic differential
Programm *n* — program
Programmierungssprache *f* — programming language
Programmschleife *f* — loop
Prozedur *f* — sub-routine
Pseudocode *m* — pseudo-code
Psychophysik *f* — psychophysics

Quant *n* — quant
Quantisierung *f* — quantification
Quelle *f* — source
Quelle, ergodische — source, ergodic
Quelle, stationäre — source, stationary

Rampe *f* — calling sequence
Rauschen *n* — noise
RC Glied *n* — R.C. circuit
Reafferenzprinzip *n* — reafferent principle
Reaktion *f* — reaction
Realisation *f* — realization

Rechenautomat *m* — computer (digital)
Rechenwerk *n* — arithmetic unit
Rechenzeit *f* — computing time
Redundanz *f* — redundancy
Redundanztheorie *f* des Lernens — informational theory of learning
Referent *m* — referent
Reflexionsmuster *n* — pattern of reflection
Refraktärzeit *f* — refractory period
Regelabweichung *f* — deviation
Regelgrösse *f* — controlled condition
Regelkreis *m* — feedback control system
Regelstrecke *f* — controlled system
Regelsystem *n* — feedback control system
Regelung *f* — feedback control; closed loop control
Regelung, biologische — biological control
Regelungstechnik *f* — control engineering
Regeneration *f*, biologische — regeneration
Register *n* — register
Regler *m* — regulator
Reihenverfahren *n* — sequential coding
Reiz *m*, physiologischer — stimulus, physiological
Reiz, psychologischer — stimulus, psychological
Reizschwelle *f* — threshold (I)
Rejektionswert *m* — rejection value
Relais *n* — relay
Repertoire *n* — repertory
Repertoire, subjectives — repertory, subjective
Requisite Variety — requisite variety
'Residue'-Phänomen *n* — 'residue' phenomenon
Rezeptor *m* — receptor
Rindenpotential *n* — evoked response
Rückkopplung *f* — feedback
Rückwirkungsfreiheit *f* — feedback, absence of
Ruderer *m* — oarsman

Schaltalgebra *f* — switching algebra
Schieberegister *n* — shift register
Schwelle *f* — threshold (II); limen
Schwingung *f* — oscillation
Selbstbeobachtung *f*, reversive — introspection
Selbstorganisation *f* — self-organization
Semantik *f* — semantics
semantisches Differential *n* — semantic differential
Semiotik *f* — semiotics
Serien-Parallelsystem *n* — series-parallel-system
Seriensystem *n* — serial operation
SHEFFERscher Strich *m* — SHEFFER's stroke; non-conjunction
Signal *n* — signal
Simulation *f* strategischer Spiele — simulation of strategic games
Simulator *m* — simulator
Sollwert *m* — index value; set point; control value
Soziotechnik *f* — social science
Speicher *m* — store; memory
Speicher nach dem Stapelprinzip — pushdown store
Speichermatrix *f* — matrix store
Speicherung *f*, mechanische — memory, mechanical
Spektrum *n* — spectrum
Spike *m* — action potential
Sprachanalyse *f*, mathematische — mathematical analysis of language
Sprache *f* — language
Sprachen *pl.f*, formalisierte — languages, formalized
Spracherkennung *f*, automatische — speech recognition
Sprachübersetzung *f*, automatische — language translation, mechanical
Sprungantwort *n* — step response
Sprungbefehl *m* — jump instruction
Sprungfunktion *f* — step function

Stabilität *f* — stability
Stellglied *n* — correcting element
Stellgrösse *f* — regulating variable
Steuermann *m* — steersman
Steuerung *f* — open-loop control
stochastisch — stochastic; random
stochastische Variable *f* — random variable
stochastischer Prozess *m*, stationärer — stochastic process, stationary
Störgrösse *f* — disturbance
Struktur *f* — structure
Stufenredundanz *f* — redundancy by steps
subkortikale Kerne *pl.m* — subcortical nuclei
Summation *f* — summation
Summenaktionspotential *n* — compound actional potential
Superierung *f* — hierarchization
Superzeichen *n* — super-character
Superzeichenbildung *f* — hierarchization
Superzeichenredundanz *f* — redundancy at the super-character level
Symbol *n* — symbol
Synapse *f* — synapse
Syntax *f* — syntax
Systemtheorie *f* — system theory

Taktgeber *m*; Taktgenerator *m* — clock; clock generator
Taktspur *f* — clock track
Technik *f* — technique
Testwertgeber *m* — test signal generator
Theta-Wellen *pl.f* — theta waves
TLD (technische Lautschrift des Deutschen) *f* — German technical phonetic script
Toposkop *n* — toposcope
Tor *n* — gate
Totzeit *f* — dead time
Transfluxor *m* — transfluxor
Transinformation *f* — transinformation; transmitted information
Transistor *m* — transistor
Transjunktion *f* — transjunction
Trigger *m* — trigger
TURINGmaschinen *pl.f* — TURING machines
Übergangsfunktion *f* — step response
Überraschungswert *m* — surprise value
Übersetzer *m* — translator (I)
Übertragungsfunktion *f* — transfer function
Übertragungsglied *n* — linear system
Überwachungsprogramm *n* — monitor (II)
Ultrastabilität *f* — ultrastability
Unsicherheit *f* — uncertainty
Unternehmensspiele *pl.n* — management games
Unterprogramm *n* — sub-routine
Unterscheidung *f* — discrimination
Unterscheidungsmatrix *f* — difference matrix
Unterschiedsschwelle *f* — differential threshold

Valenz *f* — valence
Vergessen *n* — forgetting
Verhaltenssteurung *f* — behaviour determination
Verknüpfung *f*, logische — logical connective
Verlernen *n* — extinction
Verständlichkeit *f* — intelligibility
Verstärker *m* — amplifier
Versuch und Irrtum *m* — trial and error
Verwirklichung *f* — realization
Vierpol *m* — four terminal network
Visible Speech *f* — visible speech
Vocoder *m* — vocoder
Vorgriff *m* eines Kanals — anticipation of a channel
Vorwärtsregelung *f* — feed-forward control

Wachstumsregulation *f* — growth regulation
Wahrnehmbarkeitsgrenze *f* — threshold (I)
Wahrnehmung *f* — perception
Wahrscheinlichkeit *f* — probability
Wahrscheinlichkeit, subjektive — probability, subjective
Wahrscheinlichkeitsdichte *f* — probability density
Wahrscheinlichkeitslernen *n* — probability learning
Wahrescheinlichkeitsverfahren *n* — probabilistic approach
Wahrscheinlichkeitsverteilung *f* — probability distribution
Wandler *m* — transducer
WEBERsches Gesetz *n* — WEBER's law
Wechselwirkung *f* — reciprocal action; interaction
Weitschweifigkeit *f* — redundancy
Wortzeit *f* — word-time

Zahlendarstellung *f* — number representation
Zähler *m*; Zählwerk *n* — counter
Zeichen *n* — character; sign
Zeichen, nichtideales; Zeichen, reales — type font, mutilated
Zeichenabstand *m* — pitch
Zeichenerkennung *f*, automatische — character recognition; pattern recognition
Zeichenfunktion *f* — semiotic aspects of characters
Zeichenleser *m* — character reader; reading machine
Zeichennormierung *f* — font standardization
Zeichenreproduktion *f* — reproductive storing
Zeichensatz *m* — type font
Zeichenteilung *f* — pitch
Zeichenträger *m* — signal
Zeichenveränderung *f* — type font, mutilated
Zeichenvorrat *m* — repertory
Zeichenzentrierung *f* — character centering
Zeitkonstante *f* — time constant
Zeitquant *n*, subjectives (SZQ) — moment
Zentralnervensystem *n* — central nervous system
Ziffer *f* — number
Zittern *n* — tremor
zufällig — stochastic; random
Zufallsvariable *f*; Zufallsgrösse *f* — random variable
Zufallszahl *f* — random number
Zufallszahlengenerator *m* — random number generator
Zugriffszeit *f* — access time
Zuordner *m* — translator (II)
Zweipol *m* — two terminal network
Zweipunktregler *m* — bang-bang servo
Zweitor *n* — four terminal network
Zwischenneuron *n* — interneuron

**French-English word list**

accommodation *f* informationelle — probability learning
accumulateur *m* — accumulator
action *f* réciproque — reciprocal action
adaptation *f* — adaptation; matching
addeur *m* — adder
adresse *f* — address
afférent *m* spécifique — specific system
agnosie *f* — agnosia
aléatoire — stochastic
algèbre *f* Booléenne — Boolean algebra
algèbre *f* des circuits — switching algebra
ALGOL *m* — ALGOL
algorithme *m* — algorithm
alphabet *m* — alphabet
alphanumérique — alphanumerical
altération *f* des caractères (signes) — type font, mutilated
ambiguité *f* — ambiguity
amplificateur *m* — amplifier
analogie *f* — analogy
analogue — analogous
analyse *f* de FOURIER — harmonic analysis
analyse *f* factorielle — factor analysis
analyse *f* harmonique — harmonic analysis; FOURIER analysis
analyse *f* mathématique de langage — mathematical analysis of language
analyse *f* mathématique musicale — mathematical analysis of music
anticipation *f* d'un canal — anticipation of a channel
antivalence *f* — non-equivalence
aphasie *f* — aphasia
apperception *f* — apperception
apprentissage *m* — learning
apprentissage *m* mécanique — didactics, mechanical
approche *f* probabiliste — probabilistic approach
approximation *f* informationnelle — informational approximation
apraxie *f* — apraxia
arbre *m* de HUFFMAN — HUFFMAN's tree
association *f* — association
ataxie *f* — ataxia
automate *m* — automaton
automates *pl.m* d'apprentissage — learning machines
automate *m* finalisé — automaton, finite
automation *f* — automation
autoorganisation *f* — self-organization
axone *m* — axon

bande *f* passante — band width
bande *f* perforée — punched tape
béhaviorisme *m* — behaviourism
binaire — binary
bit *m* — binary digit; bit
boucle *f* — loop
boucle *f* de régulation — feedback control system
bruit *m* — noise

calculabilité *f* — computability
calculatrice *f* — computer (digital)
calculatrice *f* analogique — analogue computer
canal *m* — channel
canal *m*, stationnaire — channel, stationary
capacité *f* — capacity (I)
capacité *f* de mémoire — capacity (II)
capacité *f* du canal — channel capacity
capitaine *m* — captain
caractéristique *f* — characteristic curve
carte *f* perforée — punch card
cellules *pl.f* (informatives) de GABOR — GABOR information-cell
centrages *m* des signes — character centering

cerveau *m* — brain
cerveau *m* mécanique — electronic brain
cervelet *m* — cerebellum
chaîne *f* de MARKOFF — MARKOV chain
chaîne *f* morphogrammatique — morphogrammatic compound
champ *m* — probability field
chiffre *m* — number
choc *m* de réponse — step response
chorée *f* — chorea
circuit *m* à convergence-divergence — focalized-diffused-excitation
circuit *m* à valeur optimale — optimalizer
circuit *m* de porte — gate
circuits *pl.m* logiques — logical circuits
*m* COBOL — COBOL
codage *m* — coding (in nervous system); encoding
code *m* — code
code *m* d'instructions — instruction code
coefficient *m* de corrélation — correlation coefficient
cohérent — coherent
commande *f* — open-loop control
communication *f* — communication
compilateur *m* — compiler
complexité *f* — complexity
compteur *m* — counter
compteur *m* ordinal — sequence control register
computer — computer (digital)
conceptualisation *f* — concept formation
conditionnement *m* classique — conditioning, classical (Pavlovian)
conditionnement *m* instrumental — conditioning, instrumental (operant)
conditionneur *m* — gate
conjonction *f* — conjunction
conscience *f* — consciousness
constante *f* de temps — time constant
content *m* d'information — information content
coordinateur *m* — translator (II)
correction *f* d'erreur — error correction
cortex *m* — cortex
créativité *f* — creativity
cryotron *m* — cryotron
cybernétique *f* — cybernetics

déclancheur *m* — trigger
decodage *m* — decoding
degré *m* de surprise — surprise value
démon *m* de MAXWELL — MAXWELL's demon
dendrite *f* — dendrite
densité *f* de probabilité — probability density
descriptor *m* — descriptor
détection *f* des erreurs — error detection
didactique *f* informationnelle — informational didactics
différence *f* liminaire — differential threshold
différential *m* semantique — semantic differential
digital — digital
diode *f* — diode
dipole *m* — two terminal network
discrimination *f* — discrimination
disjonction *f* — disjunction (inclusive)
distance *f* de HAMMING — HAMMING distance

distribution *f* de probabilité — probability distribution
durée *f* de présence — duration
dynamique *f* des groupes — mathematical group dynamics

écarte *f* de réglage — deviation
écorce *f* cérébrale — cortex (of brain)
écriture *f* magnétique — magnetic ink font

écriture *f* phonétique (technique) allemande — German technical phonetic script
électrocorticogramme *m* — electrocorticogram
électroencéphalogramme *m* — electroencephalogram
électronique — electronic
élement *m* non linéaire — nonlinear element
engramme *m* — engram
entreé *f* — input (I) and (II)
entropie *f* — entropy
entropie *f* des groupes — entropy of groups
entropie *f* élective — elective entropy
entropie *f* élective des classes de choix — elective entropy of choice classes
entscheidbarkeit *f* — decidability
épaisseur *f* du présent — time discriminability
équivalence *f* — equivalence (material)
équivoquation *f* — equivocation
espace *m* informationnel — message space
espacement *m* des caractères (signes) — pitch
essai et erreur *m* — trial and error
esthétique *f* informationnelle — informational aesthetics
évaluateur *m* de tests — test signal generator
excitation *f* — excitation
extension *f* de domaine — open-loop amplification

facilitation *f* — facilitation
feed back *m* — feedback
ferrite *f* — magnetic core
filtre *m* — filter
filtre *m* d'amplitude — amplitude filter
filtre *m* de fréquence — frequency filter
flèche *f* de PEIRCE — nor-function
fonction *f* d'autocorrélation — autocorrelation function
fonction *f* de choc — step function
fonction *f* de corrélation — correlation (function)
fonction *f* de corrélation inverse — cross correlation function
fonction *f* de DIRAC — pulse function
fonction *f* delta — unit pulse
fonction *f* de passage — step response
fonction *f* descriptive — describing function
fonction *f* de signes — semiotic aspects of characters
fonction *f* de transfert — transfer function
fonction *f* 'en marche d'escalier' — step function
fonction *f* logique — logical connective
fonctions *pl.f* logiques — propositional functions
formants *pl.m* — formants
formation *f* de concepts — concept formation
forme *f* — pattern
fréquence *f* — frequency

gamme *f* de fréquence — frequency range
généralisation *f* — generalization
générateur *m* de nombres aléatoires — random number generator
grammaire *f* — grammar
grand *m* sympathique — autonomic nervous system
grandeur *f* d'entrée — input (I); input signal, input value
grandeur *f* de sortie — output quantity
grandeur *f* perturbatrice — disturbance
grandeur *f* réglante — regulating variable
grandeur *f* réglée — controlled condition
graphe *m* — graph

hédonie *f* — hedony
heuristique *f* — heuristics
hierarchisation *f* — hierarchization

homéostasie *f* — homeostasis
homéostat *m* — homeostat
horloge *f* — clock (generator)

icon *m* — icon
idéogramme *m* — ideogram
impératif *m* — imperative
implication *f* — implication
impulsion *f* — pulse; impulse
incertitude *f* — uncertainty
information *f* — information
information *f* esthétique — information, aesthetical
information *f* sémantique — information, semantical
information *f* subjective — information, subjective
information *f* transmise — transinformation
inhibition *f* latérale — inhibition, lateral
inhibition *f* temporelle — inhibition, temporal
installation *f* réglée — controlled system
instances *pl.f* cybernétiques — cybernetics, levels of
instruction *f* — instruction
instruction *f* conditionnée — instruction, conditional
instruction *f* de saut — jump instruction
intégrale *f* de FOURIER — FOURIER integral
intelligence *f* — intelligence
intelligence *f* artificielle — intelligence, artificial
intelligibilité *f* — intelligibility
introspection *f* — introspection
invariabilité *f* — invariancy

jeu *m* à somme nulle — zero-sum-game
jeu *m* d'entreprise — management games
jugement *m* absolu — absolute judgement

langage *m* — language
langage *m* de programmation — programming language
langage *m* FORTRAN — FORTRAN
langage *m* machine — machine code
langage-objet *m* — object language
langages formales — languages, formalized
lecteur *m* de cartes perforées — punch card reader
liberté *f* — freedom
liberté *f* d'action en retour — feedback, absence of
LIFO store *m* — pushdown store
logique *f* — logic
logique *f* mathématique — logic, mathematical
Logon *m* — logon
loi *f* de BUNSEN-ROSCOE — BUNSEN-ROSCOE law
loi *f* de FECHNER — FECHNER's law
loi *f* de WEBER — WEBER's law
loi *f* du tout ou rien — all-or-none law

machine *f* à adresses multiples — multiple-address machine
machine *f* à calculer automatique — computer (digital)
machines *pl.f* à enseigner — teaching machines
machine *f* à lire — character reader; reading machine
machine *f* TURING — TURING machine
maladie *f* de PARKINSON — PARKINSON's disease
matrice *f* à apprendre — learning matrix
matrice *f* des distances de Hamming — difference matrix
mécanisme *m* automatique — automaton
membrane *f* — membrane
mémoire *f* — memory; store; storage

mémoire *f* à bande magnétique — magnectic tape store
mémoire *f* à disques — magnetic disc store
mémoire *f* à ligne à retard — delay line store
mémoire *f* à tambour — magnetic drum store
mémoire *f* à tores magnétiques — core memory
mémoire *f* d'un canal — memory of a channel
mémoire *f* matricielle — matrix store
mémoire *f* phosphorescente — short-term memory
mémorisation *f* mécanique — memory, mechanical
message *m* — message
mesure *f* esthétique — measure of aesthetics
metalangage *m* — meta language
méthode *f* des groupes — group coding
méthode *f* des séries — sequential coding
méthode *f* Monte-Carlo — Monte-Carlo method
métronome *m* — clock (generator)
modèle *m* neuronique — neuron model
modification *f* d'adresse — address modification
modulation *f* — modulation
monitor *m* — monitor (I) and (II)
monoflop *m* — monostable multivibrator
morphogramme *m* — morphogram
multivibrateur *m* — multivibrator
multivalence *f* — polyvalence
multivibrateur *m* monostable — monostable multivibrator

négation *f* — negation
négentropie *f* — negative entropy
nerf *m* — nerve
neuristor *m* — neuristor
neurone *m* — neuron
neurone *m* intermédiaire — interneuron
nombre *m* aléatoire — random number; random variable
nombre *m* binaire — binary number
normalisation *f* des caractéres — font standardization
noyaux *pl.m* sous-corticaux — subcortical nuclei
nystagmus *m* — nystagmus

objet *m* d'un signe — referent
ondes *pl.f* alpha — alpha waves
ondes *pl.f* bêta — beta waves
ondes *pl.f* delta — delta waves
ondes *pl.f* thêta — theta waves
opérande *m* — operand
opération *f* — operation
opérationalisme *m* — operationalism
opération *f* de SHEFFER — SHEFFER's stroke
opération *f* parallèle — parallel operation
opération *f* série — serial operation
optimaliser — optimize
ordre *m* — order
organe *m* de réglage — correcting element
organigramme *m* — blockdiagram; flow diagram
organisation *f* — organization
originalité *f* — originality
oscillation *f* — oscillation
oubli *m* — extinction; forgetting
ou *m* inclusif — disjunction (inclusive)

pandemonium *m* — pandemonium
paramétron *m* — parametron
pédagogie *f* cybernétique — cybernetical pedagogics
perception *f* — perception
perceptron *m* — perceptron
période *f* réfractaire — refractory period
phénomène *m* de résidu — 'residue' phenomenon
phénomène *m* du maximum — maximum effect

pilote *m* — pilot
potentiel *m* cortical — evoked response
potentiel *m* d'action — action potential
potentiel *m* d'action mononodale — action potential at a node of RANVIER
potentiel *m* total d'action — compound action potential
predicteur *m* — predictor
principe *m* de hierarchie — hierarchical principle
probabilité *f* — probability
probabilité *f* subjective — probability, subjective
procédé *m* des groupes — group coding
procédé *m* des séries — sequential coding
processus régulateurs *pl.m* du comportement — behaviour determination
processus *m* stochastique stationnaire — stochastic process, stationary
programme *m* — program
programme *m* d'assemblage — assembler
programmes *pl.m* de démonstration — theorem proving program
pseudo-code *m* — pseudo-code
psychologie *f* de la forme — Gestalt psychology
psychologie *f* des groupes — group dynamics
psychologie *f* informationnelle — information psychology
psychophysique *f* — psychophysics

quadripole *m* — four terminal network
quantification *f* — quantification
quantum *m* — quant
quantum *m* subjectif de temps — moment
quotient *m* intellectuel — intelligence quotient

rameur *m* — oarsman
réaction *f* — reaction
réafférence *f* — reafferent principle
réalisation *f* — realization
récepteur *m* — receptor
reconnaissance *f* — recognition
reconnaissance *f* automatique des signes — character recognition
reconnaissance *f* automatique du langage — speech recognition
redécouverte *f* d'information — information retrieval
redondance *f* — redundancy
redondance *f* de niveaux — redundancy by steps
redondance *f* des supersignes — redundancy at the super-character level
régénération *f* — regeneration
registre *m* — register
registre *m* coulissant; registre *m* de décalage — shift register
registre *m* index — index register
réglage *m* — feedback control
régle *m* du minimax — minimax process
régulateur *m* — regulator
régulateur *m* à deux paliers — bang-bang servo
régulation *f* — feedback control
régulation *f* biologique — biological regulation
régulation *f* de la croissance — growth regulation
régulation *f* par impulsions — sampled data control
régulation *f* par l'amont — feed-forward control
relais *m* — relay
relais *m* RC — R.C. circuit
répertoire *m* — repertory
répertoire *m* subjectif — repertory, subjective
réponse *f* de début — on-effect
réponse *f* de fin — off-effect
réponse *f* harmonique — frequency response

représentation *f* des chiffres — number representation
reproduction *f* des caractéres (signes) — reproductive storing
requisite variety *f* — requisite variety
ressemblance *f* — similarity

saut *m* — jump instruction
schéma *m* fonctionnel — blockdiagram
sciences *pl.f* informationnelles — informational sciences
sémantique *f* — semantics
semi-conducteur *m* — semi-conductor
semiotique *f* — semiotics
séquence *f* d'appel — calling sequence
série *f* de FOURIER — FOURIER series
seuil *m* — threshold (II)
seuil *m* absolu — absolute threshold
seuil *m* de différenciation; seuil *m* de séparation — differential threshold
seuil *m* d'excitation — threshold (I)
seuil *m* différentiel — differential threshold
signal *m* — signal
signe *m* — character
signe-type *m* — type font
signification *f* — meaning
similitude *f* — similarity
simulateur *m* — simulator
simulation *f* de jeux stratégiques — simulation of strategic games
sociotechnique *f* — social science
sommation *f* — summation
sortie *f* — output (I) and (II)
source *f* — source
source *f* ergodique — source, ergodic
source *f* markovienne — MARKOV source
source *f* stationnaire — source, stationary
sous-programme *m*; sous-routine *f* — sub-routine
spectre *m* — spectrum
spike *m* — spike
stabilité *f* — stability
standardisation *f* des caractères — font standardization
stimulus *m* — stimulus
stochastique — stochastic
structure *f* — structure
substance *f* réticulée — non-specific-system
substitution *f* d'adresse — indirect addressing
super-signe *m* — super-character
symbole *m* — symbol
synapse *f* — synapse
syntaxe *f* — syntax
système *m* d'afférents non spécifique — non-specific system
système *m* endocrinien — endocrine system
système *m* nerveux centrol — central nervous system
système *m* série-parallèle — series-parallel-system

tableau *m* de réflexion — pattern of reflection
tambour *m* — magnetic drum store
technique *f* — techniques
technique *f* de régulation — control engineering
temps *m* d'accès — access time
temps *m* de calcul — computing time
temps *m* de latence — refractory period
temps *m* de propagation — transit time, propagation time, delay time
temps *m* d'un mot — word-time
temps *m* mort — dead time
tête *f* magnétique — magnetic head
théorème *m* d'échantillonage — sampling theorem
théorème *m* de FEINSTEIN — FEINSTEIN'S theorem
théorème *m* de McMILLAN — McMILLAN'S theorem
théorie *f* de l'information — information theory

théorie *f* des décisions — decision theory
théorie *f* des systèmes — system theory
théorie *f* du comportement — behaviourism
théorie *f* informationnelle de l'apprentissage — informational theory of learning
théorie *f* mathématique de la dynamique des groupes — mathematical group dynamics
théories *pl.f.* de l'apprentissage — learning theories
timonier *m* — steersman
tonus *m* affect — hedony
toposcope *m* — toposcope
tore *m* magnétique — magnetic core
trace *f* d'impulsion — clock track
traducteur *m* — translator (I) and (II)
traduction *f* automatique — language translation (mechanical)
traitement *m* de l'information — information processing
traitement *m* des données — data processing
transducteur *m* — transductor
transfluxor *m* — transfluxor
transinformation *f* — transinformation
transistor *m* — transistor
transjonction *f* — transjunction
transmittance isochrone — transfer function
tremblement *m* — tremor
trigger *m* — trigger
tube *m* électronique — vacuum tube; valve
typographie *f* de l'information — informational typography

ultrastabilité *f* — ultrastability
unité *f* arithmétique — arithmetic unit
unité *f* de contrôle — control unit

valence *f* — valence
valeur *f* d'acception — acceptance value
valeur *f* à atteindre; valeur *f* de consigne — index value; set point
valeur *f* d'entrée — input signal
valeur *f* de rejection — rejection value
valeur *f* de sortie — output quantity
valeur *f* instantanée — actual value
valeur *f* liminaire — absolute threshold
valeur *f* logique — logical value of occupancy
valeur *f* réelle — actual value
variable *f* aléatoire — random variable
visualisation *f* du discours — visible speech
vocoder *m* — vocoder
voie *f* spécifique — specific system

## Russian-English word list

автокорреляционная функция *f* — autocorrelation function
автомат *m* — automation
автоматизация *f* — automaton
автоматический перевод *m* — language translation (mechanical)
автоматическое узнавание речи *n* — speech recognition
агнозия *f* — agnosia
адаптация *f* — adaptation
адрес *m* — address
азбука *f* — alphabet
аккумулятор *m* — accumulator; store; memory
аксон *m* — axon
алгебра Буля *f* — Boolean algebra
алгебра логики *f*; алгебра релейных схем *f* — switching algebra
алгоритм *m*; алгорифм *m* — algorithm
алфавит *m* — alphabet
альфа-лучи — alpha waves
амплитудный селектор — amplitude filter
аналогичный — analogous
аналогия *f* — analogy
аналоговая машина *f*; аналоговое устройство *n* — analogue computer
аналоговый — analogous
апперцепция *f* — apperception
апраксия *f* — apraxia
арифметическое устройство *n* — arithmetic unit
ассоциация *f* — association
атаксия *f* — ataxia
атомность *f* — valence
афазия *f* — aphasia

бета-лучи *m* — beta waves
бинарная единица *f* — binary digit; bit
бинарный — binary
биопотенциал *m* — action potential
биорегулирование *f* — biological regulation
биоэлектрический потенциал *m* — action potential
бит *m* — bit
бихевиоризм *m* — behaviourism
блок-схема *f*; блочная схема *f* — block-diagram
болезнь Паркинсона *f* — PARKINSON's disease
буквенно—цифровой — alphanumerical
валентность *f* — valence
ввод *m*; ввдное устройство *f* — input (l)
величина помех *f* — disturbance
вероятностный подход (способ) *m* — probabilistic approach
вероятностный подход *m* — probability learning
вероятность *f* — probability
вероятность, субъективная *f* — probability, subjective
везаимодействие *n* — reciprocal action; interaction
видимая речь *f* — visible speech
внутрисекреторная система *f* — endocrine system
возбуждение (физиол.) *n* — excitation
возмущающее воздействие *n* — disturbance
вокодер *m* — vocoder
восприятие *n* — perception
воспроизведение информацин (сведений) *n* — information retrieval
воспроизведение образов *n* — reproductive storing
временная память *f* — short-term memory
время выборки *n* — access time
время задержки *n*; время запаздывания *n* — transit time
время исчисления *n* — computing time
время осознанного восприятия *n* — moment
время пробега *n*; время пролета *n* — transit time
время существования *n* — duration
вход *m* — input (ll)
входная величина *f* — input signal
выбор информации *m* — information retrieval

вывод *m*; выдача *f* — output (l)
выработка понятий *f* — concept formation
выход *m* — output (ll)
выходная величина *f* — output quantity
выходное устройство *n* — output (ll)
вычислимость *f* — computability
вычислительная машина *f* — computer (digital)
вычислительное устройство непрерывного действия *n* — analog computer

гармонический анализ *m* — harmonic analysis; FOURIER analysis
генерализация *f* — generalization
гештальтпсихология *f* — Gestalt psychology
главные электрочасы *m* — clock (generator)
гомеостазис *m* — homeostasis
гомеостат *m* — homeostat
грамматика *f* — grammar
граф *m* — graph
график *m* — characteristic curve
гребец *m* — oarsman
групповая динамика *f* — group dynamics
групповая динамика (матем.) *f* — mathematical group dynamics
групповая энтропия *f* — entropy of groups

датчик пробной велчины *m* — test signal generator
датчик случайных чисел *m* — random number generator
двоичная цифра *f* — binary digit; bit
двоичное число *n* — binary number
двусмысленность *f* — equivocation
двухполюсник *m* — two terminal network
двухпозиционный регулятор *m*; двухступенчатый регулятор *m* — bang-bang servo
действительная величина *f* — actual value
декодирование *n* — decoding
декодирующее устройство *n* — translator (ll)
дельта-лучи *m* — delta waves
дельта-функция *f* — unit pulse
демон Максвелла *m* — MAXWELL's demon
дендрит *m* — dendrite
дерево Хуффмана *n* — HUFFMAN's tree
дескриптор *m* — descriptor
детальная блок-схема программы *f* — flow diagram
дешифратор *m* — translator (l) and (ll)
дешифровка *f* — decoding
диапазон частот *m* — frequency range
диафрагма *f* — membrane
дизъюнкция *f* — disjunction (inclusive)
диод *m* — diode
дискриминация *f* — discrimination
диссипация *f* — ambiguity
длительность слова *f* — word-time
дрожание *n* — tremor

емкость *f* — capacity (l)
емкость канала *f* — channel capacity
емкость памяти *f* — capcaity (ll)

забвение *n* — forgetting
заданное значение измеряемой или регуируемой величины *n* — index value
задающий генератор *m* — clock (generator)
задержка *f* — transit time
закон Бунзена-Роско *m* — BUNSEN-ROSCOE law
закон Вебера-Фехнера *m* — FECHNER's law; WEBER's law
закон 'все или ничего' *m* — all-or-none law
замкнутый контур регулирования *m* — feedback control system
запоминающее устройство *n* — store; memory
запоминающее устройство на магнитной ленте *n* — magnetic tape store
запоминающее устройство на магнитном барабане *n* — magnetic drum store
запоминающее устройство на магнитном диске *n* — magnetic disc store
запоминаюцее устройство на ферритах *n* — core memory
запрещение *n* — inhibition
знак *m* — character
значение *n* — meaning

игра с нулевой суммой *f* — zero-sum-game

идеограмма *f* — ideogram
иерархический принцип *m* — hierarchical principle
избыточность *f*; излишняя часть сообщения *f* — redundancy
изменение адреса *f* address modification
икон *m* — icon
имитирующее устройство *n* — simulator
императив *m* — imperative
импликация *f* — implication
импульс *m* — pulse; impulse
импульс Дирака *m* — pulse-function
инвариантность *f* — invariancy
индексный регистр *m* — index register
интеграл Фурье *m* — FOURIER integral
интеллигенция *f* — intelligence
интенсификатор *m* — amplifier
интроспекция *f* — introspection
информационная аппроксимация *f* — informational approximation
информационная дидактика *f* — informational didactics
информационная психология *f* — information psychology
информационная типография *f* — informational typography
информационная эстетика *f* — informational aesthetics
информационные ячейки Габора *f* — GABOR information-cell
информация *f* — information
инхибиция *f* — inhibition
искажение образа *n* — type font, mutilated; noisy pattern
исключающее 'или' — non-equivalence
искусственная интеллигенция *f* — intelligence, artificial
исполнительный элемент *m* — correcting element
истинная величина *f* — actual value
источник *m* — source
источник Маркова *m* — MARKOV source
источник стационарный *m* — source stationary
исходное число *n* — operand
исчисляемость *f* — computability

канал *m*–channel
канал стационарный *m* — **channel, stationary**
капитан *m* — captain
квант *m* — quant
квантование *n* — quantification
кибернетика *f* — cybernetics
кибернетическая педагогика *f* — cybernetical pedagogics
кобол *m* — COBOL
когерентный — coherent
код *m* — code
код команд(ы) *m* — instruction code
кодирование *n* — Coding (in nervous system); encoding
колебание *n* — oscillation
команда *f* — instruction
команда безусловного или условного перехода *f* — jump instruction
командное устройство *n* — control unit
коммуникация *f* — communication
компилирующая программа *f* — compiler
комплексность *f* — complexity
комплект (набор) знаков *m* — type font
конвертер *m* — transducer
конечный автомат *m* — automaton, finite
контрольно-измерительный прибор *m*; контрольный аппарат *m* — monitor (l)
конъюнкция *f* — conjunction
коэффициент корреляции *m* — correlation coefficient
кривая геометрического места (точек) *f*; кривая концов вектора *f* — locus
криотрон *m* — cryotron
круговая диаграмма *f* — locus

линейное передаточное (трансляционное) звено *n* — linear system
линия задержки *f* — delay line store
логика *f* — logic
логистика *f* — logic, mathematical
логическая связь *f* — logical connective
логическая схема *f* — logical circuits
логическое сложение *n* — disjunction (inclusive
логическое умножение *n* — conjunction

логон *m* — logon
лоцман *m* — pilot

магнитная головка *f* — magnetic head
магнитная запись *f* — magnetic ink font
магнитный накопительный барабан *m* — magnetic drum store
магнитный накопительный диск *m* — magnetic disc store
математический анализ музыки *m* — mathematical analysis of music
математический анализ *m* — mathematical analysis of language
матрица обучения *f* — learning matrix
матрица различения *f* — difference matrix
матричный накопитель *m* — matrix store
машина-аналог *f* — analogue computer
машина Тьюринга *f* — TURING machine
машинное распознавание устной речи *n* — speech recognition
машинный перевод *m* — language translation (mechanical)
машинный язык *m* — machine code
международный язык программирования Алгол *m* — ALGOL
мембрана *f* — membrane
'мёртвое' время *n* — dead time
местная кривая *f* — locus
метаязык *m* — meta language
метод Монте-Карло *m* — Monte-Carlo method
механическая дидактика *f* — didactics, mechanical
механическое накопление *n* — memory, mechanical
многоадресная машина *f* — multiple-address machine
многовалентность *f*; многозначность *f* — polyvalence
моделированный — analogous
моделирующее счетно-решающее устройство *n* — simulator
модель *f* — model
модель нейрона *f* — neuron model
модификация адреса *f* — address modification
модуляция *f* — modulation
мозг *m* — brain
мозговая кора *f* — cortex of brain
мозжечок *m* — cerebellum
момент *m* — moment *n*
монитор *m* — monitor (l) and (ll)
морфограмма *f* — morphogram
морфограмматическая цепь *f* — morphogrammatic compound
мультивибратор *m* — multivibrator

накопитель *m* — store
накопитель на магнитной ленте *m* — magnetic tape store
негэнтропия *f* — negative entropy
неизменность *f* — invariancy
нейрон *m* — neuron
некоординированность движений *f* ataxia
нелинейный элемент *m* — nonlinear element
ненадёжность *f* — uncertainty
непрерывно изменяющийся — analogous
нерв *m* — nerve
неэквивалентность *f* — non-equivalence
нистагм *m* — nystagmus
нормирование образов *n* — font standardization

обобщение *n* — generalization
обработка информации *f* — information processing
образ *m* — pattern
образование понятий *n* — concept formation
обратная афферентация *f* — reafferent principle
обратная связь *f* — feedback
обучающие машины *f* — teaching machines
обучающиеся автоматы *m* — learning machines
обучение *n* — learning
объект регулирования *m* — controlled system
объем информации *m* — information content
однокоординатная адресация *f* — sequential coding

однонаправленность *f* — feedback, absence of
одностабильный вибратор *m* одноперекидная схема *f* — monostable multivibrator
on-ответ *m* — on-effect

оперативная память *f*; оперативное запоминающее устройство *n* — short-term memory
операционализм *m* — operationalism
операция *f* — operation
описательная функция *f* — describing function
опознавание *n* — recognition
опознавание ощибок *n* — error detection
оптимализировать — optimize
оптимальный фильтр *m* — predictor
оптимизатор *m* — optimalizer
организация *f* — organization
оригинальность *f* — originality
основные частоты (звука) *f* — formants
осуществление *n* — realization
отклонение регулируемой величины *n* — deviation
отрицание *n* — negation
отрицание однозначности *n* — non-equivalence
off-ответ *m* — off-effect
ошибка регулирования *f* — deviation
ощущение *n* — perception

память *f* — memory
память канала *f* — memory of a channel
пандемоний *m* — pandemonium
параллельная система *f* — parallel operation
параметрон *m* — parametron
переадресация *f* — indirect addressing
перегородка *f* — membrane
передаточная функция f — step response
перепонка *f* emmbrane
переработка информации *f* — information processing
пересчетное устройство *n* — counter
переходная функция *f* — step response
перфокарта *f* — punch card
перфолента *f*; перфораторная лента *f* — punched tape
перфорированная карточка *f* — punch card
перфорированная лента *f* — punched tape
перцептрон *m* — perceptron
перцепция *f* — perception
плотность вероятности *f* — probability density
плотность существования *f* — time discriminability
подобие *n* — analogy; similarity
подобный — analogous
подпрограмма *f* — sub-routine
поиск инфорации *m* — information retrieval
поле *n* — probability field
полоса пропускания *f* — band width
полоса частот *f* — frequency range
полупроводник *m* — semi-conductor
полупроводниковый триод *m* — transistor
понятность *f* — intelligibility
поправка ошибок *f* — error correction
порог *m* — threshold (ll)
порог абсолютный *m* — absolute threshold
порог возбуждения *m*; порог раздражения *m* — threshold (l)
порог различимости *m* — differential threshold
порядок *m* — order
последовательная система *f* — serial operation
последовательно-параллельная система *f* — series-parallel-system
постоянная времени *f* — time constant
потенциал коры головного мозга *m* — evoked response
предписанное значение *n* — index value
предрешение канала *n* — anticipation of a channel
представление чисел *n* — number representation
преобразователь *m* — transducer
принцип ‘все или ничего’ *m* — all-or-none law
приспосабливание *n* — matching
проба и ошибка *f* — trial and error
проводник *m* — pilot

программа *f* — program
программа для построения доказательств — theorem proving program
продолжительность хода *f* — transit time
промежуточный нейрон *m* — interneuron
пропускная способность канала (связи) *f* — channel capacity
противодействие *n* — reaction
процент внятно воспринятых слов *m* — intelligibility
прямое регулирование *n* — feed-forward control
псевдокод *m* — pseudo-code
психофизика *f* — psychophysics
пусковое устройство *n* — trigger
путь неспецифический *m* — non-specific system
путь специфический *m* — specific system

раздражитель *m* — stimulus (physiological) and (psychological)
различение *n* — discrimination
разъединяющий механизм *m* — trigger
распознавание *n* — recognition
распознавание образов *n* — character recognition
распределение вероятности *n* — probability distribution
рассогласование *n* — deviation
расстояние образов *n* — pitch
расстояние Хемминга *n* — HAMMING distance
расшифровывание *n* — decoding
реакция *f* — reaction
реализация *f* — realization
регенерация *f* — regeneration
регистр *m* — register
регистр адресов *m* — index register
регистр сдвига *m* — shift register
регулирование *n* — feedback control; closed loop control
регулирование поведения *n* — behaviour determination
регулирование роста *n* — growth regulation
регулируемая величина *f* — controlled condition
регулируемый объект *m* — controlled system
регулирующее воздействие *n* — regulating variable
регулирующий контур *m* — feedback control system
регулирующий орган — correcting element
регулятор *m* — regulator
резистивно-емкостное звено *n* — R.C. circuit
релаксационная схема *f* — multivibrator
реле *n* — relay
репертуар *m* — repertory
репродукция образов *f* — reproductive storing
референт *m* — referent
рецепторный нейрон *m*; рецептор *m* — receptor
RC-звено *n* — R.C. circuit
рулевой *m* — steersman
ряд Фурье *m* — FOURIER series

самонаблюдение *n* — introspection
самоорганизация *f* — self-organization
свобода *f* — freedom
семантика *f* — semantics
семантическая информация *f* — information, semantical
семиотика *f* — semiotics
сигнал *m* — character; signal
символ *m* — symbol
симулятор *m* — simulator
синапс m — synapse
синтаксис *m* — syntax
система дискретных данных с обратной связью *f* — sampled data control
скачкообразная функция *f* — step function
скелетная схема *f* — blockdiagram
сложение *n* — summation
случайная переменная *f* — random variable
случайное число *n* — random number
случайный — stochastic
собиратель *m* — assembler
сознание *n* — consciousness
сознательное восприятие *n* — apperception
сообщение *n* — communication; message

спайк — spike
спектр *m* — spectrum
способность создания — creativity
спусковая схема *f* — multivibrator
стабильность *f* — stability
стандартизация образов *f* — font standardization
степень интеллекта *f* — intelligence quotient
стохастический — stochastic
стохастический процесс *m* — stochastic process
стратегия минимакса *f* — minimax process
стрелка Пирса *f* — nor-function
строение *n*; структура *f* — structure
ступенчатая избыточность *f* — redundancy by steps
субкортекс *m* — subcortical nuclei
субъективная информация *f* — information, subjective
суммарный потенциал *m* — compound action potential
сумматор *m* — adder
суммация *f*; суммирование *n* — summation
суммирующее устройство *n* — adder
схема совпадений *f* — gate
сходство *n* — analogy; similarity
счетно-решающее устройство *n* —computer (digital)
счетчик *m* — counter
счетчик команд *m* — sequence control register

тактовая дорожка *f* — clock track
теорема Котельникова *f* — sampling theorem
теорема Макмиллана *f* — McMILLAN's theorem
теорема Фейнштейна *f* — FEINSTEIN's theorem
теории обучения *f* — learning theories
теория информации *f* — information theory
теория связи *f* — system theory
тета-лучи *m* — theta waves
техника *f* — techniques
техника регулирования *f*; техника управления *f* — control engineering
торможение *n* — inhibition
транзистор *m* — transistor
трансинформация *f* — transinformation
транслятор *m* — translator (l)
трансфлюксор *m* — transfluxor
трансформатор *m* — transducer
трансъюнкция *f* — transjunction
требуемая величина *f* — index value
триггер *m* — trigger
триггерная схема *f* — multivibrator

узнавание образов *n* — character recognition
ультраустойчивость *f* — ultrastability
управление *n* — open-loop control
управляемая величина *f* — controlled condition
управляющее устройство *n* — control unit
усилтель *m* — amplifier
условная команда *f* — instruction, conditional
условный рефлекс *m* — conditioning, classical (Pavlovian)
устойчивость *f* — stability
устройство ввода данных *n* — input (l)
устройство для чтения перфокарт *n* — punch card reader
учение *n* — learning

фактическое значение *n* — actual value
факториальный анализ *m* — factor analysis
ферритовый сердечник *m* — magnetic core
фильтр *m* — filter
фон *m* — noise
формальный язык *m* — languages, formalized
формант *m* — formants
формирование *n* — facilitation
фортран *m* — FORTRAN
функтор *m* — operand *m*
функция включения *f* — step function
функция корреляции *f* — correlation function
функция образа *f* — semiotic aspects of characters
функция передачи *f* — transfer function

хаотический шум *m* — noise
характеристика *f* — characteristic curve
хорея *f* — chorea

центральная нервная система *f* — central nervous system
центрирование (центровка) образов *n* — character centering
цепь Маркова *f* — MARKOV chain
цепочка задержки *f* — delay line store
цифра *f* — number
цифровой — digital

частота *f* — frequency
частотная характеристика *f* — frequency response
частотный фильтр *m* — frequency filter
четырёхполюсник *m* — four terminal network
читающий автомат *m* — character reader

шифрирование *n* — encoding
штрих Шеффера *m* — SHEFFER's stroke
штурман *m* — steersman
шум *m* — noise

эвристика *f* — heuristics
эквивалентность *f* — equivalence
эквивокация *f* — equivocation
электрокортикограмма *f* — electrocorticogram
электронная лампа *f* — vacuum tube; valve
электронная линия задержки *f* — delay line store
электронное моделирующее устройство *n* — analogue computer
электронное управление сигналом *n* — gate
электронный — electronic
электронный мозг *m* — electronic brain
электроэнцефалограмма *f* — electroencephalogram
энграмма *f* — engram
энтропия *f* — entropy
эргодический источник *m* — source, ergodic
эстетическая информация *f* — information, aesthetical
эстетическая мера *f* — measure of aesthetics
эффект максимума *m* — maximum effect

язык *m* — language
язык машины *m* — machine code
язык предмета *m* — object language